Praise for *Rapture Ready*

"Daniel Radosh writes about evangelical culture with brilliance, humor, and understanding. Everyone should read this book—with the possible exception of Stephen Baldwin [see page 143]."
—A.J. Jacobs, author of *The Know-It-All and The Year of Living Biblically*

"Very entertaining."
—Tom Perrotta, author of *Little Children* and *The Abstinence Teacher*

"Offers evaluations and insights that might be considered downright prophetic, and compassionate too. No evangelical insider could have done as good a job as Daniel Radosh. He's a witty, energetic, and insightful writer who grabs your attention and interest on page one and won't let go until he's escorted you to a powerful conclusion in the final paragraphs."
—Brian McLaren, author of *A New Kind of Christian* and
Everything Must Change

"A wonderfully funny and very, very smart book. Highly recommended as a memoir, a meditation on American religious tensions, and a perfect example of why taking popular culture seriously is so important."
—Linda Holmes, National Public Radio

"Delightful. A smart book about a surprisingly subtle subject."
—Jeff Sharlet, author of *The Family*.

"An intelligent but fun read that will have you thinking twice about what Jesus would buy, watch, or listen to . . . Deserves to be a great discussion starter in Christian circles."   —*Beliefnet*

"Radosh has discovered a world that is hilarious, unpredictable, and lucrative! It seems there's a foreign country in America and it's right down the street . . . and now I'm not so sure that I'm not the foreigner."
—Sam Seder, *Air America Radio*

"A rich exploration of the realm . . . Reading Radosh's book is like coming across another planet hidden somewhere on Earth where everything is just exactly like it is here except blue or made out of plastic."   —*Slate*

"Radosh is open about his own biases and shortcomings, and responds with astonishing intellectual and emotional honesty to the people and ideas he encounters."   —*The Boston Globe Magazine*

"Written with style and sensitivity, the book is at turns comical and spiritually uplifting."   —*The Dallas Morning News*

"[Radosh] finds plenty of trash . . . and surprises, too."
   —*The New York Times*

"I kept breaking into hysterical laughter, [but] what makes *Rapture Ready!* worthwhile is that Radosh—a secular Jew—goes beyond mockery to engage seriously with Christian believers who make, consume, and even criticize Christian pop culture."   —*The Atlantic.com*

"A fundamentally serious, sober if amusing and entertaining attempt to create a bridge between progressive Jesus-lovers and the secular world."
   —*The Onion A.V. Club*

"A fascinating and funny exploration of exactly what the title indicates, leavened with empathy."   —*McSweeney's*

"Juicy [and] fascinating."   —*AlterNet*

"The book is full of surprises and tonal shifts, and made me look at not just evangelical culture but American pop culture and Jewish culture in a new light."   —*The Forward*

"Funny, revealing, and descriptively titled."   —*Esquire*

"Quick: Name the last time you laughed out loud while reading a book. Mine's recent, with *Rapture Ready!*"   —*The Hartford Courant*

"Opening his readers to a complex subculture with an abundance of unusual characters, Radosh's traveling road show is riveting, side-splitting, and thoughtful." —*The Jerusalem Post*

"Radosh has the astute sense of a journalist and the evocative humor of a stand-up comic. He balances his rather skeptical perspective with respectful stories about the lives of people he encounters." —*Publishers Weekly*

"Entertaining, often enlightening . . . Radosh takes his role of reporter in an unfamiliar land seriously, yet he isn't afraid to use his well-honed wit to good advantage." —*Booklist*

"Deeply thoughtful, often insightful, and sometimes downright hilarious . . . *Rapture Ready!* is much more than a witty cultural critic's Christian pop odyssey. It's the best kind of travel narrative, the kind in which the storyteller comes back changed."
    —Timothy Beal, author of *Biblical Literacy* and *Roadside Religion*

"Radosh paints complex portraits of modern, spiritually engaged Americans struggling to define their faith and its role in the world at large and is his best in these encounters, proving himself a keen observer. He is skilled at teasing out the truths and contradictions of his subjects, many of whom he describes with lyrical precision." —*American Conservative*

"Readers of all backgrounds will enjoy Radosh's journal about his bizarre adventure in this parallel universe because it is informative and deeply insightful . . . The greatest lesson in the book is not in what Radosh says with words but what he teaches by way of his tremendous example. If Christians treated American pop culture with the same respectful criticism and discerning openness that Radosh employed when examining the evangelical universe . . . these two cultures could have a productive encounter."
    —*First Things: The Journal of Religion, Culture, and Public Life*

"As an outsider, he sees things that all of us who grew up in this little world either slide past, choose to ignore or shrug off . . . He isn't really kind in many ways, but here's the kicker: He's right." —*Relevant Magazine*

RAPTURE READY!

Adventures
in the Parallel Universe of
Christian Pop Culture

DANIEL RADOSH

Soft Skull Press
New York

First published by Scribner, a division of Simon & Schuster, in a hardcover
edition in April 2008.

Library of Congress Cataloging-in-Publication Data

Radosh, Daniel, 1969-
Rapture ready! : adventures in the parallel universe of Christian pop culture / Daniel
Radosh.
p. cm.
Originally published: 1st Scribner hardcover ed. New York : Scribner, 2008.
Includes bibliographical references and index.
ISBN 978-1-59376-281-0
1. Popular culture—Religious aspects—Christianity. I. Title.

BR115.C8R25 2010
261.0973—dc22

2009043841

Cover design by Adrian Kinloch
Printed in the United States of America

Soft Skull Press
New York, NY

www.softskull.com

For Margalit and Milo

Contents

In the beginning

An airfield in rural Kansas, September 2005. The last echo of guitar feedback pulsed through the afternoon air as tattooed roadies carried equipment off the stage and the mosh pit untangled. A lanky teenager made his way out of the crowd and ran to where his friends were waiting on the periphery, sweat smearing his thick black eyeliner. "Awesome performance." He grinned broadly. "They prayed like *three times* in a twenty-minute set."

I glanced around. If anyone else thought this was a strange criterion on which to evaluate a rock concert, they didn't show it. Not for the first time, I wondered what I was doing here, at a Christian music festival where the merch tables sold "Got Jesus?" T-shirts and Bibles that looked like beach novels. Dustin, the sixteen-year-old prayer fan, continued his rapid-fire appraisal of the hard-rock band Disciple. A black-clad girl named Amanda gazed at him admiringly, and I began to suspect that her T-shirt—"I'm a sucker for guys in eyeliner"—was not chosen by accident. Amanda's friend Alexis smiled mischievously at her. Alexis is my sister-in-law. These were her friends. This was her world. Teenage hormones, rock 'n' roll . . . and Jesus Christ? It occurred to me that I had never before been in a situation where everything felt simultaneously so familiar and so disorienting.

I had met Alexis only two days before. She's the much younger daughter of my wife's formerly estranged father and his second ex-wife. So it's not exactly a close relationship. The first time I saw her she was wearing a form-fitting black trench coat, studded knee-high boots, and a shoulder-less red shirt, for a look you might call neogoth meets Harajuku girl. She was as chic as any sixteen-year-old should be, and I wasn't sure why this surprised me more—because she lives in Wichita or because she is an evangelical Christian. I'm a liberal New York Jew in my mid-thirties, but we hit it off well enough, and I thought it might be fun to tag along for the trip to SHOUTfest in Neodesha, a hundred miles east.

Picking up my ticket at the gate, I looked over the dozen bands who would be performing on two stages. Jump5, ZOEgirl, Skillet, Disciple. I didn't recognize a single name. I wasn't expecting to, but it was still an unusual experience. I'm fairly pop-culture savvy. I download the latest singles from iTunes, my Netflix queue has five hundred movies in it, and I can name all seven Harry Potter books, all six James Bonds, and both of Britney Spears's husbands (at press time). And now I was getting a taste of a teeming subculture that was almost completely off my radar. Sure, I knew Christian rock existed—was Stryper still around?—and the words *Left Behind* had a familiar ring, but I'd never really given this universe much thought.

And it is an entire universe—vast, complex, and with strange rules all its own, like a mirror universe from a science fiction tale, where everything is the same on the surface, only Spock has a beard and worships Jesus. As we made our way into the field, a volunteer handed me a yellow sticker that read "The Logan Show."

"Who's Logan?" I asked.

"Omigosh, he's the host. He's *so* funny! He's like the Christian Jon Stewart."

This is a book about popular culture. It's about entertainment, leisure, and shopping. It's also about politics and the culture war that engulfs America. And it's a little bit—but not as much as you might think—about religion. True, it is by definition impossible to draw a distinction between evangelical faith and the consumer lifestyle of evangelicals, but I drew one anyway. From the beginning of my research, I made a decision not to set foot in a church, mega or otherwise, unless it was to attend an event that any neutral observer would describe as performance rather than worship (even if the people hosting it might beg to differ). While you'll hear a fair amount about

Christian faith and Christian values, both with and without scare quotes, this book is not primarily intended to be a critique of either.

By the end of SHOUTfest, I had a few reasons for wanting to write about Christian pop culture. First, I thought it would be amusing. Even people in this subculture will admit that it can sometimes seem pretty ridiculous. A few songs from the white rapper KJ-52—the Christian Eminem—persuaded me of that. But I also thought it might be important. The modern world takes popular culture seriously, after all. Pretty much anyone would agree that you can't truly understand America without knowing who Elvis Presley, Stephen King, and Oprah Winfrey are. Depending on your definition, between 44 and 126 million Americans are evangelical Christians. Christian popular culture is a $7 billion industry, and it is increasingly crossing over to the mainstream. Wal-Mart now carries some 1,200 religious book titles and 550 inspirational albums, which regularly crack the mainstream bestseller lists and pop charts. Yet for everything I'd read and heard about the rise of the evangelical movement over the past two decades, I knew next to nothing about how this movement might be shaped by, or reflected in, its pop culture.

SHOUTfest gave me a small sense of this dynamic at work: The emotional manipulation of the lead singer for Seventh Day Slumber, who wrung tears from the audience by urging them to publicly confess their suicidal impulses before inviting them to come forward and accept Christ; the hipped-up doublespeak of sixteen-year-old punk princess Krystal Meyers, whose hit song "Anticonformity" promotes obeying God as a form of rebellion; the ominous militarism of T-shirts declaring "Soldier of Christ" and "God of Elijah, send your fire"; the unabashed earnestness of Logan, the supposed Christian Jon Stewart, whose patter turned out to be along the lines of "How 'bout Jump5! But more than that, how 'bout God for that sunset!"

Alexis and her trend-conscious clique were something of an anomaly at SHOUTfest. Most of the people wore baggy jeans or cargo shorts with camo baseball caps. They had bad haircuts and extra pounds. "Other Christians think we're freaks because we wear black." Amanda laughed mirthlessly. "We've been called Satanists." The irony is that for these kids, their alternative trappings are symbolic of a deeper embrace of faith, not a rejection of it. They are theologically, politically, and socially conservative evangelicals. And, to a remarkable extent, this worldview comes wrapped up in pop-culture ribbons. Amanda's favorite teen magazine is not *Cosmo-GIRL* but *Brio,* published by the far right Focus on the Family. Alexis was reading an inspirational book called *Sister Freaks,* about female martyrs. And Dustin—don't even get him started.

"So, I'm curious," I got him started. "Why is how many times a band prays what makes a good set?"

"Because it's becoming more and more rare. A lot of so-called Christian bands are really what I call crossover bands. They write these songs where they replace *Jesus* with *You,* so you can't tell if they're singing about God or a girlfriend. They can tell Christian fans, 'Yeah, we're still believers,' but nobody else knows. I don't want to judge, but I think a lot of bands try to hide it. They don't deny their Christianity, but they don't talk about it at their shows. They claim their music should be the message, and think the music speaks for itself, but even their lyrics have very little spiritual meaning if any. And if they do, it's very, very vague and could easily be confused with other intonations."

"Um, okay, but Christians don't just have to sing about God, right?"

Dustin looked at me like I had two heads.

"I mean, I haven't heard any love songs all day. Christians fall in love, right?"

"Love songs are all a bunch of clichés," he said. "How many times can you sing 'My girlfriend left me, she broke my heart, so now I'm going to chop her up and bury her in the basement'?"

I guess some people *have* had enough of silly love songs. I thought about a Seventh Day Slumber song I'd heard earlier in the day. The chorus went, "I believe in Jesus / He rescued me." It sounded to me like, well, a cliché. Not to mention a little simplistic. Even if you believed the message, what could this formulation of it have to do with the messy real world? Dustin was clearly a bright guy, so I asked if lyrics like this didn't insult his intelligence. "The music I listen to thrives on ambiguity and irony," I explained. "What makes it rewarding is that you have to figure out for yourself what the singer is saying, or if he even means what he says."

"If they're really a Christian band, and they're trying to win people over to Christ, there's no blurry lines," said Dustin. "The truth is bold. I don't think people who hear a song should have to *do something* to find out what it means." He gave the matter one last thought. "Irony in Christian music would not be good."

"Why not?"

"The Bible says, 'Do not cause anyone to stumble.' If someone interprets a song wrongly, the band is held accountable for that."

In so many ways, Dustin reminded me of friends I had in high school and college. He was a rock snob, only instead of scorning a song for being too melodic, he kept tabs on the number of times it mentioned Jesus. As for his convictions about the music he loved—his ingrained belief that doubt was something to be banished rather than wrestled with, and that any questions must be swiftly followed by pat answers—was I wrong to see in them a path to creationism and abstinence education? Much has been written about these and other political and social movements, but what if we can only really grasp their meaning by listening to teenagers talk about hard-core rock?

Not long after I returned from Kansas I happened to exchange e-mails with a stranger—a reader of my blog—who told me that she had grown up in a strict Christian family. I mentioned my SHOUTfest observations, and she understood my bafflement. "Most people don't understand that this parallel world exists," she wrote. "I think they have the idea of fundamentalists as sort of malevolent Amish, who have completely turned their backs on secular culture. Rather, they have co-opted the forms of secular culture and turned them to their own ends. Whether this hybridization will make their version of Christianity more resilient in the long run, or whether it means that they are, in essence, losing because they are tacitly accepting the secular rules of the game, is up for debate."

Over the next year, I immersed myself in Christian pop culture. I watched movies about the end times and read novels about spunky virgins-by-choice. I saw wrestling matches, raves, and standup comedy. I averted my eyes as Bibleman, the evangelical superhero, stripped down to his underwear and pulled on his spandex. I learned not to trust my first impressions. And I came out the other side with a very different perspective than I had going in.

This book is intended to be personal and idiosyncratic rather than comprehensive. It's organized as a series of adventures, each one investigating some broad aspect of Christian pop culture by focusing on one or two particular events or a handful of interesting people. There will be enough statistics and sociology to help make sense of individuals and experiences, but no more. Some of the people you'll meet in these pages are at the center of Christian culture and some are on its fringes. While I will try to provide context for my travels, I do not pretend to offer a definitive overview or history of this entire subculture. The chapters about contemporary Christian music, for example, will discuss some of the genre's seminal artists and some of its most popular contemporary ones, but it will leave out many more of both. I won't have much to say about Christian television or talk radio, two topics that could fill books of their own. Nor is there anything in this book about Christian mimes or graffiti crews, smaller but no less fascinating subjects. The reason, honestly, is that I decided to write about something else instead.

Christian pop culture in America is largely—almost exclusively—the domain of a particular subset of Protestants. In a 2006 Gallup survey, 44 percent of American adults, or about 86 million people, identified themselves as either evangelical or born-again. The terms are fuzzy. There are basic beliefs that evangelicals share, but there is lots of room for variation. For this reason, The Barna Group, the nation's premier evangelical polling firm, does not generally rely on self-identification when examining people's religious beliefs. Instead it asks whether they "have made a personal commitment to Jesus Christ that is still important in their life today and . . . believe that when they die they will go to Heaven because they [have] confessed their sins and [have] accepted Jesus Christ as their savior." Broadly speaking, those who would answer *yes* are the same 86 million people who call themselves evangelicals and are the ones I am writing about in this book.

But Barna does not classify everyone who answers these questions as evangelicals, no matter what they call themselves. The vast majority of them Barna calls "born-again Christians." To qualify as an evangelical, in Barna's judgment, people must meet the criteria for born-again Christian plus seven additional requirements.

Those include saying their faith is very important in their life today; believing they have a personal responsibility to share their religious beliefs about Christ with non-Christians; believing that Satan exists; believing that eternal salvation is possible only through grace, not works; believing that Jesus Christ lived a sinless life on earth; asserting that the Bible is accurate in all that it teaches; and describing God as the all-knowing, all-powerful, perfect deity who created the universe and still rules it today.

According to a 2006 Barna survey, only 8 percent of Americans, or 18 million people, meet these standards. Based on other Barna surveys about the disparate attitudes between "evangelicals" and "born-agains," it's reasonable to posit that the people Barna calls evangelicals are what many non-Christians would call fundamentalists (e.g., 66 percent of "evangelicals" favor a Constitutional amendment to make Christianity the official religion of the United States, versus 44 percent of "born-agains"). While 67 percent of Barna's evangelicals are politically conservative, only 38 percent of born-agains are; more born-again Christians are Democrats than Republicans.

One reason for this is that fully two-thirds of black Americans describe themselves as born-again or evangelical, double the share of whites.* Blacks, of course, are far more likely to be liberals and Democrats. Remove them from the sample, and the data shifts significantly. Sixty-three percent of white born-agains say they are Republicans; only twenty-nine percent are Democrats.†

And for the most part I *am* going to remove African Americans from the sample, because as I learned early on, Christian pop culture, the focus of my exploration, is an almost exclusively white affair. Not that there aren't prominent black authors and artists in the Christian sphere—pastor-turned-novelist T. D. Jakes, comedian Steve Harvey, filmmaker Tyler Perry—but overall, blacks remain underrepresented in Christian pop culture. Black gospel music sells well, but not in Christian bookstores. Almost everyone I asked about this offered the same observation: "The most segregated hour in America is eleven o'clock Sunday morning." It was true when Martin Luther King Jr. said it, and it's true today when the church hour is

---

*ABC News poll, 2002.
†Pew Research Center, 2006; includes "leaners."

extrapolated to the entire Christian culture. In the last fifteen years, organizations like Promise Keepers have done admirable work in casting racism as one of the most intolerable sins, but whatever effect this has had in reducing personal bigotry, it has done little to erase the cultural divide between black and white Christians.

The people I am writing about call themselves by many names: traditional Christians, conservative Christians, orthodox Christians, Bible-believing Christians, or even the saints. But mostly they just say Christians, and for the sake of simplicity, I've chosen to follow their lead. If you're a mainline or liberal Christian who has a problem with this, take it up with them. One word I'll use only very judiciously is *fundamentalist*. Not only because it's now considered largely pejorative but because it's hard to even nail down what it means. Three aphorisms I heard on my travels get at how tricky this terminology is. I was told that "an evangelical is a fundamentalist with a college degree" or, similarly, that "a fundamentalist is an evangelical who is angry about something." But I also heard that "a fundamentalist is anyone who is more conservative than you are." It's all a matter of perspective. When I do have to use this label, I try to make clear what I mean by it. Most likely something pejorative.

Every conversation and scene in this book took place as described. However, I have frequently changed the sequence of events and trimmed and rearranged dialogue in order to tell my story more clearly. When taking this literary license I have been careful not to alter the meaning of any individual event or conversation or the overall accuracy of this story.

Get Rapture Ready (.com)!

Throughout this book you may find that my account raises questions that prose alone cannot answer, such as, What can a Christian Eminem possibly sound like? That's why I've created an online multimedia appendix with photos, audio, and video of key people, places, and things mentioned in these pages, along with additional information about them and links to related sites. You can find it at **getraptureready.com**.

1

As goods increase, so do those who consume them

An affable middle-aged man in a bargain-basement pirate costume—striped pantaloons and puffy shirt, vinyl boots and plastic sword—is going to save your immortal soul.

Not directly, of course. Jesus Christ will handle the actual salvation, as he has for some two thousand years. But Hugh Sparks is going to play a key intermediary role. Sparks is going to ensure that in the year to come, Christian bookstores across America will carry his company's new line of Jolly Roger auto decals, with messages like "Christian Pirates: Bound to the Code" and "Dead Man for Christ." These stickers will then be purchased by some of the 100 million Americans who shop in Christian stores, so that one day, when you are driving down the highway, you will see one on the car ahead of you. Perhaps you will have just watched the latest *Pirates of the Caribbean* sequel, and you will think to yourself, *Why, yes, being a Christian is a lot like being a free-spirited rogue who sails the seven seas in search of adventure.* By tapping into the pirate zeitgeist, the Christian in the car in front of you will have *planted a seed your heart,* and then one day—*Blam!* You're saved. And the next thing you know, you're buying a Christian decal to put on *your* car.

That's the plan, anyway. It's what brought Sparks to booth 2101 at the 2006 International Christian Retail Show in Denver, Colorado. Americans spent more than $7 billion on Christian products in 2006, according to a

survey by market research firm Packaged Facts.* Not long ago, virtually
the only places to buy Christian books, music, and gifts were Christian
bookstores—the ones served by this trade show. These days, roughly half
of all Christian goods are bought at stores like Wal-Mart, Barnes & Noble,
and Amazon.com. With the attention from mainstream retailers, sales of
Christian products jumped 28 percent between 2002 and 2005. Laugh at
the pirate all you want, but Christian retailing is serious business.

Nearly five hundred companies had come to display their wares at the
Denver trade show, which is usually called CBA, after its organizer, the
Christian Booksellers Association. They ranged from newly minted mom-
and-pop operations to multimillion-dollar publishers with decades in the
business. Together, the 9,133 people attending this show shape the practice, principles, and politics of American evangelicalism in profound and
underappreciated ways. According to a 2005 survey by The Barna Group,
more people consume Christian mass media, such as radio and television,
than attend church. Broaden that to include all Christian entertainment
and commodities, and the influence of pop Christianity on the body of
believers is even more pronounced. "For some people, these media com-
plement their church experience," says pollster George Barna. "For others,
a combination of these media forms a significant portion of their faith experience." That's the kind of thing that really makes you think—especially
when you meet the children's video star Squiggz, a six-foot purple cockroach.

The cavernous exhibition hall of the Colorado Convention Center was a
tempest of color, noise, and networking. CBA lasts for five days, and some
people still only see a small fraction of it. It is an atmosphere that jolts you
with adrenaline the moment you enter the door—so many "God is totally
awesome" T-shirts, so little time!—and then leaves you utterly spent three
hours later, forcing you to refuel with a cup of coffee from the sandwich
counter, which is called, appropriately enough, Sub Culture.

For longtime CBA attendees, the big story this year was the new respect
and attention Christians were getting from mainstream companies, especially

---

*The Christian Booksellers Association, which uses narrower criteria, puts the figure at
$4.63 billion.

book publishers. Secular publishers such as Random House, Simon & Schuster, and Hachette competed with the traditional Christian houses for retailers' attentions. "People are recognizing that the Christian community is a viable market," said Andy Butcher, the editor of *Christian Retailing* magazine. "There's money out there." Rick Warren's *The Purpose-Driven Life* has sold more than 25 million copies since its release in 2003, making it one of the bestselling hardcovers of all time. Books in the *Left Behind* series, which portrays the end of days following the Rapture, when God will sweep believers up to heaven, have sold more than 65 million copies.

In reality, Christian books have been selling well for many years, but since mainstream bestseller lists don't count books sold through Christian stores, few publishers paid attention. Even now, most people outside the Christian publishing industry have no idea that scores of Christian writers, such as romance novelist Karen Kingsbury or inspirational speaker Beth Moore, regularly outsell the authors on *The New York Times* lists.

For a newcomer like me, the books section of the CBA floor was overwhelming. There were scholarly texts, breezy advice books, and even manga, Japanese-style comics. I picked up a book for ten-year-olds called *Why is Keiko Sick?* and read the back cover. "Through the story of Emily's friend Keiko, who has been diagnosed with leukemia, children learn how the Fall in the Garden of Eden and man's sin are responsible for sickness and death in the world." Remind me never to get cancer around these folks.

I made my way back to the more accessible gifts section. *Gifts* is the official industry term for any items that aren't books, music, or videos. The unofficial term, used widely, if discreetly, is *Jesus junk*. The phrase covers a range of products. The fussy knickknacks that have graced suburban homes for decades are as popular as ever—ceramic "Footprints in the Sand" wall plaques and nativity-scene snow globes. For the people who buy these, there is no such thing as being too corny. The slogan of one company is "Our gifts aren't perfect . . . just for givin'."

I was more interested in the first-time exhibitors' booths. These are the people who have dreamed up some gewgaw—or had it given to them by God, as they often say—and are convinced that it's the blessed tchotchke the world has been waiting for. Sometimes, they're right. In 2004, a gray-haired couple from rural South Dakota introduced His Essence: candles that smell like Jesus (from Psalm 45: "All your robes are fragrant with myrrh and aloes and cassia"). Since then they have sold more than fifty thousand. Products aspiring to such success in 2006 included Virtuous Woman perfume and My Loving Jesus Doll, a sixteen-inch plush savior designed to comfort the lonely. "We targeted them to children," the maker told me, "but we also found seniors are buying them." Sometimes, God will give two people the same idea, just to watch them fight it out. BirthVerse, a line of birthday cards with a different Bible passage for each day of the year, was going head-to-head with Happy Verse Day.

At one table I met a neurosurgeon who had been inspired to create a line of products featuring a character called Smiling Cross. This was, as it sounds, an anthropomorphic cross with its horizontal beam bent up into a cheery smile. Apparently the traditional symbol of Christ's agonizing death by torture was just too depressing. For the first time, I had the experience of seeing devout Christians embrace something that I, as a non-Christian, found sacrilegious. It wouldn't be the last.

The largest subset of Christian gifts is apparel. Christian T-shirts are the uniform in which evangelicals under thirty suit up for battle, and the companies that make them are constantly scrambling to come up with slogans and designs that appeal to today's youth, generally to embarrassing effect: "God is my DJ"; "Jesus has skills"; "I'm like totally saved." The marginally more ambitious shirts attempt to impart a lesson: "Life would be so easy if everyone read the manual"; "Friends don't let friends go to hell"; "Modest is hottest." The tangled rationale of that last one—*we can persuade girls to dress in a way that does not attract sexual attention by telling them that doing so will attract sexual attention, especially if they wear this form-fitting shirt*—begins to hint at the tension in bending Christian messages to pop-culture forms.

As I walked the blue-carpeted aisles of the convention center, I mentally assembled a head-to-toe "witness wear" outfit: a baseball cap with the Intel logo altered to read "Jesus inside"; holographic glasses that project the word *Jesus* almost everywhere you look (a redundant trick in this setting); a polyester Ten Commandments tie; a leather iPod case embossed with a cross; an old-school "Smile, God loves you" fanny pack; Jesus fish cuff links and belt buckle; black leather gloves with more crosses; dress socks with more fish; and "Follow the Son" beach sandals, with die-cut outsoles that imprint the words *Follow Jesus* in the sand when you walk.

Christian women have the option of accessorizing their outfits with jewelry, but only if they like shoddy costume jewelry. At least that's what I thought until I reached the large showcase of Bob Siemon Designs. Siemon, I discovered, is the most popular maker of Christian jewelry and one of the few with genuine artistry. While most of the trinkets I saw were cheap and gaudy, Siemon's work is clean and modern. A few years ago he designed a collection to promote *The Passion of the Christ*; his rough-hewn nail pendants could be the most elegant icon of Christianity since the cross itself, or at least the Jesus fish. The gulf in quality between his work and everything else I'd seen was so noticeable that I had to ask him about it.

"There's this mediocrity that goes on in Christianity," he said. "They're focused on making money and not serving people. When I was nineteen, I walked into a Christian bookstore, and I looked at the jewelry and I said, 'Look at this crap.'" That was in 1970, and he's been going against the grain ever since. To Siemon's surprise, his success—he now employs 150 artists and craftspeople—has not converted other retailers to his high-end approach. "This is really the Christian discount industry," he told me. "The mentality is: How can we make it cheap, cheap, cheap?"

Much of the gifts section bore him out. Apparently there is an insatiable demand for the timeless message of the gospel slapped onto anything made out of plastic. Key chains, cheerleader dolls, kazoos. Want a "Jesus erases sin" pencil eraser? No problem. Good News Tattooz? Got 'em (temporary only). You won't find many WWJD bracelets, however; pop culture is ephemeral, and that trend was played out years ago. I sorted through a basket of refrigerator magnets. "One Way: Jesus." "Rapture Ready!" I picked out one that said "Pray for America." The fine print on the back said "Made in China."

Many of these products were supposed to be Christian alternatives to popular non-Christian toys. At times I could see the logic behind this approach. Life of Faith historical dolls took off after the religious right denounced American Girl for donating money to Girls Inc., which was declared a front for abortion-loving lesbians. But I was stumped by Praise Ponies and Rainbow Promise Rings ("Moods change, but God's promises don't"). Was there something Satanic about mood rings or My Little Pony?

The *ne plus ultra* of Jesus junk—the product that Christians themselves are most likely to bring up when they want to acknowledge how cheesy

Christians can be—are breath mints that come wrapped in Bible verses. They're called Testamints. I had heard about Testamints even before I began my exploration of this parallel universe—David Letterman had made jokes about them—and I was eager to find the guy responsible.

Unfortunately, he'd gone bankrupt. Blame poor management, not consumer rebellion. The candies had been wildly popular, and a rival company, Scripture Candy, had been trying desperately to buy the name for years.*

Scripture Candy has had modest success with its less catchily named Scripture Mints, but it thrives on specialized holiday candies, and not just the predictable Easter jelly beans. Standing in his lively booth, founder and CEO Brian Adkins showed me his Valentine's Day candy hearts—just like the Necco originals, except instead of "Be mine" and "UR a QT" they said "Try God" and "Love the Lord." "Valentine's is big," Adkins explained, because kids give out candy to their classmates, so "you can get a Christian message into schools without getting into trouble." Halloween is even bigger, because handing out Faith Pops makes witnessing to the neighbors so easy. "It's the only time people actually come to *your* door," he said. "You can take the pagan holiday of Halloween and reverse it."

Such clandestine proselytizing was a recurring theme at the CBA show. The pitch for Gospel Golf Balls—Top-Flite balls imprinted with Bible verses—was "Now when you lose a golf ball you will be sharing the Good News of Jesus Christ!" A pastor's endorsement added, "This golf ball is the most effective outreach tool I have ever seen in golf," raising the question of how many golf-based outreach tools there are. Does someone make a Cleansed by His Blood ball washer?

Despite how all this may sound, many of the entrepreneurs here were sophisticated about business. The woman who created Oil of Gladness anointing oil was inspired not by a message from God so much as market research. "There's only one other competitor," she said when I asked how she came up this particular item. "Also, I wanted a product people would need to use and buy again."

The most savvy dealers focused not on individual products but on

---

*Several months after CBA, the founder of Testamints announced that he was relaunching the brand.

building licensable brands. Perhaps due to the success of the Superman and Spider-Man movies, several companies were trying to start Christian superhero lines. One had created a team of heroes called E-force, around which it hoped to build comic books, action figures, and other kid stuff. The members of E-force were Moses, Samson, and Queen Esther. Instead of robes and sandals they wore vibrant capes and sexy skintight leotards. Also, Moses could fly and shoot laser beams from his staff. When I noted that E-force seemed to be missing a member, the company representative explained that the team members were selected by careful research. "*Parents* want Jesus," he said. "Kids get bored by that."

Since E-force didn't yet have any supervillains to fight, perhaps they could tangle with the Almighty Heroes, another line of young, buff Bible action figures. Almighty Heroes were the brainchild of Don Levine, the seventy-eight-year-old legend who in his youth had created G.I. Joe. "I wouldn't do military figures today, not with what's going on overseas," he told me. "In today's world, the timing is right for Almighty Heroes." I fiddled around with a Noah figure, who for some reason came equipped with a sword and bow. Then I turned back to Levine. "So, um, you *are* Jewish, right?"

"I'm Jewish," he confirmed, catching my drift. "But c'mon: There are twelve million Jews in the world and two *billion* Christians. That's the kind of niche I like."

Over and over, two conflicting ideas about what Christian products should be seemed to play out on the CBA floor. I noticed this most starkly when looking at children's games. Some were so heavy-handed and tragically uncool that the only people I could imagine enjoying them were Rod and Todd Flanders. According to the box for Salvation Challenge,

> The players get saved by landing on Calvary and making the salvation call, "Jesus save me." After getting saved the players enter a race to see who can be the first to give all their cash to missionaries.

Games like this, which turn the acquisitiveness of Monopoly on its head, suggested that Christian children were (or ought to be) fundamentally different from other children, with different interests and dispositions. Other games, however, implied that Christian kids were essentially the same as any others, at least at first glance. Redemption was a fantasy card game that could easily be confused with Magic: The Gathering. In one aisle, two preteen girls slipped off their shoes to hop on the electronic pads of Dance Praise, a Christian pop version of the mainstream video game Dance Dance Revolution. Pushing the limits of this assimilationist philosophy of Christian entertainment was Left Behind: Eternal Forces, a computer game based on the novels. I played for a few minutes, taking control of a team of Christians fighting the antichrist's one-world government in post-Rapture New York; my weapons were prayer when possible, a tank when necessary.

In his first letter to the Corinthians, the apostle Paul writes, "I have become all things to all people so that by all possible means I might save some." Purveyors of Christian pop culture invoke this passage frequently to explain their ministry to skeptics. Just as Paul said, "to the Jew I became like a Jew" and "to the weak I became weak," modern-day evangelists become like golfers to the golfers or like hunters to the hunters. The Christian Outdoorsman company sells T-shirts that say "Be a camouflage Christian . . . Hunt for God." Arguing that tacky Jesus slogans make most non-Christians snicker derisively is futile, since as far as biblical inerrantists are concerned, Isaiah 55:11 promises that God's word *never returns void*—even if it's on a trucker cap.

But evangelism isn't the only explanation for the proliferation of Jesus junk. "There's a scripture verse in Deuteronomy that says, 'Paint my sayings on the doorposts and lintels of your home,'" the owner of a Christian bookstore told me. "That's sort of the scriptural admonition for what we do with this stuff. You can say a mug is not painting it on a doorpost, but it's the modern-day equivalent." As it happens, this commandment of Deuteronomy is important in the Jewish tradition as well. Most Orthodox and Conservative Jews keep a scroll with this passage of the Bible inside an ornamental case nailed to their doorposts. My own Judaism is neither orthodox nor conservative—in either the denominational or colloquial senses of the words—but I too have a mezuzah outside my door. It's a signifier of a Jewish household and, ideally, a reminder to me that as I go out into the world each day I should stay true to my heritage and my principles.

So I understand the impulse to have and display what outsiders may simply dismiss as a souvenir of religion. And while I would make a distinction between a ritual object and a consumer one, in the evangelical mind, the blending of religion and pop culture is itself a form of religious practice. The biblical foundation of evangelicalism is the Great Commission, Jesus's injunction to "go and make disciples of all nations." By definition, evangelicals engage with the culture at large. Paraphrasing John, evangelicals often say they are called to be "in the world but not of the world." They neither protect their faith by sealing themselves off from society nor tailor their faith to society's rules. That's the philosophy, at least. In practice, almost all do a little of both. As the children's games I saw demonstrate, the Christian community is engaged in a constant implicit debate about where to come down on the spectrum. Do Christian rock and romance novels transmit evangelical ideas into the culture, thus sanctifying the mundane (and possibly winning converts)? Or do they corrupt evangelical ideas while serving to keep Christians walled off from the culture (which already has enough romance novels of its own, thank you)? Or, alternatively, do Christians simply find a personal comfort zone and construct a theological and cultural justification around it? The day of judgment on these questions may never arrive.

In the book *Material Christianity: Religion and Popular Culture in America*, religious studies professor Colleen McDannell demonstrates that the separation of sacred practice from profane culture is an idea that has never made sense in the context of American evangelicalism. "The practice of Christianity is a subtle mixture of traditional beliefs and personal improvisations," she writes.

> Artifacts become particularly important in the lives of average Christians because objects can be exchanged, gifted, reinterpreted, and manipulated. People need objects to help establish and maintain relationships with supernatural characters, family, and friends. Christians use goods and create religious landscapes to tell themselves and the world around them who they are. While some Christians accomplish the same things through the exchange of ideas, many prefer to interact with visual and sensual symbols. Religious meaning is not merely inherited or simply accessed through the

intellect. Orthodox statements of belief and formal rituals are only one part of the complicated structure of religion. Religious meaning must be constructed and reconstructed over and over. Amid the external practice of religion—a practice that utilizes artifacts, art, architecture, and landscapes—comes the inner experience of religion. We can no longer accept that the "appearance" of religion is inconsequential to the "experience" of religion. The sensual elements of Christianity are not merely decorations that mask serious belief; it is through the visible world that the invisible world becomes known and felt.

I had taken it for granted that the mingling of religion and pop culture was a relatively new and therefore suspect phenomenon. But while this alchemy is certainly more prevalent now, it is firmly grounded in the history of American Christianity. McDannell notes that the first board game manufactured in America, by the Puritans, was Mansions of Glory, a race to heaven. "Christians of the nineteenth century could drink out of glasses etched with the Lord's Prayer or 'Rock of Ages.' On Sunday, children played with wooden Noah's Arks or Bible puzzles." Catalogs from the mid-1930s advertised "He careth for you" pencil clips and Spread-the-Light Reading Lamps.

Indeed, McDannell writes, Christian artwork and decoration was very much a part of mainstream commercial culture until the early twentieth century, when American homes adopted a more restrained interior design.

> Brightly colored prints and mottoes of biblical scenes did not harmonize with Colonial Revival design. It was the change in aesthetics, more than any change in American religious life, that motivated secular producers to stop making goods with religious themes. Religious goods disappeared from ordinary stores and catalogs not because Christians rejected the commercialization of their beliefs but because religious art was no longer fashionable. The figurative image, whether sentimental or religious, was being replaced by the abstract form.

The revival of Christian consumerism came in the 1960s with the so-called Jesus movement, when the church was shaken up by the arrival of a new breed of young Christians affectionately called Jesus people or Jesus freaks. These Christian youths, a combination of hippies who found God and church kids who became hippies, transformed evangelicalism every bit as much as their secular cohorts transformed the mainstream. Above all, they wanted religious forms that were relevant to the modern world. Christian rock is their most famous innovation, but that was only one aspect of their embrace of pop culture. Just as secular baby boomers popularized the concept of a consumer-oriented *lifestyle,* born-again boomers brought a personal identification with cultural fashions into the world of the church.

And "just as some of the hippies grew up to be yuppies," writes McDannell, "so Christians became more politically and socially conservative" in the 1980s and 1990s, maintaining their affiliation for pop-culture forms, but tying it to a new moralistic social agenda. It was in this era that Christian pop culture developed into a truly parallel universe, superficially similar to the mainstream, but separate and generally hostile. One result of that separation and hostility was that evangelicals could be safely ignored by the mass media—which only reinforced their separation and hostility.

In *Shaking the World for Jesus,* an academic exploration of evangelical culture, Heather Hendershot, an associate professor of media studies at the City University of New York, writes that in the heyday of Jerry Falwell's Moral Majority and Donald Wildmon's Coalition for Better Television, Christians developed a reputation as serial boycotters. "They professed to be willing to not buy cars, food, clothing, whatever it took to get objectionable shows off television. They were willing to be non-consumers with a vengeance." As a result, the thought of trying to create mainstream entertainment that would appeal to evangelicals never occurred to anyone. "Followers of Wildmon and Falwell were not seen as consumers so much as people you didn't want *not* to consume." It has only been in the last decade or so that the mainstream has recognized Christians as a market, and the implications of that are still being discovered.

○　○　○

A buzzword I heard a lot at CBA was *postmodern*. I hadn't heard the term thrown around so much, meaning so many different things, since my senior year of college in 1991. The church has been late to come to terms with postmodernity. A status quo of transformation and deconstruction is inevitably confusing, if not threatening, to large institutions, especially one with such a stake in authorial intent. Lately, however, some evangelicals have warmed to the idea. In his 2001 book *Eyes Wide Open,* evangelical professor William D. Romanowski argues that "postmodern pluralism has created a climate that is perhaps more open" to the Christian worldview than the more dichotomous modernist society was.

> For example, if race is considered an acceptable framework for Spike Lee's films, and the Eastern spirituality of songwriter Alanis Morissette is understood as an important part of her work, then shouldn't Christian perspectives also be afforded a place in our public discourse? [In postmodern society] Christian artists and critics should not adopt an attitude of "This is what we believe and it's true. Take it or leave it." But something like, "This is what life looks like from our perspective. What do you make of it?"

Screenwriter Craig Detweiler and theologian Barry Taylor go further. In the 2004 book *A Matrix of Meanings,* they write that postmodern pop culture

> offers a refreshing, alternative route to a Jesus who for many has been domesticated, declawed and kept under wraps. As the Christian church has often adopted the role of moral policeman, pop culture has assumed the role of spiritual revolutionary, subverting and frustrating those religious authorities who desperately cling to black-and-white answers in an increasingly gray world . . . Jesus spent a lot of time in public places, engaging people, hearing their stories, and telling his. He developed his theological approach within the marketplace, telling stories that made God's kingdom relevant to the people he encountered . . . Pop culture is our marketplace—the arena we visit daily to encounter issues of life and death, to discover

what it means to be human, to hear the questions society asks, to meet God. The marketplace can (and must!) inform our theology.

Other observers of postmodernity aren't so sure. Kenneth A. Myers argues that Christians cannot forget Marshall McLuhan's insight that "the medium is the message." In *All God's Children and Blue Suede Shoes* he asks, "How useful is it to borrow a cultural form if that form effectively cancels out the content you're using it to communicate?"

Myers adds that the emulation of mainstream pop culture sends an "implicit message . . . that Christians are successful to the extent that they mimic the models established by the world." The ultimate manifestation of this inferiority complex may be the adoration that evangelicals lavish on any mainstream entertainer who becomes born-again and, crucially, abandons their place in the secular entertainment firmament to serve the Christian bubble. This outside validation is so important to the parallel universe that forgotten C-listers are treated like superstars. This occurred to me when I saw hundreds of CBA attendees lining up to meet Stephen Baldwin and Kirk Cameron.

Cameron, the former *Growing Pains* kid who now stars in the *Left Behind* movies, was on hand to promote *The Way of the Master,* a "reality show" about witnessing to strangers. "There's so many people walking up and down the streets, and I can't help but think of how many of these people," he marvels in one episode, "are actually going to spend eternity in hell." Clips from *The Way of the Master* have become ironic hits on YouTube. In one, Cameron's cohost, minister Ray Comfort, describes a banana as "the atheist's worst nightmare," because it is so perfectly designed for human consumption that only God could have created it.*

Appropriately, Cameron's table at CBA was set up inside a mock "Museum of Evolution." A "schedule of events" listed items such as "Q&A session with Dr. Wemak Upstuff," "The Ascension of Man (cancelled)," and "The Ascension of Woman (rescheduled due to hair appointment)." The display's attempts at actual edification were only more embarrassing. "Evolution teaches that man evolved from apes," said one plaque. "Unfortu-

---

*An atheist's response video points out that the modern banana is a product of selective breeding that bears little resemblance to its much less palatable wild ancestor.

nately our DNA, although close, is different. Interestingly enough, DNA research has proven that all humans came from one woman." The layers of ignorance, inaccuracy, and irrelevance in those three sentences alone made me wonder what a real antievolution museum would be like.

The political and social agenda of CBA exhibitors was usually less blatant, but subtly pervasive nonetheless. T-shirts that say "Arrest me. I prayed at school today" are pretty straightforward, but others had messages that their manufacturers probably didn't even realize would alienate outsiders. To a Christian, it may be a simple declaration of fact to say "Resistance is futile . . . The King is coming back," but did no one stop to consider the undertone of a dominant religious and political movement adopting a phrase commonly associated with genocidal science-fiction aliens? Other seemingly innocuous choices revealed how evangelicalism's modern social mores can even trump biblical teachings. One fashion company had a shirt with a quote from Philippians, "Let your gentleness be evident to all." It's a fine sentiment, which Paul addressed to men and women alike. But the shirt was only available for girls. Today's Christians know that gentle boys are pussies.

I found one of the most direct sociopolitical statements at a new-exhibitor table near the front of the hall. Anthony Buie, an air force veteran from Alaska, was one of the few black exhibitors whose product was not specifically aimed at a black audience. It was a design, which he had put onto shirts, jackets, hats, and other items, showing a cross superimposed on top of an American flag. "It's the American Christian logo," he told me. "I came up with it after 9/11 when all of a sudden everyone was displaying the flag, and I said, 'Well that's fine, but where's the cross?'"

Buie is a large man with a gleaming shaved head and an apparently pathological ignorance of the concept of personal space. As soon as I approached, he was all over me, thrusting into my hands a business card and an American Christian lapel pin. "Put it on!" he boomed, smiling broadly.

"Thanks," I said, "but it's not really for me."

"You're an American," he insisted.

"Yes."

"You believe in the cross."

When I set out to explore Christian culture, I knew I would have to explain my own background to people, but I had hoped this could be done casually, without quite so much pressure. "I'm not a Christian," I said tentatively.

A look of pure astonishment flashed over Buie's face. "You're not? I thought everyone was an American Christian!"

I couldn't resist laughing. "There are still a few of us left," I assured him.

Buie looked down at me, no longer smiling. "Well, who do you think made you?"

"I'm Jewish," I said, dodging the question.

Suddenly he brightened again. "Bless you!" He threw his arm around my shoulder and proclaimed, "I love the Jewish people." I nodded and tried to wriggle free. He tightened his grip. "Don't be so uptight," Buie commanded, adding, with blissful unself-consciousness, "One of my best friends is Jewish."

Andy Butcher was on to me. The *Christian Retailing* editor had agreed to spend some time browsing exhibits with me, but he began with a friendly warning. "The easiest, cheapest shot to make at the convention is to walk around and snootily say, 'I recall reading something about Jesus driving the money changers out of the temple.' Yawn. Everybody says that and sounds incredibly righteous and pious."

I threw up my hands in surrender. I found Butcher easy to talk to. He struck me as mild-mannered, urbane, and sophisticated, traits aided no doubt by his British accent. A native of Manchester, Butcher looks and sounds remarkably like the actor Jonathan Pryce.

"Okay," I said, "but *didn't* Jesus drive the money changers out of the temple?"

"There's an element of truth to it," Butcher acknowledged. "Fundamentally it's tied to commercialism and capitalism, so there's always going to be an inherent tension. But for the most part, the people here are not out here to make a quick buck. They have something that they believe, that they want to share, and they're doing it to the best of their abilities. It's very easy if you are uninformed, or wary of faith of any kind, to talk only about money."

"Well, I'm pretty uninformed," I admitted. "Maybe the best thing to ask is, when you think about people who are totally unfamiliar with this world, what other misconceptions do they have?"

"I think they would think it's weird stuff for weird people, and the reality is that while you may fundamentally disagree with their worldview, these are commonly acceptable things for commonly accepted people. Twenty-five million people have bought *The Purpose-Driven Life*. That's not just niche groups of fundamentalists who are buying up plots of land in North Carolina to wait for the Rapture."

Butcher suggested that precisely because of such cultural and commercial successes, America's image of Christians is being transformed. "The idea that *evangelical* means *crazy nut* is fading. Hey, I've moved around the church world—we have crazy nuts. But increasingly people would recognize that a lot of this stuff is on the shelf at Barnes & Noble, and your friends and neighbors are buying it."

Meanwhile, this attention from mainstream retailers has put pressure on Christians to improve the quality of their goods. "Another thing that would be a common misconception," said Butcher, "is that Christian products are second-rate, amateurish, and cheesy. Historically that's more true, but I think that's changing remarkably, especially with books. I mean, Barnes & Noble doesn't carry hokey stuff. They're not in it for philanthropy."

Another factor driving up the quality of Christian entertainment, said Butcher, is that the days when Christians shunned secular culture are over—which means many Christian products are competing against the best of the general market, although Christians still cut them lots of slack. While the Christian pop-culture bubble does a good job of keeping non-Christians out, it no longer functions to keep Christians in. "They're not in a hermetically sealed environment," Butcher said. According to one 2006 study, while 78 percent of churchgoers listen to Christian music, it accounts for less than half of their overall music consumption. Only 7 percent listen to Christian music exclusively and only 1 percent watch only Christian television.

I mentioned that a lot of what I'd seen seemed to reflect the culture of contemporary Middle America even as it presented itself as the timeless message of Jesus.

"This is definitely American Christianity," Butcher replied. "There is a very individualistic emphasis on a lot of the material. It's *me and my God; me and my life.* Which is a true and relevant and appropriate aspect of Christian life, but from a European perspective that would be overemphasized. Some people would question too the emphasis on prosperity. And hey, it's America—it's bigger and brighter and brasher."

On cue, our walk around the hall brought us past the Christian pirate, who gave a cheery wave. When I'd first met him, I'd been flabbergasted at the shamelessness of jumping onto the pirate trend, but later it occurred to me that it only was a trend because lots of people—not just Christians—jumped on it shamelessly and without a shred of integrity. That also got me thinking about some of the musicians I'd seen with my sister-in-law and her friends in Kansas. One was a singer whom I'd pegged as a Christian Ashlee Simpson, but now I realized that the general market was also filled with girls trying to be Ashlee Simpson. To a great extent, imitation is inherent in all pop culture.

"I'm glad you mentioned that," Butcher said. "Sometimes external observers who look at our industry are a little unduly critical of that. They don't recognize that it happens everywhere." He added that embracing trends to spread the gospel didn't have to be seen as sneaky. "If you are trying to communicate to people, it makes sense that you want to find a common currency, a bridge that you can communicate across." He glanced around. "Now, having said that, you can do it with style or you can do it tackily. But that's true in any endeavor, not just the Christian retailing world."

I nodded. "That's true, but I have to say that from what I've seen, it kind of looks like tacky is winning."

Butcher sighed ruefully. "When you are born again, God gives you a new heart and a new opportunity. He doesn't necessarily give you new taste."

When the week at CBA came to an end, my suitcase was bulging with Jesus junk and my head was equally overstuffed with questions. If I wanted to make sense of everything I had found here, I'd need context. My next excursion, I decided, would be to the birthplace of Christian pop culture: first-century Jerusalem.

2

The new Jerusalem

In the lobby of any hotel in Orlando, Florida, you will find a rack of tourist brochures enticing you to visit not just Disney World, Universal Studios, and SeaWorld, but dozens of specialty destinations as well: Dolly Parton's Dixie Stampede, Pirate's Cove Adventure Golf, Arabian Nights dinner theater. In among these is a glossy, exclamation-point-filled pamphlet bearing the royal purple and gold logo of the Holy Land Experience, America's most elaborate, expensive, and popular "Bible adventure park." A re-creation of first-century Jerusalem "that brings the world of the Bible to life." Leprosy and incest, here we come.

Driving north on I-4, the first sign of the Holy Land Experience is the gold-tipped crown of Herod's Temple—the Cinderella Castle of the park, as the real temple once was of ancient Jerusalem. The actual edifice, built some 20 years before Christ, was 150 feet tall and would have loomed over the billboards for discount furniture outlets and local radio stations. This 5/8-scale replica merely peeks. If you weren't looking for it, you'd never know it was there. But people are looking for it: church groups in buses, tourists in rental cars, devout locals with yearlong Jerusalem Gold Passes. Some two hundred thousand pilgrims visit every year.

When the Holy Land Experience opened in February 2001, it raised a few eyebrows. Not so much because it cost $16 million to build, covered 15 acres, and was designed by leaders in manufactured reality who had worked for Disney, Six Flags, and World of Coca-Cola. That was all par for the course, both for Orlando and Sun Belt evangelicalism. What surprised people was the park's decidedly Jewish flavor. The way cast members greeted guests with a full-on "shalom!" before guiding them into the Shofar Auditorium. The explanation, and controversy, quickly spread from the Florida papers to *Time* magazine to Bill O'Reilly: the Holy Land Experience was the vision of a man named Marvin Rosenthal—born Jewish, converted to Christianity as a teenager, and on a mission ever since to persuade those he still considers his fellow Jews that Jesus is their messiah. Rosenthal calls himself a Messianic Jew or Hebrew Christian, but he insisted that the Holy Land Experience was not created for the purpose of converting anyone. Local rabbis weren't buying it, and they raised a fuss, generating a wave of publicity for the theme park and inadvertently helping Rosenthal score the "PR Play of the Week" in *PR Week* magazine. But the debate fizzled away after a protest on opening day attracted only four people, and it officially became irrelevant in mid-2005 when the Holy Land Experience's board of directors forced Rosenthal out of office over falling revenues and disagreements about focusing attention on Jews, who weren't buying many tickets anyway.*

Which is not to say that for a Jewish visitor, the Holy Land Experience isn't still unsettling. Rosenthal's departure hasn't changed the Hebraic emphasis of the park, it's just that now all the Jewish trappings are said to be for the purpose of helping Christians better understand their roots. "Christianity has often emphasized the New Testament and has been neglectful of what the Old Testament has contributed," explained Dan Hayden, who replaced Rosenthal as executive director. Hayden is a dapper Southern radio minister with a precise manner and equally precise moustache. "Jesus was a Jew," he continued. "All the writers of the New Testament were Jewish." The problem is, Christians and Jews have very different ideas about what the contributions of the Old Testament are. For starters, Christians—or at least the ones who build theme parks based on it—tend to see the Old Testament as an elaborate game of connect the dots. Do it right and it spells out J-E-S-U-S. Jews like to think that it stands pretty well on its own, which is why we call it not the Old Testament but the Bible. Passing through the convincingly ancient gates of the Holy Land Experi-

---

*In June 2007, more than a year after my visit, HLE was acquired by the Trinity Broadcasting Network, a major Christian cable network.

ence expecting these differences to be understood and respected is just asking for abuse.

As Hayden led me past the pottery stands and meticulously weathered walls of the Jerusalem Street Market—where cast members in flowing tunics tuned their lyres and adjusted their handlooms for a day of providing ambience and, if engaged in conversation, in-character testimony regarding the miracles of a certain itinerant rabbi—he tried to impress something very important upon me: "We are not a theme park." If I was to refer to the Holy Land Experience as anything, it should be "themed ministry," "biblical attraction," or "living biblical attraction."

Hayden paused momentarily to show off the Plaza of Nations, a checkerboard courtyard of imitation marble that fronts Herod's Temple. I suppose it was meant to be impressive, but up close, the six-story building looked squat and the golden door that marked the entrance to the sacred inner sanctum (or that would if it actually opened) failed to glow with holy mystery. Also, it was an excessively sunny South Florida morning and the unbroken expanse of off-white was hurting my eyes. Though not yet 11 a.m., the thermometer had already passed fire and was climbing toward brimstone, so I was grateful when Hayden offered me a seat in the shaded royal portico, where we could look out at the cool blue pond that separates the Holy Land Experience from the highway access road. On the far shore, the pistachio-green hedges were trimmed into the forty-foot message "He Is Risen."

Hayden's insistence on avoiding the words *theme park* was not a matter of pride or semantics but law. A few weeks before my visit, the Holy Land Experience had finally triumphed in a four-year court battle to qualify for tax-exempt status as a religious institution. While not a church per se, Hayden explained, the Holy Land Experience is a not-for-profit "parachurch organization." The $35 admission fee? No different from having to buy a ticket for your local church's nativity play. The ruling saves the ministry some $215,000 a year in property taxes. As miracles go, it may not be on par with loaves and fishes, but it's got to be up there with water into wine. Hayden did admit that this designation imposes some unfortunate limits. "We have to be very careful about the kind of entertainment we would bring in that wouldn't have genuine ministry value, but that would just be dressing," he said. "You know, 'There were animals on Noah's Ark, so let's have a carousel.'" Not that these limits are never tested. Early on, administrators were surprised when so many people brought their children only to find that there wasn't much for them to do. Hence the hastily conceived mascot, Qaboo the camel, and his "archeological" sandbox. "What does that have to do with the Bible?" Hayden asked rhetorically. "Well, it doesn't, but it does attract the kids."

Hayden hustled me back to the Qumran Caves, where one of the park's periodic dramatic vignettes was about to begin. In real life, the caves were the hiding place of the Dead Sea Scrolls. Here, they are a storage space for the maintenance staff, though Hayden hopes to install an exhibit in the future; perhaps even the scrolls themselves if he can get a loaner from Israel. Though dollhouse-sized compared to the real thing, the cliffs' striated orange undulations go a fair way toward imbuing the Holy Land Experience with whatever Middle Eastern charm it has, as do the mildly fragrant olive trees, aloe, and pomegranate interspersed among the native Florida flora. As at Disney, hidden speakers filled the sticky air with constant background music, an inspirational symphony of soaring strings and triumphal brass that very nearly concealed the hum of twenty-first-century traffic just beyond the walls.

The vignette began with a blind beggar in a fraying but clean cloak and a scarf of rags pulled over his eyes. A hundred and fifty tourists began snapping digital pictures, and I wondered if the New York City subway couldn't reposition itself as an attraction and up the price of a MetroCard by $33. Then, to my surprise, several members of the audience walked up and pressed real American money into the beggar's hands, almost as if they thought he might really be needy (the money is set aside for charity, a cast member told me later). Soon other characters emerged. Civilians in cinched, ankle-length tunics, Roman officials in slightly more authoritative versions of the same, and a sinister black-clad Pharisee, looking miserable from the heat and the denying of the messiah.

A few uncharitable pedestrians tried to hustle away the unsightly blind Bartimaeus, only to be stopped in their tracks when *he* appeared—Jesus himself, resplendent in snow-white tunic, red velvet robe, leather Tevas, and shoulder-length blond hair. Also, he was wearing a headset microphone of the kind favored by pop stars and fast-food jockeys. It was not clear whether he planned to restore Bartimaeus's eyesight or offer him fries with that.

Once the healing of the blind man was dispatched, Jesus smiled serenely and began to tend his flock. "He touched me!" a little boy squealed in delight to his beaming mother. The Holy Land Experience has not only a dress code (no halter tops, short shorts, or bathing suits) but a "worship code," under which the management "reserves the right to remove anyone from the facilities if their religious activity, in our judgment, causes a disturbance." Visitors to the real holy land have sometimes been known to come down with Jerusalem syndrome, the delusion that they are biblical figures or prophets who must proclaim the word of God loudly, incessantly, and dressed in togas fashioned from their hotel linens. Now that Jesus was preaching, I watched carefully for smaller-scale manifestations of Jerusalem syndrome here, but had to settle for the excited whisper of one woman who grabbed her girlfriend and gushed, "He looks so beautiful with that hair!"

Jesus's ministry amounted to a medley of his greatest hits—a whirlwind spin from "render unto Caesar" to "the lilies of the field." It was solid material, though when he asked, "Why do you care about the clothes you wear?" I wondered if he had noticed the woman in the polka-dot shirt and rainbow umbrella hat, who didn't seem to care in the least. There was no overturning of the moneychangers' tables, which was probably for the best, as it might not have gone over well with the nearby vendor selling milk-and-honey ice cream and Thirsty Camel Coolers.

Offstage, Jesus is Les Cheveldayoff, a forty-year-old Saskatchewanian who had been starring in South Florida Passion plays for nearly a decade before the Holy Land Experience discovered him. It was easy to see why. People see Les at the mall, or driving his car, and they yell, "Hey, Jesus!" Or else they stare at him and say, "You remind me of an actor or somebody." At Blockbuster, the guy at the counter wants to know what Jesus is renting. "It's amazing how much people are listening or watching," he told me during a break. "I have to keep saying, 'Someone's watching you all the time.'"

But while I was mesmerized by how much Les looked like Jesus, it occurred to me that of course I didn't really know what Jesus looked like at all. All I knew was what Americans think Jesus looked like, which is by and large Warner Sallman's 1941 painting *Head of Christ* (Les isn't quite such a pretty boy; he more resembles the Del Parson portrait that is the official Jesus of the Mormons). I broached this with Hayden, nervous about what he'd say to my gentle suggestion that a Semite from the Middle East might have looked a touch more Middle Eastern and Semitic. To my surprise, he copped to it readily. "It may not be accurate, but it's what people expect, so it doesn't distract them," he explained. "We don't want any obstacles to the message, people saying, 'Well, that's not what Jesus looks like.' With Les, people will accept him without questioning." I soon found that despite repeated claims to the accuracy of the Holy Land Experience, this philosophy—sacrificing authenticity for ease of use—was pervasive here. When leading people to the truth, you can't let reality get in the way.

"Because we're living in a postmodern world where people are very sensory, they're not so much interested in the cerebral aspect of things: they want to feel it," said Hayden, sounding suspiciously like those French philosophers I tried to avoid studying in college. "The Holy Land Experience is like a historical novel, where the novel is not authentic but the history is. The simulation helps you realize that Jesus was a real person, he really did die. So that enhances the understanding and turns it from a theological understanding to an experiential one. It's like the difference between understanding marriage as an institution and enjoying your wife." He pointed out that the park's scale model of ancient Jerusalem—that is, a miniature model inside the larger, more impressionistic model that is the park itself—is actually in more than one scale, so that nothing is rendered too small. Also, the piped-in music resembles the soundtrack to a 1950s Bible film, not AD 1 flutes and lyres.

But this isn't a museum or a textbook, after all; it's a theme park. Sorry, a living biblical attraction. Hyperreality is its métier. This is why Hayden brushes off snickers about his chosen method of sharing the gospel. "People see that there has been change in the methodology of presentation, so they think the message is changing. But just like you as a person can put on different clothes, you change the way you present yourself, but who you are does not change. Methods will change because culture changes, and if you're going to communicate to a culture, you don't want to be looking archaic." To see this change in action, Hayden encouraged me to check out the show that was about to start at the Shofar Auditorium, *Praise Through the Ages*.

As I found a seat in the sleek, gently lit, blessedly cool theater, I recognized a middle-aged black woman nearby as one of the people who gave alms to the simulated blind beggar at Qumran. I asked her why she gave, when she knew he didn't really need it. Raquel thought it over. "I guess it wasn't for him," she said. "It's more the feeling you get from giving to someone." It was Hayden's postmodernism again. At the Holy Land Experience, you can feel more deeply charitable by pretending to help the poor. This was Raquel's first time here, and she was enjoying it just fine, but it turned out she and her husband had been to the real Jerusalem. I asked how the Holy Land Experience compared, and she gave me an *are you serious?* stare. "It doesn't."

Praise Through the Ages, said my "Scroll of Events," is "a unique union of music and art and how they have been used to praise God." I wasn't sure how projecting paintings onto screens and then singing songs from roughly the same time period was either unique or a union, exactly, but that was the basic idea. The emcee was apparently some kind of Renaissance painter. He carried a wooden brush and pallet and wore a beret, black leggings, and a lace-up shirt.

As the show got under way, the two most bewildering aspects of the Holy Land Experience—the appropriation of Judaism and the accuracy-lite simulations of reality—suddenly merged. The first age of praise was represented by a buxom Hebrew woman swinging a water jug and chanting cantorially, "*Kadosh, kadosh, kadosh Elohim Adonai tzvaot.*" Anyone who has ever been to synagogue will recognize that as standard prayer language. It simply means, like almost all Jewish prayers, "Holy, holy, holy Lord God, etc." Then the song continued in English. Audiences that don't know Hebrew might reasonably assume that the second verse was a translation of the first, but it was not. The English line was "I live to love you as I should," which is a distinctively Christian sentiment that Jews, ancient or modern, would be unlikely to sing. That may not seem like a big deal, but imagine you're a Catholic and you heard someone render *Dominus vobiscum* as "There is no God but God." You might think some Muslims were getting a little presumptuous, no matter how delicious their Thirsty Camel Coolers were.

Or perhaps I'm overly sensitive. After all, the next age of praise was Gregorian chant, and they warped that too. If you remember only one thing from Intro to Music History—and I do—it's that plainsong, by definition, has no harmony. Perhaps figuring that this would get boring after more than a minute and a half, the Holy Land Experience's monks started out monophonic, but soon shifted into three-part harmony. A music fan in front of me muttered unhappily to his wife. With subsequent leaps forward in time, the art, music, and dance became more elaborate, though not any better. For the introduction to the final age, the transitional music suddenly turned ominous and the paintings projected in the background took on a darker hue. They seemed to be pastiches of Kandinsky and Miró, only with a lot more dead bodies than the masters usually depicted. The painter emcee spoke somberly, to the extent that one can while wearing a beret, leggings, and lace-up shirt. "Much of modern art is abstract, confusing, and frightening," he declared. "It is, unfortunately, a sign of the moral decline of civilization. But not all music has abandoned form and beauty—like contemporary Christian music!" Thus reassured, we reached the big finale.

When describing *Praise Through the Ages* to me, Dan Hayden had chuckled over just how contemporary the show's contemporary Christian music was. "They're doing all the stuff, the choreography," he said, jerking his arms around in a manner that had me prepared for some electric boogaloo. The teenagers in my row perked up for the first time. Soon enough, however, they were slumping again. Later I would realize that the Holy Land Experience's version of contemporary Christian music is to real CCM what most CCM is to secular pop: a thin, watery rip-off. As the show let out, one woman headed to the gift counter and asked if a CD was available.

I headed for the Oasis Palms Café, an inviting evocation of a desert encampment, with rough-hewn tables and swaying electric candelabras. Before the park opened, Marvin Rosenthal hoped to serve only authentic Middle Eastern food, but his partners advised him that persuading Americans to forgo hot dogs and hamburgers would be slightly more difficult than merely convincing Jews to worship Jesus. The menu board featured Goliath Burgers, Jaffa Hot Dogs, Tabgha Tuna, and Bedouin Beef. This last was served in a pita with couscous, and was the park's only acknowledgment of the existence of Muslims. I ordered the Holy Land Sampler, featuring such exotic dishes as falafel, tabouli, and hummus, and immediately

realized that I should have stuck with the burger. Holy Land's Middle Eastern fare was no more authentic than anything else in the park, and about as
palatable as its contemporary Christian music.

Unfortunately, an even greater challenge to my stomach lay ahead. The
Wilderness Tabernacle is one of the Holy Land Experience's signature
attractions, a nearly life-size replica of the sanctuary-cum-temple where
the Hebrews kept the Ark of the Covenant while wandering in the desert.
The Israelites built the original tabernacle because they were commanded
to by God, as recounted in Exodus 26. Rebuilding it based on the precise
instructions given in that chapter has been a hobby of American Christians
since at least the nineteenth century, for no apparent reason except that the
goyim like to tinker, and when they see instructions for assembling something, that sounds to them like a fun way to spend an afternoon. "The
length of one curtain shall be eight and twenty cubits, and the breadth of
one curtain four cubits," reads the King James. "And thou shalt make loops
of blue upon the edge of the one curtain from the selvedge in the coupling;
and likewise shalt thou make in the uttermost edge of another curtain, in
the coupling of the second." Yeah, right. Jews can't even put together a
media cabinet from IKEA without mysterious pieces left over.

The entrance to the Holy Land Experience tabernacle is marked by a
lovely acacia tree, the type of tree from which the original tabernacle was
built. I asked Hayden if the Holy Land Experience also used acacia, and his
moustache twitched. "No, I think it's good old-fashioned American lum-
ber," he said. "Home Depot." Also, the outer wall was made not from
badger skin but theatrical scrim, so that when the light changes, it seems to
disappear, allowing the audience to see the priest when he steps inside.

Ironically, given the humble origins of the Wilderness Tabernacle, this
was the first time I got a sense of the money involved in creating the Holy
Land Experience. While the narration was fairly dry, the pulsing and shim-
mering sound and light effects created a divine ambience that the Holy
Spirit alone can't buy. Later I found an article about the tabernacle show in
a 2001 issue of *Entertainment Design* magazine:

Equipment included ETC Source Four Jr. Zooms, a wide range of
Altman instruments, including 6" fresnels and striplights, Q-Lites,

Microellipses, and 3" fresnels, Gam Twinspin2 Jrs., Times Square Lighting PAR-36 pinspots, ETC Sensor 2.4K dimmers, and High End Systems Technobeams®, plus Diversitronics Star Strobes and Le Maitre G300 and G150 foggers. The lights are run on an Alcorn McBride Light Cue and DMX Machine, with Pathway DMX repeaters.

I haven't the slightest idea what any of that means, but it sounds expensive.

The highlight of the show came when the priest called forth the Shekinah—the radiance of God—from the Ark. While this hasn't happened in real life for quite some time, everyone knows what it must have looked like, either because they're familiar with Leviticus 16:2 or they've seen *Raiders of the Lost Ark.* The Holy Land Experience may not have Spielberg money, but the "combination of fog from the Le Maitre units and high pressure CO_2 from Sigma Systems, which is then blasted into the air at speeds of 40mph and lit with the Technobeam" was mighty impressive.

The production closed with a traditional Hebrew prayer, offered, less traditionally, "in Jesus's name." My fellow audience members bowed their heads respectfully, but no one seemed on the verge of shouting a hallelujah, much less declaring themselves Moses and setting up camp inside the Tabernacle. The guests I talked to—all committed Christians, with the exception of one "seeking" woman who was persuaded to join a more devout colleague for a visit—were uniformly upbeat about the park but not particularly moved.

When the Holy Land Experience opened, the Tabernacle was its flashiest exhibit. But six months later, a new building was constructed at a cost of $12 million—the Scriptorium. It was created to house an astonishing collection of antique Bibles donated to Marvin Rosenthal by his spiritual mentor, Robert Van Kampen. "The rest of the park is virtual," said Hayden. "When you walk into the building on the far end, it ceases being virtual and it's real. Every manuscript you see is real. It's the largest collection of biblical manuscripts in the world," including a 1455 Gutenberg Bible fragment and a 1611 King James.

Van Kampen, who died in 1999, was an investment banker whose net worth was estimated by *Forbes* at $290 million. In his later years, Van Kampen threw himself into religion the way only one of the 400 wealthiest people in the nation can: He collected rare manuscripts, started a couple of churches, and invented a doctrine about the end of the world called the prewrath Rapture. It's way too complicated to get into here—suffice it to say that it involves the reincarnation of Adolf Hitler and it drives people who believe in normal stuff like the *Left Behind* books insane. Books and videos based on Van Kampen's home-brewed eschatology are available at all Holy Land Experience gift shops.

The Scriptorium is like Disney's Haunted Mansion, except you walk through instead of riding, and instead of ghouls, there are Bibles. You enter through ancient Mesopotamia—the black-light murals of ziggurats resemble nothing so much as a Yes album cover—and, room by room, trace the history of written scripture. Anyone even remotely interested in religious and historical artifacts will be genuinely spellbound by much of what is on display here: a 1537 Bible stained with the blood of the martyr who died protecting it, the first Bible printed in America (in 1663, in Algonquin), and an 1834 Bible printed in gold. Maybe that last one seemed gaudy and gimmicky at the time, but it's almost awe-inspiring 170 years later.

But the Holy Land imagineers chose not to gamble on large numbers of people being interested in religious and historical artifacts, so in every room, the feature attraction is not the texts on display but the displays themselves. Elaborate re-creations of a medieval monastery, Gutenberg's printing shop, and John Bunyan's prison cell come complete with moving walls and dizzying sound and light displays. Then there's the audio-animatronic figure of Bible translator John Wycliffe. That's right: John Wycliffe. In your face, Hall of Presidents. The people in my group were definitely primed when we stepped out of the building. One man looked at his watch and blurted, "Ooh! The crucifixion is starting!"

Holy Land Experience's Passion play—Passion musical, really—takes place every day at precisely 4:20. Les Cheveldayoff told me that as far as other portrayals of Jesus go, his most significant influence is *The Passion of the Christ*'s Jim Caviezel, "but more from a makeup standpoint than anything else. We used to do not as much makeup. After seeing that we said, 'We've gotta take it up a notch.'" The believers gathered outside Calvary's Garden Tomb gasped and reached for their cameras as four Roman centurions in bronze chest plates and short but manly leather-accented skirts dragged the beaten son of God into view. He was scarred, drenched in blood, laboring under the weight of his yoke, and the crown of thorns was doing nothing for his hair. As a final humiliation, he had been stripped of his headset. Jesus will not get a song and dance in this scene.*

The centurions led Jesus to the hill overlooking the garden. "He was probably not crucified on a hill," Dan Hayden volunteered preemptively, "but this gives people a better view, and it's more dramatic." Among his weeping followers I spotted a cast member I'd spoken to earlier named Makia (that's her real name; her character is Lydia, a dealer in purple cloth, which was apparently a viable career at the time). Makia used to work at Disney World, but she prefers this because her roles are more challenging, she believes in the message, and she gets to interact with guests. "The closest I had to that before was Busch Gardens, where I escorted our costumed character, which was Super Duck." And *he* never died for anyone's sins.

As the centurions raised Jesus's cross—aided by hidden hydraulics—I noticed one woman praying. Most people, though, were shooting video. If anyone was going to be overwhelmed with the need to cause a disturbance for the Lord, now would be the time, but fingers remained steadily in control of zoom buttons. In fact, no one I spoke to could recall any instances of outrageous behavior in the past either, though Les did offer that one woman briefly interrupted a scene when she ran forward to touch the hem of his garment. I half suspected that the worship code was no more than a publicity stunt to get people excited, the way 1950s horror movies would post warnings for people with weak hearts.

After the final number I made my way down to the tomb where Jesus had been laid. A blast of cold air greeted me and the simulated dankness was a relief from the 98-degree heat. I could see why someone would linger here for three days. Access to the inner chamber was off-limits, though. All I could see was a stone bed and a sign on the wall: "He is not here, for He is risen."

○ ○ ○

---

*In fact, Jesus does not get to sing in any of the park's productions, despite the fact that Les is said to have a beautiful voice and once sang in a Christian hard-rock band.

Before I stepped through the looking glass into the world of evangelical culture, I would have assumed—had it even occurred to me that such a thing existed—that a Bible theme park would be a one-of-a-kind place. But the Holy Land Experience is not the only Christian theme park in America. It was not the first. And it is definitely not the most creepy.

The most popular theme park in the United States, by attendance, is Walt Disney World. The second most popular is Disneyland. The third, with 6.1 million visitors in 2005, is Universal Studios Florida.

In 1986, the most popular theme park in the country was Disney World, followed by Disneyland. But number three on the list, with roughly the same number of visitors that Universal Studios has today, was Heritage USA, the 2,300-acre Christian playground, resort, and ultimately, fraud mechanism built in Fort Mill, South Carolina, by pioneering televangelists Jim and Tammy Faye Bakker. More than any other individuals, the Bakkers can take credit, or blame, for inventing modern Christian pop culture. Although Pat Robertson started the Christian Broadcasting Network in 1961, it was the Bakkers who infused it with entertainment—and made it a hit. The Bakkers joined CBN in 1964, and helped transform a dry fundraising telethon called *The 700 Club* into TV's first Christian talk show. They went on to cofound the Trinity Broadcasting Network, which eventually became the largest religious television network in the world, and then launched their own TV ministry, PTL.*

A delirious mix of prayer, music, weeping, comedy, greed, eyeliner, and pastels, PTL's programming was the pinnacle of 1980s Christian kitsch. Though remembered today chiefly for the scandal that led to its demise, PTL was extraordinarily influential in its embracing of pop-culture forms for spreading the gospel. Heritage USA opened in 1978 with the Bakkers' TV studio as its centerpiece. Before long it had grown into a massive $200 million leisure complex. Disney-esque touches included a soaring castle—housing an arcade and go-kart track—and a fantasy Main Street

---

*Alternately said to stand for "Praise the Lord" or "People That Love."

with three-story Victorian facades (on one-story shops with names like Heavenly Fudge and Der Bakker's Bakkery). The main attraction—other than Jim and Tammy Faye themselves—was an enchantingly landscaped water park: a five-acre island of beaches, wave pools, and waterfalls. The most enduring image from Heritage USA is of Jerry Falwell plunging stiffly down the five-hundred-foot Typhoon Slide in a dark blue suit after he took control of PTL. Periodically, revelers would be asked to climb out so the pools could be used for baptisms. "People ask me why a Christian complex needs a water park," Jim Bakker told *The New York Times* in 1985. "Well, if the Bible says we are to be fishers of men, then a water park is just the bait, and I don't see anything wrong in using some pretty fancy bait."

On the weekend of July 4, 1987, sociologist Thomas O'Guinn and business professor Russell Belk visited Heritage to conduct field research. Their insights, published in the *Journal of Consumer Research,* reveal much about the appeal of the Bakkers' theme park and, though they could not know it at the time, about the twenty years of Christian pop culture that would follow.

"A central theme of Heritage Village is the idealized past and its associated values," write O'Guinn and Belk. It was a theme perfectly in synch with the mytho-politics of the new religious right: "The intense yearning of millions of Americans to return to a simpler, more innocent time when there was no limit to America's resources, power and influence; when conformity prevailed and there were few challenges to value systems and to authority." As a living model of this idealized past, Heritage served an important role in the rise of the movement.

O'Guinn and Belk were particularly fascinated by the "perpetual twilight" lighting of Main Street, where the vaulted ceiling showed a projection of clouds during the day and stars at night. "Dramatists use such lighting when they are attempting to convey detachment from reality, dream and fantasy states, and heaven," they write. The effect was only one way in which Heritage reinforced the idea of separateness from the corrupt world. One teenager told them, "You can talk to people here about anything, but not in the 'real' world because you are a Christian. Everybody makes fun of them." It was heaven defined in part as a refuge from hostile, secular others.

Most incisively, O'Guinn and Belk note that by suggesting to patrons that Heritage is a slice of heaven on earth, the park liberated visitors to indulge in luxuries that more traditional forms of Protestantism might have frowned on.

> The creation of a metaphorical heaven greatly facilitates indulgent consumption through the removal of normal restraints. Heaven is a place of reward, where the long suffering children of God are to want no more. At Heritage Village, consumption is encouraged by a retail environment that matches the shared associations (i.e., heaven and reward) of visitors and that couples this consumption imperative with the explicit model and sanction, via television advertising and direct mail marketing forms, of a luxury-loving spiritual leader.

As a sign of how thoroughly Heritage had turned consumerism into a sacred pursuit, the shopping mall, not the church, was the physical and social center of the complex. "The religious and the secular have so inter-penetrated one another that a real question emerges as to where sacredness resides at the site—in God or in goods." It is a question people are still asking twenty years later.

The mystique of Heritage among many Christians is so strong that although the abandoned and decaying site has changed hands several times since Jim Bakker's humiliating fall, it has almost always remained "within the church," as various people have schemed to recapture its former glory. Today, the largest portion is owned by a wild-eyed prophet named Rick Joyner, who has made a career of predicting apocalyptic disaster and who believes that Jesus will only return once Christians conquer the world in his name. Joyner plans to build a new conference center and Christian retail complex on the site, along with studios for recording worship music—which he calls "war ship music." There will be a "refirement" community for senior citizens and a kids' ministry in the old castle.

One of the stores on the old Heritage Main Street was a clothing emporium called J. Charles, Ltd. It was named after Jim and Tammy Faye's son Jamie Charles, a delicate, moon-faced boy who grew up on the air and was beloved by the Bakkers' flock. Every year, the ministry mailed copies of his school picture to six hundred thousand members. Jamie's life was like something out of a dark fairy tale: He grew up as a prince in a magical land—his very own amusement park—but the price he paid was parents who were largely absent from his life, and a near-biblical expulsion at the age of eleven when his father was caught in an extramarital affair and arrested for selling time-shares in hotel rooms he hadn't built.

As an adolescent, Jamie grew to believe that God hated him—if there was a God—and that Christians were a bunch of hypocritical elitists. He turned to drinking, drugs, and punk rock. Eventually, Jamie started reading the Bible again, and decided that only the hypocritical elitists part was true. The scriptures didn't say all that stuff he'd been taught: that you had to behave a certain way or you wouldn't be good enough for God. Instead, he decided, what the Bible says is that Jesus loves you and forgives you no matter who you are or what you do. He sobered up and started his own tiny church, Revolution. He made up T-shirts with the church's slogan, "Religion kills," and advertised it with stickers that said, "As Christians, we're sorry for being self-righteous judgmental bastards." Not long ago, I found out that Jay Bakker, as he is now known, was expanding his church from Atlanta to Brooklyn, where I live. I sent him an e-mail welcoming him to the neighborhood, and he invited me to come hear his first sermon, at a bar in the hipster mecca of Williamsburg.

"I enjoy hanging out in bars," Bakker said when I met him. "I've been sober for almost eleven years now, but there's just something about a bar." Like many new residents of Williamsburg, Bakker looked like he belonged nowhere else. The cuffs of his dark blue Diesel jeans were rolled up precisely three inches. His T-shirt—a cigarette-smoking skull wearing an aviator's helmet beneath the words "It's only a matter of time"—was both ominous and obscure. Intricate tattoos covered both his arms. His boyish face was framed by chunky black Ray-Bans and topped with a gray Izod cap. He had holes in each ear, and his lip appeared to be stapled.

Jay hadn't exactly been run out of the South—he moved here so that his wife could attend med school at NYU—but he did hope that New York would be more receptive to his message of grace, which includes the understanding that homosexuality is not a sin. On the other hand, New Yorkers tended to be much more suspicious of evangelicals in general, even progressive ones. "We're kind of in the middle," he said. "We're too Christian for a certain group and not Christian enough for another group. Which is the dumbest thing I've *ever* heard in my life—being 'not Christian enough.' But you start accepting gay people, you're a heretic."

We stepped outside so Jay could light an American Spirit cigarette, and I asked him about Heritage. He said he had a lot of fond memories, although in retrospect it had been bizarre. He used to threaten to have employees fired if they upset him. "At one point, I thought could fire somebody in *any* place, because I thought my dad owned the world."

Jay came to decide that the whole idea of Heritage—and of Christian pop culture in general—was a ghastly mistake. "It's all about us going into our own little world, and it's Us and Them. I don't think that's a very Christ-like view of the world." He used his father's ministry as a classic example. "'We have a church, but now we have to have a water park that people can hang out at. We've got to have stuff as good as the world.' But I think that's where we make a mistake, that *we've* got to be as good as *them*. We keep on missing it: It shouldn't be all about private places, or a private pop culture."

Jay stubbed out his cigarette on the stoop. "I hate holding regret in my life," he said, "but if I could go back and change it, I don't think I would have been raised in a Christian bubble. I think it opens you up to being judgmental and naïve. I remember the first time when I was at Heritage USA and I saw a guy with earrings. He must have been a biker or an old hippie or something, he was wearing all this turquoise stuff. I was like, 'That guy's got earrings! It's crazy!' Like, I was almost *scared*. It just seems like that's not a healthy place to grow up, where you're constantly protected and constantly taught 'Well, this is how everybody thinks.'"

He continued, "We've created this culture and these big events and these big things, and it seems like these things sort of take on a mind of their own. It becomes bigger than people."

"Bigger than the faith?"

"I don't think bigger *actually* than the faith, but it definitely becomes a distraction. We forget that we're supposed to love people and build rela-tionships, and take care of the sick and the poor and the suffering, and the basic things of Christianity. All of a sudden, the next thing you know, we're out there preaching the gospel of get-rich-quick because we want to build this grand thing for everybody to come in, and in order for us to do that, we have to say"—he slipped into a televangelist voice, sounding eerily like his father—"'God will bless you if you donate.' See, then it's not about the people anymore. It's about feeding a monster that we've created."

Just before we parted ways, Jay told me a story. "There was this preacher who was a friend of my dad's, and he used to say, 'Jim, you just became in love with the box rather than what was inside it,' and Heritage was the box. But now that I reflect on it, I don't think it was so much that my dad was in love with the box. It was that the people he wanted to reach became in love with the box rather than what was inside of it. That's what's dangerous with pop culture, is that we become in love with this box."

3

He will act deceitfully

When Jim Bakker opened Heritage USA, he cited two great inspirations. One was Disney. The other was a park in Eureka Springs, Arkansas, called New Holy Land, created by a man named Gerald L. K. Smith. New Holy Land has lost much of its newness by now, but unlike Heritage, it is still open to the public. The fifty-acre park features a ramshackle collection of "thirty-eight historically accurate exhibits" from the world of Jesus: the inn where he was born; the Sea of Galilee, where tourists can snap pictures of him walking on the water; the tomb, with its "He is not here, for He is risen" sign. And if it's all a little shabby—if the first-century innkeeper forgets to remove his gold watch, or the Sea of Galilee is more like a pond, or the concession stand at the tomb sells only one flavor of ice cream—it hardly matters, because no one is really here for any of that anyway. The New Holy Land is only a side attraction, something to do while waiting for the main event in Eureka Springs: *The Great Passion Play*. Ambitious as the New Holy Land is, the play is Gerald Smith's greatest accomplishment.

Gerald L. K. Smith ran for president of the United States three times, in 1944, 1948, and 1956. The first time, as the candidate of the America First Party, he won 1,780 votes. The second time, running under the banner of the newly formed Christian Nationalist Party, he won forty-two. In his final campaign, Smith received eleven write-in votes, and packed it in.

World War II had not been good to Smith, but he never expressed any regrets about backing, at least philosophically, the losing side. Smith stood by his principles. Principles such as shipping all black Americans to Africa and "the preservation of our Christian faith against the threat of Jew Communism." But he must have felt some pangs about being reduced to just another kook. Not too long before, he had been famous and influential. A fourth-generation Midwestern preacher, Smith had captivated radio audiences with his powerful sermons. In the 1920s, he became a top aide to Louisiana populist Huey Long, and after Long's assassination in 1935—which Smith witnessed from inches away—he anointed himself Long's successor, teaming up with Father Charles Coughlin in a frenzied campaign to drive "Franklin D. Jewsevelt" out of the White House. An appalled and awestruck H. L. Mencken declared him the greatest orator of all time. "Not the greatest by an inch or a foot or a yard or a mile, but the greatest by at least two light years. He begins where the best leaves off."

The fall from grace—or at least notoriety—gnawed at him. "How did I, Gerald L. K. Smith, get this way?" a melancholy Smith asked in a 1959 issue of his newsletter, *The Cross and the Flag*. "Am I just an opinionated fanatic operating from a heart of bitterness and contempt? Or am I a warm-hearted Christian overwhelmed with love for my country and determined to pay any price in the battle to preserve this Christian civilization, this magnificent America, this Constitutional tradition?" Determined to prove that "the last thing that I want in this world is to do injury to any human being regardless of his race, creed, or color," Smith continued to write prolifically on subjects ranging from integration (a plot to "liquidate the white race") to the media ("a Jew-controlled propaganda machine"). And yet his reputation only continued to dwindle.

And so, in 1964, at the age of sixty-six, Smith set out to create a new legacy for himself. He would put politics aside (or at least at a distance) and rededicate himself to the humble calling of spreading the gospel. With his wife, Elna, Smith moved to Eureka Springs and began construction of a seven-story concrete statue of Jesus Christ.

The sleepy former spa town was reinvigorated by the Christ of the Ozarks statue, which drew tourists like a beacon to its 1,500-foot perch at the top of Magnetic Mountain. A few years later, the grateful town raised little objection to Smith's next proposal, a permanent staging of the nation's largest outdoor Passion play, "the Oberammergau of America." It would unfold on a stage the length of two football fields and feature a cast of hundreds, not counting the live animals. Writing about Smith's expanding empire in *The New Yorker* in 1969, Calvin Trillin noted that

> The *Arkansas Gazette* took the trouble of reminding everyone that the Passion play, a rendition of Christ's last week on earth, was a device that had been used by antisemites for centuries, and that it might not be a coincidence that the one proposed for Eureka Springs was being sponsored by Gerald L. K. Smith. But people in Eureka Springs, most of whom knew nothing about Passion plays except that they are based on the New Testament, preferred to consider the play the same kind of religious project as the statue— maybe even another act of old-age repentance for all that political controversy.

The townspeople were correct that Passion plays are "based on the New Testament." The problem, as the National Council of Catholic Bishops and numerous other Christian and Jewish bodies have elucidated over the years, is that many Passion plays manage to use authentic gospel texts in a manner that distorts what most people accept as the authentic gospel message, not to mention authentic history. These productions emphasize passages that suggest Jewish perfidy and group guilt, downplay or ignore passages that affirm the essential Jewishness of Jesus and the apostles, and exaggerate suggestions that the Roman authorities were doing the bidding of the Jewish leadership.*

Anyone holding out hopes that Smith might take a different tack had to be unaware that his interpretation of Jesus's death was already a matter of record. "Herod and Pilate did not want to crucify Him, but they yielded, as many men are doing in this world today, to what is called Jewish pressure," Smith had written in *The Cross and the Flag*. After the crucifixion, Christ's tormentors

---

*It should be noted that most modern churches stage Passion plays or read Passion gospels without any malice.

continued to perpetuate the doctrine of the synagogue of Satan. They continued to represent the seed of Abraham [i.e., Jesus] as a fraud and an imposter. They perpetuated this blasphemy and this denial, and they took on to themselves the label "Jew," and they launched a worldwide propaganda campaign which they have continued until this hour boasting to the world, "We are God's chosen people." There is nothing in the Scripture to establish the theory that Christ's worst enemies are God's chosen people.

It should not have been surprising that upon the opening of *The Great Passion Play,* many observers were aghast. Trillin graded the production using the Bishops' Council's checklist of things not to do in Passion plays and marked nearly every box.

Smith shrugged. Criticism was to be expected, he said, of "the only presentation of its kind in the world which has not diluted its content to flatter the Christ-hating Jews."

The Great Passion Play was an immediate hit. Before long, the Institute of Outdoor Drama had acknowledged it as the most-attended open-air show in the United States, an achievement due in part to its proximity to Branson, Missouri. Since its opening, "over seven million people have enjoyed this portrayal of The Greatest Story Ever Told," according to a 2006 tourist brochure.*

Today, *The Great Passion Play* runs most evenings from May through October. It has been rewritten several times since Smith's death in 1976, and I wanted to see if the show still reflected its antisemitic roots. And if not, what was left. The production allows volunteers to serve as extras, and I decided that the most interesting way to see the show would be from the inside. My plan for my exploration of Christian pop culture had been to

---

*Smith began work on the New Holy Land addition a few years later, but after his death the project was scaled back, both physically and theologically. Smith's aesthetic inspiration was Disney World, but his ambition was more profound. "The enemies of Christ are in possession of the original Holy Land," he wrote in a 1970 fund-raising letter. "[They] will use the despoiled areas to glorify the antichrist instead of our Savior." Arkansas's New Holy Land would not only be fun for the whole family, it would be the spiritual home of Christianity in exile.

always identify myself and my intentions honestly, including the fact that I am Jewish. But *The Great Passion Play* has had some bad experience with the media (what kind of name is Trillin anyway?), and I really wanted to be chosen as an extra, so I decided, just this once, to go incognito. I figured I could live with myself as long as I avoided any outright lies. I called the 800 number and asked if there were any openings.

"I can check," said the man in charge of such things. "Have you seen the play before?"

"No, I haven't."

"Oh." Silence. "We usually ask people to be familiar with the play first."

Seeing my opportunity slip away, I considered saying that I had, of course, seen *The Passion of the Christ,* a film I was confident would have met with Gerald L. K. Smith's approval. But what if he wanted to talk about it? *My favorite part? Oh, probably the scourging. Or maybe the gouging. Really it was all wonderful!* That was a conversation I didn't feel like having.

"I understand," I said, "but I was really hoping to do this." And then I heard myself say, "It's something I felt called to do."

"Do you have your own sandals?" he asked.

A canopy of leaves scattered the sun into a Rorschach of dots across the winding mountain road in front of me. At a fork, I passed a small country store. A sign out front said, "If Christians praised God more, maybe the world would doubt Him less." Scanning the postcard-perfect vistas for a 67-foot, 340-ton statue of Jesus, I wondered if insufficient praise was really the problem.

Art critics have not often been kind to Christ of the Ozarks. One famously likened it to a milk carton topped by a tennis ball. It is a massive, blocky piece of work; a snow-white figure with arms outstretched—sixty-five feet from fingertip to fingertip—as if backed by an invisible cross. If Rio's Christ the Redeemer married Mount Rushmore's George Washington and had a retarded child, it would be Christ of the Ozarks.

And yet when I finally saw it for myself, I was strangely moved. The ridiculous disparity between physical size and artistic refinement seemed not offensive but delightfully playful and naïve, like the outsider art made by grizzled old men in these parts and sold for thousands of dollars in

SoHo galleries. The contemplative mood of the statue park was sullied by tinny speakers mangling a pompous orchestral arrangement of "Amazing Grace"—and by the tomb of Gerald and Elna Smith, pleading coyly for undeserved respects—but Jesus didn't seem to care. The expression on his face (fifteen feet long) was disarmingly serene, as if he had transcended the attempt to turn him into kitsch.

Elsewhere in Eureka Springs, he would have less success.

That evening, I grabbed dinner at the Daily Bread Café and milled around the gift shop waiting for my call to join the regular cast in *The Great Passion Play* amphitheater. Browsing the children's section, I found a book about the Passion for preschoolers.

The people just grew angrier.
"We ALL want Jesus dead!
And if His death makes you feel bad,
We'll take the blame instead!"

Pontius Pilate feared the crowd.
He wanted to keep peace.
He washed his hands, and then he gave
Barabbas his release.

I began to get worried.

You the fella from New York?" A man wearing a security badge gripped my hand and led me through a gate into first-century Jerusalem. The effect was stunning. I thought I had a sense of what "two football fields" meant, but I was picturing empty green lawn and evenly spaced white lines. The set of *The Great Passion Play,* even without any people on it, looked packed. Sand and grit swirled around a dense row of buildings. In between a "marble" temple and a "sandstone" house, an alleyway snaked off into the "distance." Jars of clay rested alongside a stone well. It was as if an entire street had been lifted out of time and plopped down at the base of an Arkansas hill. Upwards, on the side of that hill, I could see other locations: a tomb, a row of wooden crosses.

The guard pointed me backstage to dressing room number three, where the cast was getting ready. The small, bunker-like room was crowded with men and women in period dress sipping Diet Cokes and doing Sudoku. The room's matron—horn-rimmed glasses on a chain around her neck—greeted me crisply and sized me up for a costume. While I waited for her to dig one out, I skimmed an article from the local paper that had been tacked on a bulletin board. The boosterish spin of the story was about how *The Great Passion Play* was making plans to attract younger people by becoming more modern and "interactive." (Would they be handing out whips?) But the subtext was clear: After nearly forty years, the play was in danger of dying out. The 4,100 seats were rarely even half full. In 1992, 300,000 people had bought tickets; in 2006, only 87,000 had. Officially the play still had a cast of 200, but on an average evening only 120 showed up. On school nights—or game nights—there might be as few as ninety-eight.

The matron handed me a pile of rough, earth-toned linen and rope. "We'll have to find someone to pair you up with," she said.

"I'll take him." A big man with a warm, snaggletoothed smile clapped me on the back. "My name's Danny."

"I'm Daniel."

"Well how about that!"

Danny began introducing me around and putting me at ease. He was cheerful and friendly, and I liked him immediately. While I pulled the tunic over my jeans and T-shirt, Danny explained that as an extra, my job would be to enhance the illusion of a bustling city, carrying props from one end to the other and making appropriate gesticulations in crowd scenes. I would not have any lines, but then, nobody would, really. All the dialogue in *The Great Passion Play* is prerecorded and played through loudspeakers at the front of the seats. Actors lip-synch their dialogue with broad gestures. The audience, twenty feet above the set and at least four hundred feet from where most of the action takes place, is too far away to actually hear anything, so Danny can talk me through scenes as we do them. "Some nights I play King Herod," he said wistfully as I belted my mantle. "Tonight I'm just a traveler, so you can be my assistant or some-thing."

When I'd finished getting into my assistant traveler's robes, I was left holding a mysterious kerchief and a small cord. I tried draping them around my neck.

"How does this go?"

"You wear it on your head," said Danny. "Kind of like an A-rab. Or a Jew."

Sensing that this might be a good time to change the subject, I glanced around at the small group seated nearby, and said I'd never done any acting and asked if they had any tips. "This is the only acting any of us do," said Danny, laughing. "I'm a custodian at the middle school."

Danny's cavalier disregard for his craft put me off a bit. Perhaps he saved his intensity for his King Herod nights. Since my small role would be the only one I would ever have, I was determined to give it my all. What would Sean Penn do?

"From now on, I would like everyone to call me by my character's name," I announced. The other performers looked at me like I was from New York. "So, um, what's my character's name?"

King Herod—tonight's King Herod—chuckled over his coffee mug. "You don't have a name. You're a red shirt."

A *Star Trek* joke! I smiled at this unexpected shared cultural reference. Maybe this wouldn't be so bad.

"Okay, your attention please, everybody." The matron came out from behind her counter. "A few quick announcements. We're a small group again tonight, so when Jesus comes out, *please* do not all run over to him. We need to keep the stage *populated*. If you feel the need to go to Jesus, at least *try* not to bunch up." After a little bit, she went on to an apparently related issue. "The office has made an important decision about next season." The actors shifted in their seats. "Starting in the spring, we're only going to be doing four nights a week, not five. In addition to Sunday and Wednesday, we'll have Monday nights off too. If you have any questions, come see me later. Now let's pray."

A few minutes later I was outside, waiting with Danny at the dark end of an alley for the music that would cue us to stride onto the set and begin bustling. "We'll follow the sheep," said Danny. A couple of giggly children in shepherd costumes slapped each other playfully.

The music began and Jerusalem sprang to life. The kids chased a dozen sheep onto the set and we set off after them. Around us, women fetched water from the well, priests climbed the temple steps, and everyone made way for a man leading a camel. I followed Danny confidently through this chaos to the far side of the stage, where we stepped into the semidarkness and stopped again. My first scene was over.

While we waited offstage again, a spotlight came up on a palace, where the Sanhedrin, the council of Jewish priests, was holding an urgent discussion.

"What are we to do? This man does many miracles." The priests waved their arms for attention as their lines played through the loudspeakers.

"If we do not intervene, all men will believe in him!" The line readings were stilted and bombastic. Considering that the dialogue needed to be recorded only once, you'd think it would have been done by professional actors. This did not seem to be the case.

Danny nudged me. "When this scene is over, we're on again. I have one line, then we walk over to that rack of pots and we try to sell them to the king and queen."

I craned my neck looking for the pots, but they were too far away. "So are we salesmen or travelers?"

"Both. Traveling salesmen."

That made sense. "Where are we traveling from?"

Danny seemed momentarily stumped. Then he grinned. "From afar," he said. "Come on, this is us."

We stepped out through a stone arch and were confronted by two teenage centurions in red cloaks and crested helmets. "Halt!" boomed a voice over the loudspeaker. The unamplified soldiers pawed at our satchels. "What do you got in there, drugs?" one asked.

"Who goes there?" continued the voice.

Danny lifted his arms in the patented *Great Passion Play* gesture for *I'm speaking now*. "Only a traveler from afar," came his words. He gave me a wink. We ambled over toward Herod's palace where we pantomimed a sales pitch for earthenware-look pots until the king and queen threw oversized wooden shekels at us. "I want a receipt," the queen joked. The main action, of course, was taking place elsewhere. But it was difficult to hear the speakers from where we were, so I had very little idea what was going on until Jesus entered and everybody ran over to him, just as we had been instructed not to do.

He was riding on an ass, but when the crowd gathered, he hopped down and began grasping outstretched hands like a politician working a rope line. "Hosanna!" boomed the voices over the loudspeaker, and more than a few of the actors. "Did you touch him?" Danny asked me. From his gestures, I gathered this was meant to be in character.

"I couldn't get close enough."

Danny nodded. "He's our best Jesus. We've got three, but he's the one who really looks the part." The crowd dispersed as Jesus began healing lepers. "That's a good role," Danny continued. "He gets a lot of lines."

"Hi, Danny. Haven't seen you in a while." A thin, older woman fell into step alongside us.

"I know. Say, this Daniel. He's down here from New York City."

I smiled hello and she smiled back. "From New York?" she said to Danny. "You better watch out. I used to work with one of them."

As the action moved back to the temple we stayed off to the side, populating the stage. Danny decided to make casual conversation. "So, do you go to church up there in New York?"

"Uh . . . Yeah, sure." *It's not exactly a lie*, I told myself. *We just call it "synagogue."*

"What kind?"

"Nondenominational." Okay, that was a lie, but at least it would end this line of questioning.

"Church of Christ?"

Fuck. I mentally riffled through the books I'd been reading about evangelicalism. Wasn't Church of Christ a denomination? If he asked, does it mean he's Church of Christ? Which means I should definitely say no. But what do I say after that? "No . . . uh . . ." Danny smiled kindly, waiting for me to go on. And then, just at that moment, Jesus saved me. Not in his usual manner, but by causing a distraction—kicking over tables on the temple steps. We ran over to join the throng of gawkers and the conversation was forgotten.

When the scene was over, the extras drifted offstage and the spotlight came up again on the villainous Sanhedrin. Danny and I were heading back to the dressing room when his friend, the woman with previous New

Yorker experience, stopped us. "Can I borrow him?" she asked, meaning me. Danny handed me off and the woman explained that we would need to walk past the Jewish priests as they plotted. "Throw a little scare into them." She handed me a shapeless sack to throw over my shoulder. We would be townspeople on some early morning errand.

As we began our walk across the empty stage, Caiaphas, the high priest, made his case over the loudspeaker. "We must conceive some cunning plot to seize this Jesus and put him to death!" Another priest jerked his head in our direction. "But enough! Some passerby might overhear our plot." I stared at the ground.

By my next scene, the tide had turned against this Jesus. Danny found me again and told me it was angry mob time. "Shake your fist or something." Jesus was paraded past us in chains, and it fell to Danny's character to turn to a neighbor and deliver the line that would express our growing antipathy toward this false prophet. Raising his arms, Danny caught a buddy's eye. "I just realized," he mock shouted, as the loudspeaker blared his actual dialogue. "With the new schedule, not working Monday nights, we're going to get to see *every single NFL game!*"

We hounded Jesus until the Romans moved in to break it up. Two centurions planted themselves in our path. They looked about eleven years old and four and a half feet tall. "I think we can take 'em," I said to Danny.

Offstage again, we watched a guilt-ridden Judas hurl his blood money to the floor. "He's a pilot for Wal-Mart," Danny said. "Whenever one of the executives wants to fly somewhere, he's the guy that takes them. He makes good money doing that."

"Well he's making good money here tonight."

Perhaps for the best, Danny missed my lame thirty-pieces-of-silver joke. "Nah, not so much," he replied. "He makes maybe twenty, thirty dollars a night. The Christ figures, they make a hundred and twenty."

"Why do you do it?" I asked.

"Ministry," he said quickly and earnestly. We looked back at the stage. "And put a little extra money in my pocket," he added. "Plus we get free tickets to all the shows in Branson."

Danny stood. "Big scene coming up," he told me. We navigated toward the alley where we would make our next entrance, avoiding the audience's sight lines. Along the way, we passed three women in their early twenties gossiping happily. "These girls are from Texas," Danny said as we stopped to say hello. "Daniel here is from New York."

"New York?" gasped one, laughing. "Get a rope!" Much later I found out she was probably quoting an old regional TV commercial mocking East Coast salsa, but in my increasingly paranoid state I was convinced she'd just proposed a lynching, if only as a joke.

A palace in Jerusalem, two thousand years ago, night. A handsome man paces the portico. He wears white robes trimmed in scarlet and a gold band on his head.

"What have you done to make these people so angry?"

The other man does not answer. He remains slumped on the steps. There is blood on his tunic.

A priest steps forward. "He claims to be the messiah—a king!"

"A king?" Pontius Pilate is bewildered. "Are you the king of the Jews?"

"The words are yours." Jesus's voice is hushed and broken.

"What an extraordinary reply," marvels Pilate. "What charges do you bring against him?"

The priest spits. "If he were not a criminal, we should not have brought him before you."

"Yes, I would hope not, Caiaphas." The Roman governor continues his patient questioning of the prisoner, but Jesus does not speak.

"There is nothing he can say," shouts another priest. "He is guilty!"

Pilate spins around. "Guilty?! Guilty of what? Certainly nothing that concerns Rome. Take him and try him by your own law."

"We are not allowed to put any man to death."

"To *death*?! You want to put him to death over these matters?"

Early the next morning, Pilate goes to Jesus in private. "Are you the king of the Jews?" he asks again.

"Is that your own idea, or have others suggested it to you?"

"What kind of an answer is that?" Pilate demands. "Am I a *Jew* that I should be concerned with such matters? Your own nation and their chief priests have brought you before me. I repeat, what in the world have you done?"

"My kingdom does not belong in this world. If it did, my followers would be fighting to save me from my arrest by the Jews."

Outside, a crowd has gathered. Pilate steps forward as his soldiers drag Jesus behind him. "As you can all see, this poor man has been punished severely. Therefore it is my desire, in expression of the goodness of Rome, to release him."

The crowd explodes. "No! No! He must be crucified!"

"But why? Again I ask you, What wrong has he done? I have not found him guilty of any capital offense. Clearly this man has done nothing to deserve death. Therefore, I propose to let him off with a flogging."

Two soldiers tie Jesus to a post and begin lashing him as the crowd screams for blood. When it is over, Pilate stands above him. "Behold your king. He has been flogged, beaten, ridiculed, spit upon. What more can you want?"

"He must be crucified!" The crowd shrieks as one. "Crucify him!

Still, the compassionate Pilate cannot believe his ears. "*Crucify* him?"

"Crucify him!"

Pilate calls for a bowl of water. "I am washing my hands. My hands are clean of this innocent man's blood. Let it be recorded that it is on the eve of *your* Jewish Passover. It is on the sixth hour as I sit here on my tribunal. Behold, here is your king, the man called Jesus. I ask you one last and final time, what would you have me do with him?"

"Crucify him!"

I don't know how this scene played in the audience. No doubt the hammy acting, the stiff dialogue, the church-pageant costumes, and cornball music all worked mightily against any emotional engagement. But as I stood in the jostling crowd on that dusty set, some strange alchemy took place. From this position, I could see nothing that was not the scene around me. There were spectators up there somewhere, but looking up in their direction, all I could see was inky darkness. No modern buildings were visible beyond the set. The sky, far from any city, was black and dizzy with stars, exactly as it must have been two thousand years ago.

All around me, dozens of presumably well-meaning Christians were representing themselves as Jews and acting out a scene that for centuries has been used to justify hatred and oppression. Not only was I feeling sick about being along for the ride, but I started to have this mad hallucination that I had fallen into some eternal retelling of this story—that I was back at the actual moment of Jesus's ordeal; or rather, at the moment when whatever in fact happened on that day was first reexperienced as a story of persecution by a Jewish mob. I was under the gaze not merely of a few hundred contemporary Americans but of all past and future generations. I was at a linchpin of history, and I had a choice: be complicit in this grotesque distortion of events—or try to change it.

"Maybe we should reconsider this!" I shouted desperately. "Maybe a flogging is enough!"

Danny laughed. He hadn't heard that one before.

The audience couldn't hear me, of course, but they could see me. The rest of the cast shouted and shook their fists. From behind me, four Jews emerged with masks over their faces and cudgels in their hands, pushing through the crowd to get in a few more shots at the fallen Jesus. I waved my arms for them to stop. I turned away, burying my face in my hands. I exaggerated every movement so that even from four hundred feet away the audience might see something they had never witnessed before, never considered: a compassionate Jew who was not willing to accept Jesus as the messiah, but who didn't want him tortured to death either. I mean, if they can believe in a sensitive Pontius Pilate, this shouldn't be too much for them.

Although I hadn't truly expected any other outcome, I was genuinely saddened at being unable to halt the crucifixion. The jeering crowd followed Jesus offstage as he dragged his heavy cross and set off up the hillside to Golgotha of the Ozarks. Danny put a hand out to stop me. "It's pretty steep up there, and we don't have insurance for volunteers."

I found a flight of metal steps around the back of Herod's palace to watch the end of the drama unfold. I felt glum. My silly gestures hadn't made the Passion play any less offensive, and as for dispelling the stereotype of cunning, manipulative Jews—I fiddled with the digital recorder I'd hidden in my pocket and tried to count the lies and half-truths that had brought me here. I imagined the look of disappointment on Danny's face.

But I don't think I deserved to be lynched.

○ ○ ○

It is hard to imagine that *The Great Passion Play* will still be around forty years from now. The show hails from the prehistory of Christian pop culture, when local spectacles mattered because there was no mass culture. When Gerald Smith conceived of the show, Christian television was still in its infancy, there was no Christian popular music or Christian entertainment radio to play it on. Believers could book Christian films for their churches, but they could not find them at the local theater or rent them from Blockbuster. Christian bookstores sold precious little fiction, if any. In the mainstream, mass culture had long superseded popular theater by the 1960s. *The Great Passion Play* hung on longer than its secular counterparts, vaudeville and burlesque, only because it lacked the same competition. It cannot be a coincidence that the popularity of *The Great Passion Play* began to wane in the early 1990s, just as Christian pop culture finally caught up with the mainstream in its ability to reach a national audience with homogenized product.

But could Passion plays adapt and survive? The rise of Christian mass culture also posed a challenge for another pre-pop religious artifact. The Bible may have survived for two thousand years, but that didn't mean it wasn't vulnerable to more flashy competition and changing tastes in the twentieth century. How the holy scriptures managed to survive the transition into entertainment-saturated, ADD-addled postmodern America is perhaps the quintessential story of faith-based consumerism.

4

To each province in its own script and to each people in its own language

In a sixth-floor conference room of an office building near Nashville International Airport, Rodney Hatfield's BlackBerry buzzed with an incoming e-mail: "The Lord placed a vision on our hearts of a skaters' Bible. We really love the NKJV and would love to use this version. Who can I talk to regarding this? We hope to pack the study Bible with testimonies from pros, devotions, skating tips, etc."

Hatfield is the vice president of marketing for the Bible division of Thomas Nelson, by some measures the largest Christian publisher in America, the second-largest publisher of Bibles, and the ninth-largest publishing house of any kind (the NKJV—New King James Version—is Nelson's bestselling translation). The e-mail was from a Florida skateboard ministry, and Hatfield read it impassively but not dismissively. After all, one of the company's lead titles for the fall, *The Family Foundations Study Bible*, had its origins in a similarly unsolicited suggestion from an outsider. True, that source was more estimable (a major Christian retailer) and the idea less fanciful. But the general principle—that scripture can be repackaged to meet the demands of an increasingly segmented market—is at the heart of the modern Bible-publishing industry.

The familiar observation that the Bible is the bestselling book of all time obscures a more startling fact: the Bible is the bestselling book of the year, every year. Getting a fix on exactly how many Bibles are sold in the United

States is a virtually impossible task, but a conservative estimate is that in 2005 Americans purchased some 25 million Bibles—twice as many as the sixth Harry Potter book. The amount spent annually on Bibles has been put at more than half a billion dollars.

In some ways, this should not be surprising. According to The Barna Group, 47 percent of Americans say they read the Bible every week. But other research has found that 91 percent of American households own at least one Bible—the average household owns four—which means that Bible publishers survive by selling 25 million copies a year of a book that almost everybody already has. And not just survive, thrive. Bible sales were up 25 percent between 2003 and 2005. While the industry is dominated by a half dozen Christian houses, the money involved has begun to attract mainstream interest. In 2006, the Penguin Group published two editions of the Bible, and HarperSanFrancisco, part of HarperCollins, announced the creation of an entire Bible division. Also in 2006, Thomas Nelson, which last changed hands 37 years earlier, for $2.6 million, was purchased by a private investment firm for $437 million.

This is an intensely competitive business, and, despite the provenance of *The Family Foundations Study Bible,* publishers can hardly afford to rely on mere inspiration. Another new Nelson release, *The Grace for the Moment Daily Bible,* had a more typically strategic genesis: It is an extension of one of the publisher's most popular brands, a series of devotional books by Max Lucado, a Texas minister whose many titles have sold nearly fifty million copies. Nelson has seventeen imprints in addition to the Nelson Bible Group, and when it has a popular writer like Lucado it will spin him off into as many different lines as possible. *The Daily Bible* features scripture portions paired with short essays excerpted from other Lucado titles. In the absence of such ready-made material, Bible publishers formulate projects using classic market research. Every year, Nelson Bible executives analyze their product line for shortcomings, scrutinize the competition's offerings, and talk with consumers, retailers, and pastors about their needs.

Nelson categorizes *Grace for the Moment* as an everyday-life, or devotional, Bible. *Family Foundations* is a study Bible. The distinction points to one way in which publishers sell multiple copies of the Bible to the same customers. "They each have a different purpose," Hatfield told me. "It's kind of like a tool chest. All the tools are tools, but they're designed for doing different things." And there are distinctions within each category. There are study Bibles that focus on theology, on historical context, or on practical applications of biblical teachings. There are devotional Bibles for new believers, couples, brides, and cowboys. On an airplane one day, I saw a woman reading a surfers' Bible very similar to the proposed skaters' one. The variety is seemingly limitless. Nelson Bible Group's 2007 catalog lists more than a hundred titles.

"I almost liken it to what happened in radio," Wayne Hastings, the publisher of Nelson's Bible division, said. "Look at satellite radio—what is that, a hundred and seventy-eight stations? And it's all niched. We're doing the same thing in Bibles." In this process, style is nearly as important as content. Bible publishers depend heavily on focus groups, surveys, and trend-spotting firms. For cover designs, they subscribe to fashion-industry color reports. Tim Jordan, a Bible marketing manager at B&H Publishing Group, an arm of the Southern Baptist Convention, said, "It doesn't have to be a King James Bible in black bonded leather, and we might offer it to you in burgundy. In years past, that might have been okay, but the game has changed."

Perhaps more than any other aspect of Christian pop culture, Bible publishing in the twenty-first century embodies the intersection of faith and consumerism that defines contemporary American evangelicalism. Peter Thuesen, a religious historian and the author of *In Discordance with the Scriptures,* a history of Bible translation controversies, sees in Bible publishing "a growing comfort with commercialization." He explained, "Different kinds of packaging can always be seen by true believers as having an evangelical utility. If it helps reach people with the Word, then it's not bad. You can consecrate the market."

As with so much of American popular culture, the modern era of Bible publishing has its roots in the 1960s. Through the first half of the twentieth century, the Bible, literally hidebound, had been synonymous with the establishment. Though there had been two major American translations— in 1901 and 1946—they were scholarly and dense, and the archaic King James Version, of 1611, remained dominant.

Into this world came *Good News for Modern Man.* Published by the

American Bible Society in 1966, *Good News for Modern Man* was a Bible for the young and disaffected. It resembled a mass-market illustrated paperback novel. A year later, 5 million copies were in print. Other publishers were quick to follow this lead. Tyndale House published the Living Bible, a freewheeling paraphrase. The spirit of the era is best captured by an edition of the Living Bible put out under the title *The Way*, which features psychedelic lettering and photographs of shaggy-haired young people and describes Jesus as "the greatest spiritual Activist who ever lived." The success of these accessible, culturally relevant Bibles alerted publishers to a new world of possibility. They introduced women's Bibles in pastel colors, recruited celebrity pastors to write exegeses, and made room for breezy spiritual pep talks alongside, or instead of, the scholarly commentary.

Good News for Modern Man was revolutionary not just in its packaging but also in its text. Until then, major Bible translations in English had taken an approach now known as "formal equivalence," striving to maintain the sentence structure, phrasing, and idioms of the original Hebrew and Greek. The Good News Translation, as it's usually known, followed the precepts of "functional equivalence"—translating not word for word but thought for thought, with the goal of capturing the meaning of the original text, even if that required massaging the words or reordering sentences. Walter Harrelson, a Bible scholar who served on the committee that produced the relatively formal New Revised Standard Version, in 1989, likes to say that formal equivalence carries the reader back to the world of the Bible, while functional equivalence transports the Bible into the world of the reader.

Harrelson is a proponent of formal equivalence and argues that preserving the linguistic qualities of the ancient text reminds readers that the Bible is "a document from another world that is luminous and transforming of our world." Proponents of functional equivalence counter that, to the original audience, the Bible would have sounded contemporary and vernacular, and that translators should preserve these qualities.

The popularity of the Good News Bible proved that there was a following for functional equivalence, and other publishers began tinkering with the formula. By far the most successful has been the New International Version, a moderately functional text published by Zondervan in 1973. Highly readable, it was more accurate than its '60s predecessors and more theologically conservative than the 1946 Revised Standard Version. These qualities enabled it, by 1986, to supplant the King James Version as the bestselling translation in America. Since then, publishers have pushed functional equivalence to its extremes. In 1996, Zondervan published the New International Reader's Version, an adaptation of the NIV appropriate for six-year-olds. (Well, linguistically appropriate anyway. It still contains verses such as, "She will eat what comes out of her body after she has a baby. Then she'll even eat her baby. She won't share it with anyone in her family. She'll plan to eat it in secret.")

The effect of the functional-equivalence approach on the message of the scriptures is most striking when it comes to rendering metaphors. A literal translation of God's words to straying Israelites in Amos 4:6 reads, "I gave you cleanness of teeth." The NIV eliminates the potential misreading that God was punishing the wicked with dental hygiene, and translates the phrase as "I gave you empty stomachs." Functionally equivalent translations, at their most radical, often bypass the exotic metaphors of the Bible entirely. Matthew 3:8, in the NRSV, reads, "Bear fruit worthy of repentance." The Contemporary English Version (1991) reads, "Do something to show that you have really given up your sins."

It is estimated that there have been more than five hundred English translations of the Bible, and there has never been a time in American history when so many translations have been in widespread use at once. A large Christian bookstore may carry as many as 15, although the top 6 account for 95 percent of sales. Considering that the King James Version lacked a significant rival for three centuries, I wondered if we really need so many versions. Publishers say yes. For one thing, scholarship advances more rapidly today. New archeological discoveries are constantly shedding light on the best way to reconstruct the piecemeal documents that make up scripture. For another, language changes faster than most people realize. When the NIV was published, few readers would have been confused by Psalm 1:1's "Blessed is the man who does not walk in the counsel of the wicked or stand in the way of sinners or sit in the seat of mockers." Today's readers are arguably better served by the 2004 Holman Christian Standard Bible's "How happy is the man who does not follow the advice of the wicked, or take the path of sinners, or join a group of mockers!"

Still, it's hard to argue that anything truly significant changed between the publication of the English Standard Version (2001), Today's New International Version (2002), and the HCSB. A more important factor, it seems, is market demand for more choices. Different denominations want translations tailored precisely to their needs, and the more translations are available, the greater readers' desire for yet further variety. The liberties taken by The Message, a popular 1993 paraphrase,* help readers look at more staid translations with fresh eyes.

There are also commercial incentives. The King James Version is in the public domain, but if a company wants to publish a study Bible or a devotional Bible using a modern translation, it will have to pay royalties to the owner of that translation. Commissioning a proprietary translation is often more cost effective in the long run, especially since it can be licensed out to other publishers. Kenneth Barker, a theologian who ran the committee that translated the NIV and has worked on three other translations, told me that he doesn't think a new version will be needed for at least twenty-five years, but he doubts there will be such a long break. "We like to think that the motivation is all holy and pure," he told me, "but finances do enter the picture, and publishers and Bible societies like to have their slice of the pie."

The popularization of the Bible entered a new phase in 2003, when Thomas Nelson created the BibleZine. Hastings described a meeting in which a young brand manager, who had conducted numerous focus groups and online surveys, presented the idea. "She brought in a variety of teen-girl magazines and threw them out on the table," he recalled. "And then she threw a black bonded-leather Bible on the table and said, 'Which would you rather read if you were sixteen years old?'" The result was *Revolve,* a New Testament that looked indistinguishable from a glossy girls' magazine. The 2007 edition features cover lines like "Guys Speak Their Minds" and "Do U Rush to Crush?" Inside, the Gospels are surrounded by quizzes, photos of beaming teenagers, and sidebars offering Bible-themed beauty secrets.

Have you ever had a white stain appear underneath the arms of your favorite dark blouse? Don't freak out. You can quickly give deodor-

---

*Psalm 1:1: "How well God must like you—you don't hang out at Sin Saloon, you don't slink along Dead End Road, you don't go to Smart-Mouth College."

ant spots the boot. Just grab a spare toothbrush, dampen with a little water and liquid soap, and gently scrub until the stain fades away. As you wash away the stain, praise God for cleansing us from all the wrong things we have done. (1 John 1:9)

Revolve was immediately popular with teenagers. "They weren't embarrassed anymore," Hastings said. "They could carry it around school, and nobody was going to ask them what in the world it is." Nelson quickly followed up with other titles, including *Refuel,* for boys; *Blossom,* for tweens; and *Real* for the "vibrant urban crowd" (it comes bundled with a CD of Christian rap). To date, Nelson has sold well over a million BibleZines.

The success of the BibleZine was all the more notable for occurring in a commercial field already crowded with products and with savvy marketing ideas. At the Christian Booksellers Association show in Denver, I saw such innovations as *The Outdoor Bible,* printed on indestructible plastic sheets that fold up like maps, and *The Story,* which features selections from the Bible arranged in chronological order, like a novel. There is a *Men of Integrity* Bible and a *Woman, Thou Art Loosed!* Bible. For kids, there's *The Super Heroes Bible: The Quest for Good Over Evil* and *Psalty's Kids Bible,* featuring "Psalty, the famous singing songbook." In the *Rainbow Study Bible,* each verse is color-coded by theme. *The Promise Bible* prints every one of God's promises in boldface. And *The Personal Promise Bible* is custom-printed with the owner's name ("The LORD is Daniel's shepherd"), home-town ("Woe to you, Brooklyn! Woe to you, New York!"), and spouse's name ("Gina's two breasts are like two fawns").

There are Bibles covered in duct tape, faux fur, simulated diamond plate, and holographic paper. *The Battlezone Bible* has a scarred metal cover. *Immerse* has waterproof pages and a zip-up cover in lime green or orange. *TruGlo* glows in the dark. Tyndale has a line of Bibles that come with matching pocketbooks "reminiscent of such upscale brands as Coach, Dooney & Bourke, and Brighton," and B&H offers Build-a-Bible, which has removable covers that can be swapped out depending on your mood or the dictates of fashion.

There is also a renaissance in the field of audio Bibles. This category has long been dominated by stentorian readings by prominent ministers, and by such famous believers as Charlton Heston, Johnny Cash, and James Earl Jones ("The Darth Vader King James," the distributor calls it among friends). The latest audio versions, by contrast, are sophisticated dramatizations that feature sound effects, original music, and large professional casts. In Denver, Zondervan showcased *The Bible Experience,* featuring just about every black actor in Hollywood, from Denzel Washington to Garrett Morris, and starring Blair Underwood as Jesus and Samuel L. Jackson as God. The publisher of Zondervan, Scott Bolinder, spoke with excitement about the possibilities for distributing the book on iTunes: "A person hears about it, says, 'I don't know, I'm not parting with thirty-four dollars. But I'll try the Book of Revelation for a dollar-ninety-nine.'" Thomas Nelson has a rival version, in which Jim Caviezel reprises the title role in *The Passion of the Christ.* Jason Alexander, of *Seinfeld,* is signed on for an unspecified Old Testament character.

My first reaction to all this was that publishers were cynically embracing half-baked trends to make a buck. Tim Jordan, of B&H, conceded, "You do get some folks that say you shouldn't treat the Bible as a fashion accessory or a throwaway." Nonetheless, he argued that serious religious publishers can't ignore fashion as a way of reaching new audiences. The point, he said, is "to expose as many people as you can, because we believe that it's God's word, we believe that it's life-changing, and we don't take that lightly."

Rodney Hatfield invited me to sit in on a Nelson Bible strategy meeting in Nashville. The staff members radiated the efficient good cheer of marketing professionals everywhere. Hatfield, his thick hair mostly gray, sat at a corner of the conference-room table while Scott Schwertly, the marketing director, got things rolling. "If we're going to start with the *Family Foundations* Bible, let's go ahead and pull out the five-by-five matrix for that title," Schwertly said. The matrix is a chart of twenty-five squares; an axis along the top identifies "Target Audiences/Needs," such as "Churches/Pastors," and an axis down the side shows "What you will do to reach them."

Kelly Holt, a marketing specialist, took a swig from her twenty-ounce Diet Mountain Dew and briefly laid out the core appeal of the title for target audience number two, young Christian families. "There's a lot of interactive discussions in this Bible. It's designed to help Christian parents apply God's word to every life situation, and find out ways to answer tough questions your children will undoubtedly ask about the world, faith, and God."

"Think about how intimidating that is," mused Hatfield, putting himself in the shoes of a new parent. "All of a sudden you are now going to be a teacher. Now you have to be on your game."

"And for traditional Christians," added Jennifer Willingham, who will handle publicity, "you've got to make sure that the doctrine you're teaching your family isn't going to send all of you straight to hell in a handbasket."

Schwertly asked, "Do you guys have any ideas as far as looking for endorsements?" Endorsements are absolutely crucial for Bible marketing. With no living author, these are often the only names that will go on the cover. A few ideas were tossed around. "How do you guys feel about Franklin Graham?" asked Willingham.

"Eh, he's okay," Hatfield deadpanned. That got a nice laugh. Graham, the heir apparent to the crusades of his father, Billy Graham, is one of the most influential people in America.

Hatfield asked about targeting well-known pastors—David Jeremiah, Rick Warren. "Maybe there's even a customized version of this that they can brand for their ministry." The megachurch movement has been a godsend for Bible marketers. Get the right pastor to recommend your title from the pulpit and that's ten thousand potential sales.

With the book's marketing budget set at $60,000, ads in mainstream publications are out of the question. But Holt had started to brainstorm ideas for a campaign to run in several Christian magazines, including *SpiritLed Woman, MOMSense,* and *Rev!,* a magazine for pastors. Holt said, "The imagery would be the tired family at Disney World who's waiting in line all sweaty and nasty, and the tagline would be, like, 'There's a better way to spend quality time together.'" In addition to the Christian press, Nelson has the advantage of being able to place ads for its own products in its BibleZines. Ads for Christian horror novels and a reality show about missionaries ran in *Refuel.*

Next, the meeting proceeded to the *Grace for the Moment Daily Bible.* The marketing budget for this was only about half that of *Family Foundations.* Nelson was counting on star author Max Lucado's name to do most of the selling, especially when Lucado himself put in appearances at Women of Faith. Women of Faith is a distaff Promise Keepers, a traveling ministry that holds two-day "spiritual spas"—what used to be called revival meetings—attracting as many as twenty thousand paying worshippers. Thomas Nelson purchased it in 2000, and it now brings in 12 percent of the company's revenue. Events like this are only one way in which Bible marketers benefit from the robust infrastructure of the evangelical subculture. Other ideas for promoting the *Grace for the Moment* Bible include giveaways on Christian radio and partnering with DaySpring, a Christian greeting card company owned by Hallmark, for a line of Max Lucado cards.

The largest chunk of the budget was going toward consumer ads. "I need some feedback," another marketing specialist said. She pulled out an early print ad that had been created to run in *Redefine,* a BibleZine for baby boomers.

"For men, is this feminine?" she asked, holding up the ad—a white orchid on a satiny black background

"Is it feminine?" drawled a man from the software division. "Yeah, it's feminine."

"It looks like a tampon commercial to me," said Willingham.

Hatfield made a suggestion: "I guess what it doesn't say enough of is Max Lucado."

"That should be huge," Willingham agreed. "Drop out your image, white sheet of paper, and 'Max Lucado Bible.'"

Although Bible sales in America have been robust for the past decade, the business is still fraught with anxieties. For one thing, Bibles are expensive to produce—two to four times the cost of a typical hardcover book—and retail at prices that often leave a very small profit margin. (*The Family Foundations Study Bible* lists at $39.99 for the hardcover and $59.99 for the bonded-leather edition.) The expense begins with the page count: most Bibles are nearly two thousand pages long. Publishers must often commission custom fonts that are thin enough to keep the Bible compact and dark enough to read, but not so dark that they bleed through the thin (and expensive) paper. Internal design is complicated, too, with footnotes, study notes, center-column references, charts, maps, and illustrations.

Gilding, a labor-intensive process, can be halfheartedly faked with a spray stain, but costs remain high. Thomas Nelson stitches most of its bindings, though other publishers have moved toward glue. Red-letter Bibles require two-color printing. Tabs, ribbons, and boxes add to the cost. Facing tight margins, publishers usually order large print runs and console themselves that at least they're in a backlist business.

There is also concern that Bible publishers, for all their marketing ingenuity, have outsmarted themselves. Tim Jordan said, "There's been research that has shown that half the people who come into a Christian bookstore intending to buy a Bible, with money in their pocket, leave without one, because they get overwhelmed."

In an auditorium at the CBA show, Nelson's Wayne Hastings, a slender man, nearly bald with a metrosexual Friar Tuck hairdo and a trim moustache, took the stage for a seminar on this issue. For half an hour, he laid out his company's new research into customers' "felt needs." According to Nelson's findings, people don't come into a store looking for a specific translation—the criterion by which most retailers arrange their Bible shelves—but, rather, to meet a need. More than 60 percent of Bibles are purchased as gifts. Others are bought by people with scenarios in mind: I'll study it before breakfast; I'll read it on the bus. Hastings's message was that booksellers need to orient their displays to this need. "So what does the future look like?" Hastings concluded. "Start with my friend John." A photo of John Lennon appeared on the screen behind him. "He wrote a song called 'Revolution,' and one of the lines in that song is 'we all want to change the world.' So my question to you is, are you willing to change the world? Are you willing to break some paradigms?"

Behind a curtain, his company had set up a prototype for the Bible department of tomorrow. It consisted of color-coded shelves and packaging, organized not by translation but according to Nelson's six felt needs. Nelson says that 95 percent of retailers have responded positively, but the reaction from other publishers has been lukewarm. Zondervan wants to stick with a translation-based system, which, perhaps not coincidentally, benefits its popular New International Version. Tyndale and B&H accept the felt-need premise but are quibbling over the specific categories, and are skeptical about the feasibility of industry-wide color-coding. Tim Jordan said, "You're not going to go to all the potato-chip companies and tell these people, 'You've got to change your packaging to reflect some common color for the potato-chip aisle.' I don't think Frito-Lay is going to go for that."

The most obvious solution would be fewer choices, but, given the enthusiasm that consumers have shown for a diversified market and the investment that publishers have made in satisfying this demand, that's out of the question. The situation worries some people. Phyllis Tickle, a former religion editor of *Publishers Weekly* and the author of popular prayer books, told me, "There's a certain scandal to what's happened to Bible publishing over the last fifteen years." Tickle, an Episcopalian, contributed to a new Bible paraphrase for Nelson called *The Voice*, which is intended for the progressive emergent church, so she is not entirely opposed to modern repackaging. The problem, as she sees it, is that "instead of demanding that the believer, the reader, the seeker step out from the culture and become more Christian, more enclosed within ecclesial definition, we're saying, 'You stay in the culture and we'll come to you.' And, therefore, how are we going to separate out the culturally transient and trashy from the eternal?" The consumerist culture in which BibleZines and the like participate is, to Tickle, "entirely antithetical to the traditional Christian understanding of meekness and self-denial and love and compassion." In Tickle's view, reimagining the Bible according to the latest trends is not merely a question of surmounting a language barrier. It involves violating "something close to moral or spiritual barriers."

Tickle is questioning an industry trend, not publishers' sincerity. "I have yet to meet the first head of house that wasn't in it with some sense of calling as surely as a clergyman is," she said. Sitting in the Zondervan suite during the CBA show, Paul Caminiti, the head of the company's Bible division, cited an appropriately biblical parallel, a story from the book of Acts about Philip the Evangelist and a man known as the Ethiopian eunuch. The Ethiopian eunuch "was really the chief financial officer for the Persian empire," he said. "He was a brilliant man. He was probably the Alan Greenspan of his day. But he has a text Bible—and he has been to Jerusalem, so he is one of these people who is spiritually intrigued—but he can't make head or tail of it. And it's not because he isn't smart. So God sends Philip alongside." According to the Bible story, Philip ran up to the

Ethiopian's chariot and, in the King James Version, asked, "Understandest thou what thou readest?" The Ethiopian answered, "How can I, except some man should guide me?" Philip, Caminiti explained, "provides just a little bit of color commentary, and the light comes on." After listening to Philip's explication of the passage, the Ethiopian orders his chariot to stop by some water so that Philip can baptize him. "And that's what we're doing," Caminiti concluded. "We're coming alongside the text and providing some color commentary. And some color covers."

5

For many will come in my name, claiming,
"I am he," and, "The time is near"

The Bible that changed Christianity was published in 1909 by an ex-drunkard with a forgery conviction, an embezzlement scandal, and a messy divorce in his past. Even after his jailhouse conversion to Christianity, Cyrus I. Scofield never quite shook his reputation as a shady character. Yet it was Scofield who provided the color commentary that would give conservative Christians an entirely new way of understanding God's plan for the world. Among other things, the *Scofield Reference Bible*, the bestselling Bible of the twentieth century, popularized the idea of the Rapture.

Christians have been waiting for the second coming of Jesus for roughly 2,008 years now. For the first 1,830 of those years, it was universally agreed that he would return only once, on the Day of Judgment. Scofield's Bible told a different story: Jesus would actually return twice—the first time in secret, when he'll gather his true church into heaven with him in an event called the Rapture. No one can say exactly what this will entail, but in the popular imagination, Christian believers will suddenly be lifted into the sky, or disappear into thin air, leaving the rest of humanity to suffer through dire times of disaster and war. Only later will Jesus return publicly for the official Second Coming.

The word *Rapture* appears nowhere in the actual, pre-Scofield Bible. Nor, say many theologians, does the concept. To understand how it got into Scofield's elaborate notes and commentary, why most Christians eventually came to believe it, and how it eventually inspired one of the best-selling series of novels of all time, requires an overview of Christian eschatology—the study of the end of the world.

In the period immediately after Jesus's death, most of his followers believed that Jesus would return during their lifetimes to save them from persecution by the Roman Empire—probably because he had promised them as much. ("I tell you the truth, some who are standing here will not taste death before they see the Son of Man coming in his kingdom.") As decades went by and the persecution continued unimpeded, Christians turned to the book of Revelation for answers. In this last book of the Bible, John of Patmos describes a vision of the end times that is bizarre and frightening and an endless source of inspiration for heavy metal bands. A key passage mentions a coming thousand-year reign of Christ, commonly known as the millennium.* As the early Christians read it, John's depiction of a great *tribulation* (in the King James translation) described the Roman oppression; it would end when Jesus came back to usher in his thousand-year kingdom of peace and joy. This doctrine—that the second coming takes place before the millennium—is known as *pre-millennialism*.

But the persecution ended before Jesus returned, and Christianity became the official religion of Rome. As evangelical humorist Jason Boyett writes in his *Pocket Guide to the Apocalypse*, "premillennialism gradually fell out of favor. Which is a nice way of saying it was condemned as heresy at the Council of Ephesus in 431." For fourteen hundred years or so after that, most Christians adhered to a doctrine now known as *amillennialism*, which holds that John was speaking symbolically. Not surprisingly, there was no heavy metal music during most of this period.

Today, most Catholics and mainline Protestants believe some form of amillennialism. But in the nineteenth century, a new theory arose called *postmillennialism*. Participants in the growing evangelical movement believed they were witnessing the birth of a new golden age. Christianity

---

*Folklore eventually linked the biblical concept of the millennium to the calendrical one, leading many people to speculate that Christ would return in the year AD 1000 or 2000, but this has nothing to do with accepted eschatology.

was spreading rapidly, technology and medicine were extending and enhancing life, slavery was on the way out, the world was largely at peace—*maybe*, they thought, *the church will bring about the glorious millennium itself, and Jesus will return after we've paved the way for him.* World War I pretty much crushed that idea, although lately postmillennialism has reemerged in a somewhat grimmer form called *Christian reconstructionism.* Reconstructionists believe that Jesus will return after Christians take control of the planet on his behalf. Theocrats, you might call them.

Around the time the first wave of postmillennialism was gaining steam, an Irish minister named John Nelson Darby came up with a new theory called *dispensational premillennialism.* Darby's insight was that the Bible divides history into separate eras, or dispensations. This turned the Bible into a kind of code book that, when properly deciphered, would reveal when history was about to shift from the current dispensation into the next one, which will be the great tribulation. It also explained exactly what the tribulation entailed and how long it would last (seven years) before Christ came back to start the millennium. But Darby's most popular discovery was the Rapture, a Get Out of Tribulation Free card for Christians. Much of what people believe about the end times today—the Rapture, the antichrist, the one world government—was first proposed by Darby in the 1830s.

Darby brought dispensationalism to the United States in the 1860s, but it didn't really catch on until Scofield made it the basis for his 1909 Bible. Annotated Bibles had been around for a long time, but the density and single-minded focus of Scofield's exegesis was unprecedented. Paul Gutjahr, the author of *An American Bible: A History of the Good Book in the United States, 1777–1880,* told me, "All of a sudden, people are reading Scofield's notes, and they're confusing it with scripture itself."

By the middle of the twentieth century, dispensational premillennialism had become the default theology of American evangelicalism. According to a 2006 survey by the Pew Forum on Religion & Public Life, 63 percent of all American Christians believe in some form of Rapture. Since few Catholics and mainline Protestants do, that means the vast majority of evangelicals must. These already high numbers apparently don't include an offshoot of dispensationalists who accept most of Darby's theory but believe the Rapture won't happen until after the tribulation (as much as that would seem to defeat the purpose). Philosophically, advocates of a post-tribulation Rapture—Pat Robertson is the most well-known—tend to join reconstructionists in a broader theocratic or quasi-theocratic movement known as dominionism. In the bestselling 2006 book *Kingdom Coming,* Michelle Goldberg argues that although this group is small, it has a disproportionate influence on modern evangelicalism.

The modern eschatology craze began in 1967, when the Six-Day War ended with Israel in control of the Old City of Jerusalem and the Temple Mount, where the ancient Jewish Temple once stood. The Temple features prominently in dispensational calculations, and many Christians were convinced that the end-times clock had begun ticking. In 1970, a populist preacher named Hal Lindsey published *The Late, Great Planet Earth,* which correlated Darby's biblical analysis with current events. It became the bestselling book of the decade, and cemented Bible prophecy as a growth industry. Today, the hottest outlet for up-to-the-minute dispensationalist prophecy is the web site RaptureReady.com.* RaptureReady.com maintains a Rapture Index, which tracks news stories to determine how close we are to the end of the world. Since 2004, the index has fluctuated between "heavy prophetic activity" and "fasten your seat belts." The site also features a "post Rapture survival guide" for the rest of us:

> Since you have decided to reject Christ's offer to join in the Rapture, your concern is how to maintain good health in the post Rapture era. You must build a supply of multiple vitamins with particular emphasis on anti-oxidants such as C and E and minerals. It will also be necessary to have a supply of disinfectants, particularly one that can be added to water to make it potable. Above all, do not accept the mark of the beast on your right hand or forehead.

Various polls over the last few years have found that between 36 and 59 percent of Americans believe that the events described in the book of Revelation will come true.† Here is a typical passage from Revelation:

---

*Not to be confused with the online companion to the book you're reading now, which is at GetRaptureReady.com.

†E.g., *Newsweek,* 2004; *Time*/CNN, 2002.

A great and wondrous sign appeared in heaven: a woman clothed with the sun, with the moon under her feet and a crown of twelve stars on her head. She was pregnant and cried out in pain as she was about to give birth. Then another sign appeared in heaven: an enormous red dragon with seven heads and ten horns and seven crowns on his heads. His tail swept a third of the stars out of the sky and flung them to the earth. The dragon stood in front of the woman who was about to give birth, so that he might devour her child the moment it was born. She gave birth to a son, a male child, who will rule all the nations with an iron scepter. And her child was snatched up to God and to his throne. The woman fled into the desert to a place prepared for her by God, where she might be taken care of for 1,260 days.

It goes on like that for pages and pages. There is no way that between 36 and 59 percent of Americans have ever read this, much less understood it. So what is it that Americans believe will come true? Most likely, a particular interpretation of Revelation offered by dispensationalist pastor Tim LaHaye and novelist Jerry Jenkins in *Left Behind*, the most colossal phenomenon in the history of Christian pop culture.

The *Left Behind* books may be as influential in our generation as the *Scofield Reference Bible* was a hundred years ago. The 12 books in the core series—which cast the events of the tribulation as thrillers in the mode of Robert Ludlum—have sold well over 65 million copies since the first was released in 1995. The seventh installment in the series was the first Christian novel to reach the top of *The New York Times* bestseller list. The core books follow a team of new Christians as they battle the forces of the antichrist following the Rapture. There is also a sequel and a trilogy of pre-Rapture prequels. Then there are two spin-off series, which follow the same story from different perspectives, and forty slim books for teenagers called *Left Behind: The Kids*. Throw in the computer game I saw at the CBA convention, audio dramatizations, a board game, study guides, graphic novels, and downloadable wireless applications, and *Left Behind* has undoubtedly moved more than 100 million products. Obviously some people may enjoy the books as nothing more than spiritually themed fantasies, but researcher Amy Johnson Frykholm, who profiled the *Left Behind* audience for her book *Rapture Culture*, found that the most common response to the series is that it "brings the Bible to life," and that most people read and discuss it in groups, as if they were doing Bible study. It is also widely used as a "witnessing tool" to give to unsaved friends. Not surprisingly, the *Left Behind* books are the one facet of Christian pop culture that most nonevangelicals have at least heard of.

To say the *Left Behind* books are badly written is like saying the Great Wall of China is long. I use this analogy—clichéd, unhelpful, and awkward—because LaHaye and Jenkins use it themselves in the first book: "To say the Israelis were caught off guard, Cameron Williams had written, was like saying the Great Wall of China was long." The comparison is even worse in this context—what does China have to do with Israel?—but what is most revealing is that the Cameron Williams character who wrote this sentence is supposed to be a brilliant and famous journalist. "To say the Israelis were caught off guard was like saying the Great Wall of China is long" is not just a random bad sentence, it's LaHaye and Jenkins's idea of Pulitzer-winning prose.

Cameron Williams is one of *Left Behind*'s two main heroes. His friends call him Buck, "because they said he was always bucking tradition and authority." The other hero is Rayford Steele, an airline pilot. That's right, Buck Williams and Rayford Steele. There's also Steve Plank, Bruce Barnes, and Dirk Burton. Apparently, having a porn star name is enough to keep you from getting raptured. The villain is a Romanian politician named Nicolae Carpathia, who brings the world together under a single government as the head of the United Nations. A charming and outwardly altruistic leader, he seems an unlikely candidate for the antichrist—don't they always! Only in the prequels do we find out that he's the genetically engineered offspring of two gay men.

The first book opens on Rayford's plane minutes before the Rapture removes dozens of his passengers from their seats and clothes, along with billions of other people around the world, including all the children, "born and unborn." Those left behind include atheists and agnostics, who will almost universally align themselves with the antichrist, and Christians and Jews, who will fight them. The Christians who are left behind were not *true* Christians. They may have attended church and obeyed the Ten Commandments, but they were not genuinely born again. The demarcation of true versus false Christianity is one of the main themes of *Left Behind*. For-

tunately, one of the raptured true Christians has left a videotape of instructions for the unraptured, so they can all become true Christians, even the
Jews. Even more fortunately, readers can buy copies of this exact tape from
LeftBehind.com to leave in a conspicuous place for their unsaved loved
ones to find after the real Rapture. Alternatively, believers can use a web site
like RaptureLetters.com to send an automated post-Rapture e-mail.

Early in the series, the Tribulation Force, as the heroes call themselves,
fight most of their battles with the weapon of prayer. Eventually they get
guns. Really cool guns. "The thin, jagged, spinning bullet bores through
anything in its path, gathers the gore around it like grass in a power-mower
blade, and turns itself into a larger object of destruction." In the fourth
book, Buck feels mildly guilty about killing a guard at an abortion clinic,
but his partner tells him to shake it off: "If you shot an enemy soldier during battle would you turn yourself in?" In the final volume, a horrified Jesus
returns and admonishes the Tribulation Force, "Put your swords away, for
all who draw the sword will die by the sword." Just kidding. Actually, what
Jesus does is this:

> [M]en and women soldiers and horses seemed to explode where
> they stood. It was as if the very words of the Lord had superheated
> their blood, causing it to burst through their veins and skin . . . Their
> innards and entrails gushed to the desert floor, and as those around
> them turned to run, they too were slain, their blood pooling and ris-
> ing in the unforgiving brightness of the glory of Christ.

> *Gloria in excelsis Deo,* motherfucker.

The most common dismissal of *Left Behind* is that it takes the prophetic
books of the Bible too literally. This is also, of course, the most common
defense of it. Either way, it's untrue. As Lutheran minister Barbara Rossing
writes in *The Rapture Exposed,* dispensationalists' supposedly literal readings are

> convoluted and complex, relying on dubious "gaps" of thousands of
> years. To make sense, their biblical chronology must combine bits

and pieces of the Bible written many centuries apart and under very different circumstances into one overarching narrative.

Go back and read that passage from Revelation and you'll see it doesn't even make sense to speak of reading this book "literally." LaHaye and Jenkins know that. In the seventh *Left Behind* novel, their fictional Bible scholar observes of the sun-clothed woman, "Clearly she was symbolic, as no woman was that large or had a child in space." And yet the authors have no problem conjuring up an army riding horses with the heads of lions and tails like serpents—exactly as described in Revelation 9—even though other pop dispensationalists say that *clearly* those fantastical creatures are symbolic of tanks. One of these other authors says his approach is "Take it literally unless the symbolism is obvious," which really just means, it's all true except the stuff that isn't.

On a more basic level, Rossing notes,

Prophecy does not mean prediction of the future. The Bible is not like a horoscope . . . When biblical prophets preached destruction, the purpose of their threats was almost always to warn of the consequences of destructive behavior, not to furnish play-by-play information about events in the future.

But there are more concrete problems with the series as well. Evangelical blogger Fred Clark has written one of the most effective (and hilarious) critiques of *Left Behind,* a page-by-page dissection of the first book that has taken him, at the time of this writing, about four years. The level of detail gives Clark space to build a devastating case that the book's glaring absence of sympathy for anyone other than its main characters is not just a failure of imagination on the part of the authors but a form of hatred. The heroes of the book, Clark declares, are sociopaths. They are men who arrive at an airport an hour or so after billions of people have vanished without a trace—with countless hundreds or thousands more dead or dying in the wreckages of suddenly pilotless planes—yet who make no attempt to help, or even inquire about the feelings of, a single person they meet. Instead they focus relentlessly on their own travel plans, jobs, and lives.

If nothing else, you might think the sudden disappearance of every child

on earth would have some implications for society, or at least for their parents, but LaHaye and Jenkins can't concern themselves with this, because
John Nelson Darby said that once the tribulation begins, certain events
must happen on a fixed timetable, and damn it, they're going to follow that
schedule. "The authors behave as they imagine God behaves," Clark writes.
"They have a plot that must move forward, and they will advance that plot
even if it means causing, then callously disregarding, the suffering of billions of people. Plot trumps—and tramples on, and violates—character.
Here, once more, Bad Writing and Bad Theology intersect."

Left Behind describes a post-Rapture world in which a liberal govern-
ment (universal health care is mentioned) is hunting down and killing
Christians. This is not just any science fiction dystopia, it is—*clearly*—
symbolic. *Left Behind* isn't really about the future, it's about the present. In
*Skipping Towards Armageddon: The Politics and Propaganda of the Left Behind
Novels and the LaHaye Empire,* Michael Standaert writes,

> Essentially about power and not faith, these books can be read as a
> guide to understanding this battle for the mind of America: the battle
> between a moderate secular society, built on tolerance over the past
> century for any number of views, and a new brand of quasi-pop-
> culture fundamentalist absolutism.

This might strike a casual reader as liberal paranoia, but it makes sense if
you know anything about Tim LaHaye. Born in 1926 to a working-class
Detroit family, LaHaye is one of the most important figures of the modern
religious right: an original board member of the Moral Majority and the
founder of several influential behind-the-scenes organizations such as the
Council for National Policy and the American Coalition for Traditional Values. His wife, Beverly, is the founder of Concerned Women for America, an
antifeminist organization known among critics as Ladies Against Women.
"No one individual has played a more central organizing role in the religious right than Tim LaHaye," Larry Eskridge of the Institute for the Study
of American Evangelicals told *Rolling Stone* in 2004. "More than any other
person," Jerry Falwell once said, "Tim LaHaye challenged me to begin
thinking through my involvement in the political process."

Historian William Martin credits LaHaye with popularizing, along with

Falwell and Francis Schaeffer, "the idea of secular humanism as a destructive, anti-Christian religion." LaHaye devoted several bestselling books to the subject, declaring flatly in the first one, 1980's *Battle for the Mind,* "We must remove all humanists from public office and replace them with pro-moral political leaders." LaHaye was also one of the first evangelical leaders to speak out against the growing acceptance of gay people. In his 1978 book *The Unhappy Gays: What Everyone Should Know About Homosexuality,* LaHaye reminded readers that the book of Leviticus makes homosexual acts punishable by death. "This may seem cruel and unusual by today's standards," he wrote,

> but our leniency has caused widespread problems. This is not to suggest that Christians advocate the death penalty for today's homosexuals, but I do have a question that needs consideration. Who is *really* being cruel and inhuman—those whose leniency allows homosexuality to spread to millions of victims who would not otherwise have been enticed, or those who practiced Old Testament capital punishment.

An active associate of the John Birch Society in the 1960s and '70s, LaHaye has a conspiratorial outlook that serves him well in crafting his apocalyptic fictions. In a 1992 book he wrote that the Illuminati is a real "Satanically-inspired, centuries-old conspiracy to use government, education, and media to destroy every vestige of Christianity within our society and establish a new world order." As just one example of how this conspiracy works, LaHaye believes that "the Chinese Communists" purchased the presidency for Bill Clinton in 1996, a transaction that was "downplayed or ignored by our socialist Marxist-loving media."

Before he began work on *Left Behind,* LaHaye linked his theories about the coming great tribulation to "the pre-tribulation tribulation—that is, the tribulation that will engulf this country if liberal humanists are permitted to take total control of our government." He urged his followers to struggle against this with all their power. Thus, Standaert writes, *Left Behind* is a futuristic fantasy, but it is also "an account of current political preoccupations."

LaHaye and Jenkins did not invent the end-times thriller genre. According to *Books & Culture* magazine, the first dispensationalist novel was written back in 1913, and various critics have noted that *Left Behind* draws heavily on a minor 1970s bestseller called *666*. There have also been at least twenty-five Christian end-times films, including adaptations of *Left Behind* so abysmal that LaHaye actually sued the producers for turning his masterworks into "church basement" movies. LaHaye's anger may have had something to do with the fact that the first *Left Behind* movie bombed. It came to theaters not long after the surprise success of a similarly themed low-budget Christian film called *The Omega Code,* and LaHaye no doubt expected that the *Left Behind* movie, starring Kirk Cameron, would do even better. But the producers marketed it badly and watered down the evangelistic message, which turned off Christians while failing to fool non-Christians. The sequels have all gone direct to video, alongside other films such as *Six: The Mark Unleashed,* starring Stephen Baldwin, and *Tribulation,* which features Gary Busey, Howie Mandel, and Margot Kidder, making it a sign of the apocalypse itself.

The 1990s saw a plague of end-times novels, as dispensationalists anticipated the arrival of the year 2000. At least a half dozen titles beat *Left Behind* to the market. Most sold respectably, though none approached *Left Behind* levels of success, possibly because they are actually not as good. Seriously, to say the pre–*Left Behind* end-times thrillers are badly written is like saying that something even longer than the Great Wall of China is long. Here's a typical sentence from *The Illuminati,* by Larry Burkett, articulating the thoughts of one villain: "*God, how I hate Christians. No wait,* he thought, *not God*—he didn't believe in God. *Anyway, I hate them,* he concluded."

The person doing all this precise atheistic thinking is the head of an organization Burkett calls the National Civil Liberties Union. Perhaps the most interesting thing about the apocalyptic fiction of the early 1990s is that it is even more explicit than *Left Behind* about its political agenda. One of these books is Pat Robertson's *The End of the Age.* A cynic might suggest that the busy Robertson had the aid of a ghost writer, but there is no evidence that a professional writer was ever in the room with this manuscript. Writing in the Clinton era, Robertson introduces a cast of characters that includes the president of the United States (an alcoholic womanizer), his first lady (a power-hungry lesbian), the editor of *The New York Times* ("a Sixties Marxist") and Percy DuVal, the gay chief of White House personnel (who "used every trick in the book to fill the highest government positions with those who shared his lifestyle"). In a novel by Paul Meier called *The Third Millennium,* an angel announces that "judgment has engulfed San Francisco" and Los Angeles, "yet other portions of Orange County stand." Yes, the Four Horsemen check voting records. And when *The Third Millennium's* one world government legalizes euthanasia, a character intones, "It started this way in the Third Reich. First there were abortions on demand, and then one thing led to another."

Another chief motivator of the *Left Behind* authors and their immediate predecessors is wish fulfillment—imagining a world in which conservative evangelicals get to stick out their tongues and say, "I told you so." In Robertson's book, a repentant agnostic tells his new friends in the resistance, "We thought you Christians were no better than right-wing thought police. It never occurred to me that you were trying to protect us from the wrath of God." What is decidedly unimportant is anything that could be called Christian values. Between the killing and the taunting, there is nary a second spared for mercy, charity, redemption, or brotherly love. Late in *The Third Millennium,* the hero surveys the plains of Armageddon and exclaims, "Thank God we're the good guys!" For end-times thrillers, this is what being a Christian is all about.

It was not always this way. Before *Left Behind,* the most well-known pop apocalypse fiction was a 1972 film called *A Thief in the Night,* which was shown in churches and Christian camps for more than a decade. The terror inspired by *A Thief in the Night* was personal, not political. Focusing entirely on a handful of ordinary Americans, the most frightening scenes involve children who mistakenly think they've missed the Rapture when they come home to find their parents away. While scaring children may not be the most noble way of spreading the gospel, it's worth noting that the film's attitude toward its unsaved characters is markedly different from that of *Left Behind*: It feels sorry for them.

When people are sent to hell in *A Thief in the Night* and its sequels, viewers are meant to mourn the loss of their souls, not celebrate their defeat at the hands of the righteous. The theme song of *A Thief in the Night* is an eerie ballad by pioneering Christian rocker Larry Norman called "I Wish We'd All Been Ready."

Children died, the days grew cold,
A piece of bread could buy a bag of gold.
I wish we'd all been ready . . .
A man and wife asleep in bed,
She hears a noise and turns her head, he's gone.
I wish we'd all been ready . . .
There's no time to change your mind,
The Son has come and you've been left behind.

The final lyrics later provided a title for LaHaye and Jenkins, but the rest of the song would be out of place; there is no sense in the *Left Behind* books that the authors *actually* wish we'd all been ready. They're far more invested in having someone around to get their asses kicked. Journalist Adam Davidson argues that the differences between *A Thief in the Night* and *Left Behind* reveal a disturbing trend in American evangelicalism.

The progression (or regression) is the move from rural towns to the halls of power. It's the expansion of the evangelical sphere of concern from the very local (my friends, my church) to the national and global (my president, my international policy). It's a move from a complex view of the individual to an oversimplification that identifies everyone as either good-believer or bad-heathen. It's also a change in sentiment towards the unbeliever from sadness, caring, and invitation to triumph, judgment, and dismissal. It's a chilling mutation, and has entrenched evangelical Christianity in an antagonism to secular America that borders, at times, on cruelty.

LaHaye and Jenkins protest vehemently when critics accuse them of bloodlust. They preach the unvarnished truth, they say, because they love non-Christians and want them to be saved. They take no glee in anyone's demise. Suffice it to say that these claims are hard to square with what's in their books.

Many critics have been particularly concerned with the representation of Jews in *Left Behind*. Jewish characters in *Left Behind* are given three choices: join the antichrist and go to hell; resist the antichrist and go to a concentration camp (and eventually to hell); or become a Messianic Jew who believes in Jesus. And although it's a relief that Jews are not actually cast as villains—though there is some cryptic talk of conspiratorial gatherings early on—there is a definite sense that they lack any real worth. The Anti-Defamation League does a credible job of teasing out the trouble.

> While Christians are not mandated to consider other faiths as having equal claim to the truth, of course, LaHaye and Jenkins's utter lack of respect for Judaism is a significant problem. They can blithely imagine a world without Jews because, once Judaism is proved meritless, it is not difficult to dehumanize those who refuse to discard it. They do so not out of malice but unreflective certainty in their beliefs.
>
> Jews are not hated in the Left Behind books. They are merely different: not-quite-human pawns in God's plan, cosmic curiosities.

Israeli journalist Gershom Gorenberg has written that for a Jew reading *Left Behind*,

> The experience is jarring, like meeting someone who calls you by your name, insists he knows you, remembers you from a high school you didn't attend, a job you never had. I'm reading a book set largely in the country where I live—but not really, because the authors' Israel is a landscape of their imagination, and the characters called "Jews" might as well be named hobbits or warlocks. Israel and Jews are central to *Nicolae* and the other books of the hugely successful *Left Behind* series—but the country belongs to the map of a Christian myth; the people speak lines from a script foreign to flesh-and-blood Jews.

The most disconcerting thing about this is that, remember, the message of *Left Behind* is meant to be applied to today's world, and dispensationalists' passionate but obtuse embrace of Israel has been an unnecessary irritant in Middle Eastern affairs. To some extent, evangelicals tend to support Israel because they believe it is God's favored nation.* But they also have an interest in advancing an agenda in the Middle East that fits their understanding of biblical prophecy. Their interpretation of Revelation says that before Jesus returns, the antichrist will defile the Temple. Since there hasn't been a Temple in Jerusalem for about 1,940 years—and the antichrist is unlikely to settle for Orlando or Eureka Springs—they believe the Jews must first rebuild it—a thorny proposition given that for about 1,300 years now, the Temple Mount has been home to the Dome of the Rock, one of the most sacred sites in Islam. While only a small fringe of evangelicals is actually working to fund and promote a new Temple, most filter Israeli affairs through the belief that such a project is inevitable.

"Their convictions," writes Timothy Weber in *On the Road to Armageddon: How Evangelicals Became Israel's Best Friend,* "have led them to support the aims and actions of what most Israelis believe are the most dangerous right-wing elements in their society, people whose views make any compromise necessary for lasting peace impossible." Not that that matters to them. Their reading of the Bible convinces them that there will never be lasting peace in the Middle East until Jesus returns. "Dispensationalists," continues Weber, "have increasingly moved from observers to participant-observers. They have acted consistently with their convictions about the coming Last Days in ways that make their prophecies appear to be self-fulfilling."

Most evangelicals do not obsess over apocalyptic prophecies. Unlike Tim LaHaye, they do not spend their time poring over elaborate charts of the last days; when asked, they will usually respond that making predictions is a folly. "No one knows about that day or hour," Jesus taught. Nonetheless, most can't help but absorb the essence of dispensationalism through entertainment, and it gives them a palpable sense of importance that reverberates through all evangelical culture. At the festival I attended in Kansas, one of the rock singers announced from the stage, "I really believe that ours is the generation" that will see the Second Coming, and the crowd seemed to

---

* "I will bless those who bless you, and whoever curses you I will curse." (Gen. 12:3)

agree. In a poll conducted at the end of 2006, nearly half of white American evangelicals said Jesus was somewhat or very likely to return the following year. Pop culture may not be the cause of that belief, but it certainly contributes.

Perhaps the best thing to say about *Left Behind* is that its success seems to have killed the end-times thriller genre, at least for the foreseeable future. Rather than encourage imitators, it has scared them away. LaHaye and Jenkins's version of the Darby narrative has become so widely accepted that any other would strike readers as unnecessary and possibly inauthentic.

While the political and theological influence of *Left Behind* will be felt for many years to come, its status as a pop-culture icon has largely come to an end. The first book came out in 1995, long enough ago that some of the real people who make cameo appearances in its future world are now dead in the real one, and some of its futuristic technology is obsolete. As I discovered when I asked Christians about it, the secular world's continued fascination with *Left Behind* is seen as a sign of how out of touch we are with evangelical culture. Imagine thinking that *The Real World* still defined American TV. Yet secular culture was able to quickly follow *The Real World* with *Big Brother, The Simple Life,* and *The Hills.* Christians, on the other hand, are still struggling to figure out how to follow an act like the end of the world.

6

And books were opened

I f the end really is near, the people of Spartanburg, South Carolina, will have no excuse for being unprepared. The signs of the apocalypse are hard to miss here, especially the one that is an actual sign: a billboard greeting motorists on I-85 North with the message "Ready or not, here I come—Jesus."

If the billboard doesn't do the trick, the radio might. There are the usual Christian music stations, of course, but even the mainstream country radio here has no trouble incorporating ominous, if catchy, religious prophecy. On my drive into town, I found myself humming along to a song about how "the lawyers" have taken prayer out of schools and banned "under God" from the Pledge of Allegiance. "I wonder how much He will take," crooned the singer. "I just pray it's not too late."

Having no training in theology, I do not feel capable of evaluating the implication that God will base his judgment of humanity on an overturned 2002 ruling of the Ninth Circuit appellate court. But it did strike me that country music may be the only element of American pop culture that does not have a thriving Christian counterpart, simply because it doesn't need one.

And then, of course, there are the churches. The guest services book at my hotel listed no fewer than forty-five in the immediate area, from the Bible Way Community New Life Deliverance Church to the Power of Prayer Miracle Faith Temple to Gospelight. Mostly, however, what's going to keep Spartanburg Rapture ready is that it is home to Christian Supply, the world's largest Christian bookstore. Motto: "Over thirty-five thousand square feet of faith."

There are at least 2,100 Christian bookstores in America, and almost certainly a lot more—possibly as many as 10,000. Nobody knows for sure because most are tiny mom-and-pop outfits that don't bother to join the Christian Booksellers Association. As in the secular world, though, most of the money flows through a handful of big chains—Family Christian is the largest, with more than 300 stores in 37 states and $312 million in annual sales. The smaller stores tend to come and go pretty quickly.

In this environment, Christian Supply is a rarity: a thriving independent superstore that has been in business for half a century. Back in 1953, when Charles and Margaret Wallington opened Christian Supply—then only six hundred square feet of faith—the Christian retail industry was still in its infancy. By the mid-1980s, Christian Supply had expanded six times, and Christian bookstores had become a center of evangelical life, "an enormous institutional and cultural infrastructure," writes Heather Hendershot in *Shaking the World for Jesus,* that, by legitimizing a role for Bible-believers outside of the church walls, helped pave the way for evangelicalism as a political force.

Christian Supply, which now serves as the anchor tenant of a Spartanburg shopping center and is run by the founders' son, Chuck, is saddled with a utilitarian midcentury name that no longer suits its thoroughly modern ambiance. While it has not yet added a café, as many Christian bookstores have in the race to keep up with Barnes & Noble, Christian Supply exudes the generically welcoming atmosphere that keeps cash registers chirping. There is a colorful children's department, with *VeggieTales* videos on an endless loop, a small music section, and a long aisle of Dayspring greeting cards.

Many of the shelves have labels you would expect to find in a Christian bookstore: Bibles, devotions, prophecy. Other categories are less obvious. The health section includes titles such as *Body by God, Fit for Eternity,* and *What Would Jesus Eat?* (which is frequently contradicted by a rival book, *The Maker's Diet,* on subjects like red meat). You can find *The Purse-Driven Life* under humor and *God Is My CEO* under business, unless it's the other way around. Not only is there a sports section, there is a subsection within that just for golf, where you can pick up *In His Grip* and *Finishing the*

Course: Strategies for the Back Nine of Your Life. A small shelf for "other reli-gions" has titles such as *A Mormon's Unexpected Journey,* billed as "a devout Mormon woman's journey from deception and bondage to true freedom in Christ."

The most space is given over to "Christian living." That's the category known in the non-Christian world as self-help—a concept evangelicals find problematic. These are the books that help you become a better Chris-tian without having to do a lot of theological heavy lifting. They range from the giants of Christian publishing—Rick Warren, Billy Graham, Joel Osteen—to more specialized titles. *Jack Bauer's Having a Bad Day* draws "unexpected faith truths" from *24. Men Are from Dirt, Women Are from Men* offers relationship advice. *Be Intolerant* extols the virtues of being intoler-ant. The author is Ryan Dobson, son of Focus on the Family chairman James Dobson.

Christian Living is the industry's largest category, but the fastest growing is fiction, which now accounts for 20 percent of the market—quadruple the figure from 12 years ago. Within this, romance is the bestselling genre—not surprising since three-quarters of customers at Christian book-stores are women, according to one survey. The most popular Christian romance novelist is Karen Kingsbury, the "Queen of Clean" (just a nick-name) who writes "Life-Changing Fiction" (a registered trademark). She has written more than 30 novels in 10 years, and sold 5 million copies. There are Christian romances set in the old West and the old South, or among Vikings or the Amish. The latter are so ubiquitous they're known in the trade as "bonnet books."

Authors of Christian romances prefer to explain their books in terms of what they offer—tales of overcoming adversity through God—rather than what they leave out. But the truth is that most readers turn to these novels for the same reason they turn to Christian music: for safety. A Christian love story is guaranteed to be free of smut, of course, but there's more to it than that. Every publisher has its own guidelines, but all are aimed at assuring owners of Christian bookstores that even their most touchy cus-tomers will not be offended by the content of its books. A few years ago, Steeple Hill, the "inspirational" division of Harlequin, sent its writers a memo regarding taboos. A friend of mine whose girlfriend worked for the company gave me a copy.

The following terms should be avoided in the text:

Arousal
Bastard
Bet/betting
Bishop
Bra
Breast (except for breast cancer
    if necessary)
Buttocks or butt (can say derriere,
    backside)
Crap
Damn (can use "blast" instead)
Darn
Dern/Durn
Devil (except in religious sense, but
    this would be rare)
Dang
Dagnabbit
Doody
Father (when used to describe
    a religious official)
Fiend
For Heaven's Sake (can use "for good-
    ness' sake" instead)
For the love of Mike
For Pete's Sake
Gee
Geez/Jeez (can use "Sheesh" instead)
Gosh
Golly

Halloween
Harlot
Heat (when used to describe kisses)
Heck
Hell (except in religious sense,
    but this would be rare)
Holy Cow
Need/Hunger (when used to
    describe non-food-focused state
    of being)
Pee
Poop (except in Mom lit,
    sparingly—but not "oh poop"
    as an expression)
Panties
Passion
Priest
Sexy
Sex
Sexual attraction
Tempting (as applied to the
    opposite sex)
St. [name of Saint]
Swear, as in "I swear"—
    Christian characters are not
    supposed to swear
Undergarments of any kind
Whore

The following are allowed only in the context mentioned:

Angel—only when used in a biblical context ("My late Aunt Edna is my
    guardian angel"—not allowed)
Miracle—only when used in the biblical context ("finding that Diet Coke
    was a miracle"—not allowed)
Oh my God/Oh God—ONLY allowed when it's clearly part of a prayer. NOT as
    an exclamation
Heavenly—only when used in a biblical context (Food, clothes, shoes, etc.
    are not heavenly)
It is acceptable to say "He cursed" or to mention cursing, but this should be
    used sparingly, for realism, not excessively. And only non-Christian char-
    acters can curse.

Situations to be avoided:

Kissing below the neck
Visible signs or discussions of arousal or sexual attraction. This includes the
    overuse of words like attraction, hunk, hottie, kisses, sparking, flames,
    getting out of control
Double entendre
Nudity
• People changing clothes "on screen"
• Any character clad only in a towel
Hero or heroine sleeping in same house without a third party, even if they're
    not sleeping together or in same room.

Also, Christian characters should not smoke, drink, gamble, play cards, or
dance, and terms associated with these activities should only be used in
connection with bad guys or disapproving of them or such. Bodily functions, like going to the bathroom, should be mentioned as little as possible
and some euphemism may be necessary but we don't want to sound quaint
or absurd.

Not surprisingly, many Christians roll their eyes at such, well, quaint
and absurd rules. A few believe them to be downright dangerous. "Secular
romance novels might diminish sexuality by detaching it from deep and
committed relationships," writes William Romanowski in *Eyes Wide Open*,
"but Christian stories of love and relationships that deny the force of sexual
passion and desire, and even avoid consideration of sex, can also distort
and cheapen human life." Romanowski disputes the conceit that sexual sin
is the worst kind, and warns that "morality too easily becomes moralism, a
list of dos and don'ts."

That list has been, if not quite thrown out, at least pared down considerably to accommodate a new subgenre of Christian romance: Christian
chick lit. The first of these books, *Sisterchicks on the Loose!*, appeared in
2003, five years after the U.S. publication of *Bridget Jones's Diary*, just as the
chick-lit craze in the secular market was reaching its peak. If the title of *Sisterchicks* echoes such mainstream chick-lit brands as *The Divine Secrets of
the Ya-Ya Sisterhood*, that's probably not a coincidence. Another popular
Christian series is called *The Yada Yada Prayer Group* and there's a nonfiction Christian chick-lit anthology called *The Divine Secrets of the Yahweh
Prayer Group*. The women in these books don't have premarital sex, but
they may enjoy margaritas and describe clothes as heavenly. Christian

chick lit is geared to younger women who are devout without being legalistic, and who, as avid readers of non-Christian chick lit too, aren't willing to sacrifice storytelling for piety. What they want most are heroines like themselves who obsess a little less about their weight and a little more about God's plan for their lives.

There are also Christian mom-lit and teen-chick books, and an author named Ray Blackston, who lives not far from Spartanburg, has even carved out a niche for himself as the Christian Nick Hornby, writing lad-lit books about single, pop-culture-obsessed young men.

Most fiction aimed at Christian men, however, is much less whimsical. After *Left Behind* opened the floodgates for thrillers, publishers expanded into nonapocalyptic themes. *Left Behind*'s Jerry Jenkins went on to write a series about a world government that has outlawed Christianity. Okay, it's basically *Left Behind* without the Rapture, but apparently there is no end to the demand for near-future stories about persecuted Christians. Somehow the more powerful the religious right grows, the more desperately Christians cling to the fantasy that they are only one act of Congress away from being herded into concentration camps.

In 2006, WestBow Press, a division of Thomas Nelson, published a thriller called *House*, the first collaboration by two of the most important names in Christian fiction, Frank Peretti and Ted Dekker. While this meant nothing in particular to me, a secular publishing magazine declared it "as big of a deal as Tom Clancy and Clive Cussler getting together to coauthor a spy novel." Peretti, I learned, is the man who more or less invented the Christian thriller. His 1986 novel, *This Present Darkness,* was rejected by fifteen publishers before Crossway took a chance on this new genre and printed four thousand copies. It has since sold more than 2.5 million. Dekker, meanwhile, is Christian publishing's hot young thing. Two of his (relatively) gory horror novels were made into (relatively) big budget films by Fox Faith. Both Dekker and Peretti are among the many Christian authors who would regularly appear on mainstream bestseller lists, except for the fact that those lists don't count sales through Christian bookstores. A joint appearance by Dekker and Peretti at Christian Supply is what brought me to South Carolina.

○ ○ ○

It has been reported that when Tim LaHaye was looking for someone to turn his end-times prophecies into fiction, the first person he approached was Frank Peretti. That Peretti said no is the reading public's loss. Though not a particularly good writer, Peretti is still a vastly better writer than Jerry Jenkins. But perhaps Peretti felt that as a career move, popularizing dubious theology would be more of the same. He'd already accomplished that with the concept of "spiritual warfare."

I'd heard that phrase for the first time at the Holy Land Experience theme park. Les Cheveldayoff, the actor who played Jesus, had admitted that he'd been distracted during his performance and was worried that the illusion would falter. I asked what distracted him. The cameras? The traffic noise? "Spiritual warfare," he said with a shrug. I nodded as if I knew exactly what he meant, which in retrospect was not the sharpest interviewing technique, since I didn't have the slightest idea.

Later I did some homework. The concept of spiritual warfare is grounded largely in the book of Ephesians, which describes a quasi- (perhaps metaphorically) militaristic battle "against the powers of this dark world and against the spiritual forces of evil in the heavenly realms." Although there is disagreement among traditional Christians about the centrality of this battle to their lives, there is general consensus about its broad contours. As humans, we are all caught up in a supernatural struggle between God and Satan. While God calls sinners to him, the enemy bombards us with lies, doubt, and temptation, impairing our ability to choose the path of Christ. At the same time, Satan attacks the body of the church, causing internal strife and the downfall of respected evangelists, thus diminishing its appeal in the eyes of the world. The Bible enjoins mortals to enlist in this war, not retreat from it.

Peretti elaborated on this idea with vivid, violent prose in his first two bestsellers, This Present Darkness and Piercing the Darkness. In his depiction, invisible demons with thick and leathery hides latch onto people and infect them with specific sins—one demon embodies lust, another greed, and so on. These demons must be exposed and cast out using specific incantations that call forth angels of God—muscular angels with glowing, bejeweled swords—to fight on behalf of the people.

One of the leading theologians of what might be called "classical" spiritual warfare—that is, before Peretti and a few others got hold of it—is Chuck Lawless, a professor and dean at the Southern Baptist Theological Seminary. In a 2001 essay, Lawless wrote that spiritual warfare, properly understood, is fought not by seeking out and attacking the forces of darkness but by embracing the power of God. "The primary task of the spiritual warrior is not to know Satan well—it is to know God so intimately that Satan's counterfeit becomes obvious in comparison." The warrior's most valuable tactics, Lawless says, are developing character, meeting ethical demands, exhibiting personal holiness, preparing for witnessing, studying the Bible, and focusing on prayer. This is a lifelong process, not a series of daily skirmishes.

As Lawless's tone suggests, this is no longer the way that many Christians understand the concept. Today, the spiritual warfare industry is greatly concerned with identifying "territorial spirits." In cities with large evangelical communities, such as Colorado Springs, Colorado, warriors spend their free time plotting the locations of demonic forces to be fought off. One online guide to "spiritual mapping" suggests looking for cults (such as Mormon temples and Unitarian churches), gay bars, and "abortuaries." As Lawless lamented in another essay, the surge of interest in spiritual warfare over the last few decades has been almost exclusively tied to this superficial interpretation of it—an interpretation that "reflects more the theology of Frank Peretti's fiction than it does the teachings of the Bible."

This Present Darkness tells the story of Ashton, an archetypal American town where a cabal of professors and other intellectual types known as the Inner Circle is luring young people into New Age spirituality in order to open the floodgates for a full-scale Satanic invasion. "We used to trip out on drugs," one teenager explains. "Now it's demons."

The heroes are a hard-bitten reporter (hack Christian novels always need one agnostic or "backslider" who will be saved in the last third) and a fundamentalist pastor (who identifies himself as such, which dates the book to an era when the religious right was less concerned with spin control). The pastor is Hank Busche, a good man whose own congregation is slowly being infiltrated by evildoers. He begins to suspect this when the church board resists his effort to expel a longtime congregant for adultery and ludicrously brands Busche "an overly moral troublemaker." The reporter is Marshall Hogan, who belongs, unenthusiastically, to Ashton's

other church, the mainline United Christian Church (not to be confused
with the real life United Church of Christ), where Something Isn't Right.
The pastor there "endorses religious tolerance and condemns cruelty to
animals." In Peretti's world, that can only mean Satan.

Religious tolerance is one thing Peretti will never be accused of. As his
characters uncover more about the Inner Circle, we learn that one member
decorates his house with "grotesque idols of the East," while others dabble
in "meditation." Eventually, a source puts them onto the group's leader.
"Well, you know, he was like a guru, or a witch doctor, or some kind of far-
out ooga-booga man." Soon Busche can tell when someone has been brainwashed because they start saying stuff like "If we're ever going to get along
like any kind of civilized family on this earth, we're going to have to learn
to respect the other man's right to his own views." Clearly, this horror must
be stopped.

That's where the spiritual warfare comes in. While Busche and Hogan
fight the Inner Circle, they can sense, but not see, the *real* battle taking
place in the air above them.

> The demon twisted about, swung at him; the air filled with red
> smoke. Destroyer wailed like an eerie siren, clutching his opened
> side, floating, withering, fading. He pushed himself backward with
> one foot, hovering on erratic wings. Tal hauled back for one more
> blow, but it wouldn't be necessary. As the demon's eyes remained
> fixed on him, ruby-red, bulging in hate, the wings fell silent.

In theory, this should all be pretty exciting, but when you're trying to
stay at least somewhat within biblical parameters, there are two more or
less insurmountable obstacles to spinning a successful spiritual warfare
yarn. The first is that the good guys not only *must win*, they *already have*;
Jesus secured victory on the cross. As a metaphysical paradox at the heart
of a religious experience, there is arguably something compelling about a
struggle between good and evil that was won in advance two thousand
years ago. But as drama, it's hard to get worked up over a war in which
nothing is at stake. Peretti's choice for how to represent this doesn't help.
His way of acknowledging that the angels could defeat the demons any
time, thus obviating the need for all the torment and trouble that the

humans in Ashton are experiencing, is to have them lament that it is *against the rules* for them to intervene until the humans pray hard enough. Hence the second obstacle: Prayer is not the most exciting activity to read about in a thriller. At one point, the action stops while Hank and Marshall pray for over an hour, and believe me, you feel every minute of it.

Still, readers clamored for a sequel. In *Piercing the Darkness,* published in 1989, elementary schools are under attack by a nefarious civil rights organization that is attempting to prevent teachers from hitting their students with paddles—even if those students are *obviously* possessed by demons, which everyone *knows* have to be beaten out of children. The organization is called the American Citizen's Freedom Association, or ACFA. Totally lawsuit proof. The initials alone are enough to make good Christians quake in their boots. "Mark and Tom looked at each other. The ACFA, that infamous association—one could say conspiracy—of professional, idealistic legal technicians, whitewashed, virtuous, and all-for-freedom on the exterior, but viciously liberal and anti-Christian in its motives and agenda." Don't worry about who Mark and Tom are or why the ACFA wants to stop them. In the words of one character, "That's just the way the system works. The little people—the Christians—get into legal tangles because the state, or the ACFA, or some other rabid, Christian-eating secularist organization decides to pick on them."

In this universe, Christians never catch a break. Mark and Tom's lawyer explains that he once tried to help Christians stop a school from teaching "relaxation techniques" that smacked of Buddhism. It didn't work. "The school simply changed all the terms and sanitized the program so it wouldn't sound like religion, and then just kept doing it." In Peretti's defense, this tactic must have then sounded more sinister to Christians than it does now, as the book was written before the intelligent design and abstinence education movements made headway in public schools by using it.

By the second *Darkness* novel, it seemed clear that Peretti's preferred form of warfare was not spiritual but cultural. In his early 1990s novel *Prophet,* he leaves the demons out altogether to take on the topic of abortion. This time the villains are ordinary humans: a Democratic governor campaigning for reelection on the transparently evil platform of "pluralism, freedom of artistic expression, cultural diversity"; the "grim-faced feminist" who runs the League for Abortion Rights; the president of the

United Feminist Front, "a woman who hated men and was never timorous in saying so"; and an "articulate black woman" who leads the Federation for Controlled Parenthood. On the copyright page, Peretti is careful to note that "while I *am* dealing with real ideas, I'm not writing about any real persons, places, or institutions."

While his ideas may be real, they play out in a fundamentalist fantasyland. Peretti describes a society in which abortion mills send a van to the local junior high schools every Friday and then coerce girls into excruciatingly painful operations, even if they're not pregnant. "Abortions are lucrative," a hero explains late in the book.

> You can bring in a lot of money in a short time with minimum effort. The more abortions you do, the more money you make, so the natural inclination is to do them as quickly as possible and cut corners if you can. You get the procedure down to just a few minutes, you get an assembly line going, and you don't hire RNs to help in the back room because they get too picky about procedure, sterilizing the equipment, sanitation.

The clinics can get away with all this, and the occasional fatalities that ensue, because there is "virtually no paper trail, no regulation, no accountability."

The idea that abortions are lucrative is absurd, but the claim that clinics are unregulated is more pernicious. In fact, reproductive rights lawyers spend much of their time fighting burdensome regulations that they believe were put in place not to benefit patients but to hassle them—and to make running an abortion clinic prohibitively expensive. According to a statement on the ACLU web site,

> In 1995, anti-choice lawmakers in eleven states sponsored bills that sought to make "mini-hospitals" out of otherwise safe, efficient, and cost-effective outpatient abortion facilities. They demanded that the facilities conform to new specifications for minimum square footage in hallways and examining rooms, costly air circulation mechanisms, intrusive record-keeping and reporting, and mandatory ultrasound testing, to name just a few.

Prophet was published in 1992, and it is almost certainly not a coincidence that it so perfectly bolsters the antiabortion movement's legal strategy at the time. Everyone acknowledges that *The Jungle* led to regulation of the meatpacking industry; was Peretti's fiction the religious right's secret weapon on behalf of nuisance regulations on abortion providers?

Peretti's last book before *House,* his collaboration with Ted Dekker, was *Monster.* On its surface, *Monster* is about Big Foot. It seems Sasquatch has emerged from 1970s *In Search Of* episodes and is romping through the forest again. Elsewhere on its surface (I was going to say underneath, but the notion of layers and textures doesn't quite apply to Peretti's fiction), *Monster* is about how, Peretti has explained, "evolution makes monsters of us all." Apparently, evolution is not merely a flawed, or even incorrect, theory. It is a fraud cooked up by a conspiracy of atheistic scientists to destroy Christianity. When the world starts to catch on to the truth, one scientist sets out to manufacture evolution in a laboratory and accidentally creates the aforementioned monster.

One of the animating ideas of *Monster* is that scientists would embrace creationism if they could only put aside their prejudices and look honestly at where the evidence leads them. In an interview with a Christian web site, Peretti suggested that this same brand of fearless inquiry could validate the real-world existence of Big Foot as well. "There's a little rule in science that says anything that has a beginning requires a cause," he said. "One day there are no footprints, and the next day there are. By that scientific rule, if you find footprints that have appeared there, well, necessarily there is a cause for those footprints. Something put them there. And I can say that only a very, very, very tiny percentage of all the footprints found are fake footprints."

After immersing myself in Peretti, it was with some trepidation that I turned to Ted Dekker, whom I had already pegged as a Peretti wannabe. So I was surprised and pleased to find that Dekker can actually write. I wouldn't make any great literary claims for his work, and I doubt he would either, but for genre fiction, he has a solid command of pacing, a way with dialogue, and most important, an appreciation of metaphor and indirection, something many pop Christian authors seem scared of.

Dekker is best known for his horror novels about serial killers and mysterious strangers, and he aspires to subtlety. Non-Christian readers will catch on pretty quickly that there's a subtext you don't usually find in these kinds of books, but Christians often complain that the subtext remains too sub. For the most part, I enjoyed Dekker's books, but I did find myself a little disturbed by one called *Obsessed*. It's about the Holocaust.

This is a tricky subject for anyone to write a thriller about. But a Christian thriller? *Obsessed* jumps between 1944 and 1973 to tell the story of a hunt for a buried treasure—the stones of David. The villain is a crazed Nazi with vampiric tendencies. The hero is an agnostic Jew, who is aided by a wise old rabbi. This rabbi is different from all other rabbis; he believes in Jesus Christ. And the stones of David? They turn out to be a metaphor for the kingdom of heaven—in Jesus Christ.

Dekker means well, but perhaps he doesn't understand how problematic this is. In the 1960s, a Jewish philosopher and Holocaust survivor named Emil Fackenheim formulated a "614th commandment" (Jewish tradition holds that there are 613 in the Torah): "Do not grant Hitler posthumous victories." The admonition "has perfectly captured the mood of vast numbers of contemporary Jews," writes Joseph Telushkin in *Jewish Literacy*. "Hitler wanted to destroy the Jews [so] one *must* live as a Jew. To do otherwise would be to . . . complete Hitler's work." You can see how a book that proposes the lesson of the Holocaust is to become a Christian would be somewhat upsetting—even if you call it Messianic Judaism. It doesn't help that Dekker sets his novel in a real concentration camp— Stutthof, in Poland—where more than 65,000 Jews were murdered. It is the only documented camp where bodies were used to make soap. This tends to diminish the pleasure of getting wrapped up in an adventure tale about God's eternal love.

When Chuck Wallington arrived at 8:30 a.m. to open Christian Supply on the morning of the Dekker-Peretti reading, people were already waiting in line for tickets. Wallington is fifty years old and boyish-looking despite his midlife belly, pleated chinos, and graying hair, in part because he wears that hair in a bowl cut better suited to a nine-year-old. Wallington began working at the store in 1971, when he was in high school. It was a time when going into the family business was simply what many young people did, but Wallington fast grew to love it. "I don't know if it's genetic, if I got it from my father, or if I just have the kind of mind that is entrepreneurial and likes retail," he told me when I met him later that morning. "When you're doing something—just on a purely secular level—where you just feel like you're putting your talents and abilities to work, you feel satisfaction. When you take that and you overlay it with a spiritual dynamic of *this is what God has called me to do and created me to do,* it's like on steroids." Today Wallington's teenage sons run the Christian Supply web site. He doesn't see them taking over the store, but he thinks his daughter and her husband may be interested someday.

Wallington greeted me graciously and took me upstairs to his office. A large desk was piled high with books and paperwork, but the shelves against the wall were reserved almost entirely for photos, framed industry awards, and golf memorabilia. Lots of golf memorabilia. Looking again at the photos, I noticed that many of them were of Wallington and his friends playing golf. I began to understand the well-stocked golf shelf downstairs.

"I enjoy talking to people who are not of the Christian faith, just because it's always enlightening to me how they view things," Wallington said as he settled into his chair. Perhaps anticipating my outsider's reaction, he added that non-Christians often have "a pretty jaded view of the church—and sometimes it's justified. What makes the headlines is Pat Robertson calling for the assassinations of so-and-so, or Jerry Falwell talking about gays. What tends to make the headlines is the outlandish and the preposterous, and I'm sure this stuff makes God cringe."

Wallington doesn't want to talk about culture-war politics, though. He wants to talk about retailing. It's the kind of mind he has. And he has more experience than almost anybody in the industry. When his parents opened Christian Supply, he said, there were fifteen publishers putting out Christian books. "Now there's a hundred and fifty." In the old days, he adds, "I could always spot a Christian book by the cover design. Instead of doing a four-color cover, it would be two-color cover. Nobody paid for a designer in the early days. You wanted a Harry Ironside book, so you bought a Harry Ironside book. The idea of *maybe if we made this cover look better, we'd sell more* really hadn't crossed anybody's mind." Today, Wallington said, he sometimes sees seven hundred new books a week, "and most of the covers would compete with anything New York is doing. Matter of fact, some of them are better."

The pages on the inside are a different story, Wallington admitted, but he does think Christian fiction is catching up with the general market in terms of quality. "There used to be a gap, and the gap was this big." He held his arms wide. "Now the gap is probably this big." He brought his hands together until they were less than a foot apart. Wallington added that too often Christian fiction can get away with not being very good because many evangelicals believe that the message automatically elevates it; that a banal Christian book is inherently superior to a banal non-Christian book. "A lot of Christians think that because it's Christian, it can be shlocky," said Wallington. "That's the opposite mindset of what I think God would expect. In our training sessions with the staff, I always say, 'We've got to be *better* because the word *Christian* is on the outside of the building in letters six feet tall.'"

If that attitude is gradually seeping into Christian literature, a similar transformation has taken place in the gift department, an increasingly substantial section of Christian bookstores. Industry experts encourage retailers to put more emphasis on gifts because that's something they sell that Barnes & Noble still does not. When Christian Supply opened, said Wallington, people didn't buy Christian art "unless they really wanted to make an almost countercultural statement about their faith, because it looked so *blah*. You *had* to love Jesus in order to hang this on your wall, because it was almost a sacrifice."

Wallington took me back to the sales floor to show me one of his best-selling gift items. "About a year and a half ago, we ran across a Christmas tree ornament," he said. A colleague told him they could probably sell about thirty-five or forty every year. "Well, when I saw it, I said, 'We will sell the socks off that thing.'" He found one of the $15 gold-plated medallions. Around the outside it said, "Merry Christmas from Heaven." On the back was space to engrave the name of a departed loved one. In the center was a short poem. "I love you all dearly, now don't shed a tear, I'm spending my Christmas with Jesus this year."

"We wound up selling thirteen hundred of that silly thing the first year," laughed Wallington. "The newspaper came in and did an article on it."

Wallington's nearly instinctive understanding of the market sets him apart from some of his colleagues. "A lot of the stores are really struggling," he said. "This is not an industry that is filled with really savvy people." The problem is, many Christians will open a store with a simple equation in mind: If you want to spread the word, sell books. They don't realize that you need a head for business. On the other hand, some people worry too much about their profit margins and forget that a good Christian business is also a form of mission—and that the only decisions that count are the ones made up above. "The sweet spot is in the middle," said Wallington. "You do everything with the most business savvy you can possibly muster, but that's not really what determines your success. You try to be a good steward, but you're not in charge."

So, to succeed in business, you have to let go and let God—do what? Check inventory? Write catalog copy? Wallington related the story about how he ended up in his new location. He had wanted to move, but for complicated reasons, wasn't able to make it work. Instead of struggling with it, he prayed. "I'm not smart enough," he told God. "You need to be in charge. If you want to leave me in that location for seven years or seventeen years or thirty-seven years—as long as it's your decision, I'll just rejoice in it." Four days later, a Realtor, a man he'd met once a year before, called him out of the blue with a proposal that allowed him to move to his current space.

One of the business-savvy decisions Wallington has made over the years is to stock any Christian book that the market will support. If this seems obvious, it's not the way many stores operate. Most Christian bookstores won't carry books that deviate from the owners' particular theological bent, whether it's premillenialism, infant baptism, or anything else. LifeWay, a large chain owned by the Southern Baptist Convention, rejects most books by charismatics or Pentecostals, seeing practices such as speaking in tongues as heretical. Many stores even refuse to carry Bible translations that use gender-neutral language (saying, for example, "let your light shine before others," instead of "before men"). These stores put faithfulness to their own dogma ahead of broader appeal.

Wallington's standards are minimal. He will carry any book that he thinks his customers will read as long as it does not deny four basics about Jesus: his virgin birth, his death on the cross, his atonement for humanity's sins, and his resurrection and eventual return. He sells books that promote charismatic gifts or Catholic theology, as well as ones that attack these as Satanic. He sells *Left Behind,* of course, as well as critiques of *Left Behind.*

"When you go to a family reunion, you get people who are intellectuals, you get people that are rednecks," Wallington explained. "But you're all related through that blood connection. You believe that the blood of Jesus has saved you from your sins, and that's the connection. We're all going to have to get along someday anyway."

As far as Wallington is concerned, that means liberals and conservatives too. Christian Supply stocks *God's Politics,* the 2005 bestseller by progressive evangelical leader Jim Wallis, as well as books by liberal pastor Tony Campolo. Not too many copies, though; that wouldn't be good business. "When you talk about red states, blue states, this is about as red as you get. South Carolina's motto is 'eighth in, first out,' because it was the eighth state in the union and the first one to secede. So this is bedrock conservatism, and you're sort of sitting in the buckle of the Bible Belt here. So we don't have a lot of demand for books that are more left-leaning politically. If we had the demand, I would have no problem carrying them. But there's just not that community here. If we brought them in, they wouldn't sell."

Creative people in the Christian pop culture world—the authors, musicians, etc.—often complain about the power of the gatekeepers, generally Christian radio and bookstores. If Christian stores won't carry it, publishers won't publish it and authors can't sell it. But in the case of Christian Supply, at least, the gatekeeper effect can't be pinned on the actual gatekeeper but on the customers. Wallington told me that he was tempted to stock a T-shirt that said "Hell sucks"—"To me, that's what a Christian believes"—but mothers and grandmothers would revolt. Instead, Wallington is left with shirts that are simply tacky, in his opinion. He particularly dislikes the ones that knock off corporate logos: A Yoo-hoo parody that says "It's YOU WHO he died for," or "Lost . . ." in the typeface of the TV series, and on the back, "Found." Wallington admitted he still liked the classic God's Gym shirt, which shows Jesus bench-pressing his cross. Of the limited selection, I thought the most clever was "My other shirt says Jesus loves you."

Several years ago, a Lutheran singer-songwriter named Jonathan Rundman released an album of wry indie rock that included a song called "Xian Bookstore."

Well, I wonder if the kids
who buy those Bible action playsets
ever stage a cleansing of the temple reenactment.
Now no one knows for sure
but I think it's safe to say
if Jesus hadn't risen
he'd be rolling in his grave

"We hear from time to time 'You guys are selling faith,'" Chuck Wallington acknowledged. "I don't really think of it that way, any more than I think of a doctor as selling health." Besides, he observed, these complaints come up most often "when somebody thought your price was too high or you wouldn't let them return something."

I said, "But you can see their point, right? You're taking something that should be the deepest core of someone's being and marketing it like it was any other product."

"I don't have a bit of problem with using the most cunning, crafty, wise ways of the world that I can use to move more product out of the front door of this place, because the product we sell—we're not just selling widgets. We're selling stuff that impacts people's lives."

"Does it, though? There are some people who would say that when Christianity engages heavily in pop culture, that the pop-culture aspect cheapens the Christianity rather than the Christianity ennobling the pop culture."

"The bottom line is, someone like Ted Dekker, his novels always have a redemptive message in them. He's promoting the truth. It's kind of like crunching up an aspirin and putting it in a candy bar for a kid."

As Wallington saw it—and a random sampling of his customers agreed 100 percent—every product in his store was a tool for evangelism. What set the better books (and CDs and T-shirts) apart, in his view, was that they played it cool. Wallington found a book called *a.k.a. "Lost"* by Jim Henderson. A blurb on the cover read, "What if sharing your faith meant just being yourself."

"His thing is '*Seinfeld* evangelism.'" Wallington flipped pages. "Evangelism in the everyday, about nothing. Instead of being so overt in our witnessing and sweating under the armpits while we're doing it, it's as simple as—he talks about how his wife was in line at the store and she overheard the cashier say she didn't have money for lunch, so she was going to have a candy bar on the break. His wife gave her a ten-dollar bill and said, 'I'm a Christian. I heard that and it really touched me. I just want you to have this money to have lunch today. I'll pray for you,' and just walked out."

I got Wallington's point. That wasn't exactly waving Bible tracts and issuing dire warnings about hellfire, but it was hardly about *nothing* either. Later I would hear a more radically laid-back Christian say that by announcing her motivation, Henderson's wife was pulling her punches; that she should have trusted her love to be its own witness instead of "handing out business cards for God." On the other hand, when I repeated *this* to a friend who happens to be a liberal evangelical, she countered that maybe the woman wasn't making a sales pitch, but simply being humble, not wanting to take credit for an impulse that came to her only through Jesus. All I knew at the time was that something in Wallington's retelling rankled me. Maybe it was the implication that a non-Christian wouldn't have done the same thing. I like to think I'd have given at least a five.

Wallington told me that a lot of times what non-Christians experience as pushy evangelism is often, if not humility, nothing worse than enthusiasm, and that, if anything, the Christian consumer who wants to express this at every possible opportunity is being underserved. "We had people coming in who wanted Secretary's Day cards, but we didn't have any, because they don't make them. I fussed to the guys from Dayspring. I said, 'Guys, we got killed on Secretary's Day. We've got to have something.' People that are bosses, that are Christian, they want to give their secretary a card with scripture in it, whether their secretary is a Christian or a non-Christian. When it's such a core part of who you are, you just want to share that. It's like if you have a grandbaby, you want everybody to know it."

"That seems a little presumptuous to me," I admitted. "If you know someone's not a Christian, why not let them be?"

Wallington looked me in the eye. "See, the thing the secular world doesn't understand about Christian beliefs is, Jesus didn't give us room for tolerance. He said, 'I am the way and the truth and the life, and no one comes to the Father but by me.' If you think heaven is where everybody ought to be, you are consumed with the desire to make sure everybody gets to heaven. If somebody says, 'Well, I don't believe that . . .' well, according to Jesus, they're not going to make it. If you believe that and embrace it, it's exclusionary in its nature, and that's hard for our society today to grasp and understand without thinking that we're trying to threaten somebody or say 'I'm better than you.' In our society, where everybody is tolerant and everything is okay—'whatever you think is fine but I want to think something different'—that just doesn't fly.

"Jesus was either one hundred percent wrong or one hundred percent right, there's no alternative. Years ago, C. S. Lewis said Jesus was either the biggest liar in history, or he was the biggest lunatic in history—the equivalent of a guy who says he's a poached egg—or he was the Lord. There's no other alternative. He was either wrong or he was right."

I thought about that for a minute, and it seemed to me that there were at least two other alternatives. One was that we can't know with any certainty how much of the beliefs attributed to Jesus were really his own. The other was that, in the context of first-century Judaism, Jesus's claims, while certainly innovative and daring, were hardly insane. If they were, how would he have attracted followers? Jews were awaiting a messiah—others before Jesus had claimed that title, or had it thrust on them, and no one was comparing them to poached eggs. The theological leap that Jesus made, in the Gospel accounts, was to locate his kingdom in heaven, rather than on earth. For a first-century Jew to say he was God would be *heretical,* certainly, but not *crazy* in the way it would later be for Jim Jones. People were willing to entertain the idea because their society gave them context for doing so, just as, six hundred years later, the people of Arabia would be prepared to accept that Mohammed was God's prophet. In other words, Jesus could have been right about a lot of stuff, and honestly mistaken about the rest.*

While I'd been working this out, Wallington stopped to chat with a cus-

---

*Later I found that Daniel Howard-Snyder, professor of philosophy at Western Washington University, has also argued that this line of reasoning is fatal to Lewis's "trilemma." He further suggests that if Jesus had first come to believe that he was the messiah, it would have been entirely rational for him to then conclude that the messiah is divine, because an innovative reading of the Hebrew Bible—now the standard Christian reading— suggests exactly that. Howard-Snyder, himself a devout Christian, offers a second "merely mistaken" option that undermines Lewis: Satan could have misled Jesus into believing he was God so that people would abandon their authentic faith and worship Jesus instead.

tomer named Jack who had brought his twelve-year-old son to meet Frank Peretti. We introduced ourselves and I told him I was there to write about "Christian pop culture from an outsider's perspective."

"What makes you an outsider?" he asked.

"For starters, I'm Jewish."

His eyes lit up. "That's great! We stand on your faith."

I tried to process that as a compliment. I thought about saying, *Well, thanks, but we like to think of Judaism as having its own value, not just as a pillar for Christianity*. But soon I had bigger fish to fry as Jack, in his efforts to establish kinship, launched into a discourse that ended with "The important thing is, we all worship the same God."

Wallington looked at me as if to say that, come to think of it, there was something he'd been wanting to ask. Jack caught on. "You're of Jewish heritage, but you're not a believer, is that it?"

"It's . . . more complicated than that," I began. Considering how much time I'd been spending recently listening to other people talk about their faith—and asking probing questions that most had been only too happy to answer—I found myself reticent to discuss my own beliefs. I could have said "I'm a secular Jew." That would have been true, but grossly misleading. What I did say was "I'm a Humanistic Jew," but that couldn't be the end of it, because 98 percent of *Jews* wouldn't know what that means. Humanistic Judaism is a nontheistic denomination founded in the 1960s by a Reform rabbi from Michigan who was kicked out of that movement for removing all references to God from his congregation's liturgy. I explained that I embrace Judaism as a human development that grants meaning to human lives, without reference to the supernatural. I stressed that unlike most secular Jews, whose identity is defined solely by their cultural heritage, I belong to a congregation, I study the Hebrew Bible, I go to services with my family and light candles on Friday nights.

"So you do believe in some form of God," Jack tried.

"Personally I don't, though some Humanistic Jews do. But I don't call myself an atheist because the fact that I don't believe in God is not central to my worldview. What's central is finding meaning and values in the natural world, through human reason, and pursuing human dignity, and doing this in a way that connects me with the culture of my ancestors and my fellow Jews around the world."

"It sounds more like existentialism than it does humanism."

It's true that I'm not very practiced at discussing my beliefs, but I was pretty sure I hadn't just described myself as an existentialist. I don't believe in the primacy of the subjective individual, or in an absurd universe. I do believe that life has inherent meaning, and that morality is objective. I simply locate the source of that meaning and those morals in the vastly complex natural evolution of humans, society, and the universe. But when Jack said I was an existentialist, he sounded absolutely certain. At least I *know* that I don't know very much about evangelicalism.

The staff of Christian Supply had set up a haunted house display for the Peretti-Dekker event. The authors would sit on a raised platform, behind a folding table covered with a spooky black cloth. Spooky bundles of black sticks were arranged in ewers on either side. Behind their chairs was a posterboard showing the cover of the book, *House,* and portraits of the two writers: Peretti, fifty-five, but looking grandfatherly with a white beard; Dekker, thirtysomething, working a mysterious dark-eyed glower with a goatee and a shock of black hair. Wallington was expecting a good crowd. Not as large as for Karen Kingsbury, who drew nearly a thousand people, or Oliver North, who pulled about 750, but perhaps as many as Sting, a pro wrestler who had written a book about becoming a Christian in the WWE.

By one thirty, people clutching stacks of books had begun claiming their spaces in a line that snaked from the stage back to the store entrance. Most were Peretti fans who had never read anything by Ted Dekker before, but the couple that had driven the farthest—two and a half hours from Elkin, North Carolina—were there for Dekker. He was the only Christian novelist, they felt, who could convincingly portray the seductive qualities of evil—something most keep at an arm's length—and who didn't end his books by having "the pure Christian hero marching in to save the day."

If that was an implicit slap at Peretti, it was one that would not have bothered most of the hundred and fifty or so people who eventually showed up. Toward the middle of the line, I stopped to speak with a woman named Terri who was carrying five Frank Peretti books in her arms. I asked what she liked so much about them. "Well I can't put them down!" she laughed. But she quickly said that there was more to it than that. "*This Present Darkness* opened my eyes to thinking about the spiritual warfare that I'm in, and actually helped me a little in my walk."*

I had read several interviews with Peretti in which he stresses that he doesn't have any theological expertise, much less personal experience with demons; that all he does is take concepts he finds in the Bible and invent fantasies about them. And yet many people refuse to believe him. Terri was one of them. "With how vivid he puts everything, I honestly think that that's something he doesn't just come up with. I think it's got to be something he experiences and walks in. I do feel like he's experienced those things."

In a review of *Tempting Faith,* the 2006 memoir of David Kuo, an evangelical who went to work for the Bush administration only to grow bitterly disenchanted, scholar Alan Wolfe writes that "unlike people from religious traditions with long histories of involvement with politics, evangelicals have no firm foundation in history, theology, or experience against which they can judge the words that so easily come out of the mouths of politicians. Sincerity, for them, is everything, which is another way of saying that facts are nothing. The proof of their faith is its credulity." In other words, the same impulse that persuades a Peretti fan that his books contain the truth about spiritual warfare—even as he himself denies it—is the one that persuades them that George W. Bush must be a great man. "A lying Christian? It is just not possible," writes Wolfe of the attitude toward Bush— though he could easily be describing the response to Peretti as well. "Born-again Christians are not merely biblical literalists. If Kuo is any example, they are existential literalists, too—so totally lacking in irony that not to hoodwink them would be to leave them disappointed."

And this is what had me worried. Terri, who seemed like a perfectly ordinary suburban mom, might well, if she could see my cancelled checks to the ACLU and NARAL, believe that I am a member of an international conspiracy of Satan worshippers—because Frank Peretti says it so vividly.

"What do you think of the villains in his books?" I braced myself for a blast of vitriol.

---

*In *The Sinner's Guide to the Evangelical Right,* Robert Lanham's glossary of Christianese defines "How's your walk?" as "Christian shorthand for 'How's your walk with God?' It's like asking 'How's it hanging?' you know, without all that scrotum."

"I think he has a little bit of mercy towards them. He doesn't really paint them as totally evil."

What?

"It's the perspective he brings," Terri explained. "They just, you know, are pawns. We wrestle not against flesh and blood but against principalities and powers."

I had been reading Peretti through secular eyes. To a Christian, the dastardly liberals are not so much villains as victims. It's not their *fault* they're possessed by demons. But if I felt a slight diminishing of hostility, I also saw any hope of mutual accommodation go up in a blast of sulfurous smoke. It may shock Peretti, but these days, much of what liberals really anguish about behind closed doors is how to find common ground with people of faith. And now I realized that for at least some people, common ground will never be possible because they don't object to specific ideas that can be reframed or adjusted. They object to Satan, whose bidding we are doing. They may not hate us—they may believe they love us—but they hate him, and they won't negotiate with him either. We want to persuade them, reason with them, listen to them, and accommodate them. They want to save us. It's not even the same playing field.

Frank Peretti and Ted Dekker arrived at Christian Supply punctually, with a young, willowy publicist in tow. Peretti, in a cozy flannel shirt, suede jacket, and jeans looked even more folksy than his head shot. Dekker, smiling instead of glowering, casually dressed in a Lucky Jeans long-sleeve T, looked less enigmatic than his photo. Chuck Wallington picked up a microphone and conducted a casual Q&A with the writers, both clearly practiced at in-store appearances. Peretti, an amateur actor, hammed it up, while Dekker played straight man and repeatedly warned people that if they'd never read his books before, they might be a little shocked by some of the explicit gore in *House*. Peretti announced to applause that he was writing another *Darkness* sequel for the first time in eighteen years. They signed books and posed for snapshots.

After about an hour and a half, the last fan had left and I went up to shake hands with Peretti and Dekker. Wallington had set up fruit and cheese plates for them in the store's conference room. The staff meets there every morning at nine to write prayer cards, which they send randomly to people who have ordered from the store.

Dekker grabbed a Diet Coke, and while Peretti fixed himself a snack, I began to tell Dekker why I was interested in Christian fiction.

"I don't write Christian fiction," he interrupted. "I'd say I do pretty much what Dean Koontz does. He writes stories about moral dilemmas and resolves those dilemmas in a way that reflects his worldview. But there's no specific agenda behind it, other than to discover. So I'm not even sure what Christian fiction is. I write fiction that Christians read."

"But one reason for that is that you're published by a Christian publisher," I pointed out.

"But when you say Christian fiction, if someone doesn't understand what you mean by *Christian,* you're actually misleading them. I grew up in a Muslim country"—his parents were missionaries in a remote corner of Indonesia—"and I recognize that there's a big difference between your faith and your culture. Oftentimes, words like Christian, Muslim, Hindu are as much statements of one's culture as they are of someone's faith. So often when you say to someone, 'I am a Christian,' you're lying through your teeth because they're identifying you as a certain culture, and what you mean is, I have a certain kind of faith, and they don't necessarily know the difference.

"For example, if I go to Hollywood right now and say 'I want to make Christian movies,' what I mean by those words is very different from what the producer hears. They might hear I'm a bigot who hates homosexuals and thinks we should all carry guns to arm ourselves against the left-wing liberals who are out to kill us. But look at *The Matrix. The Matrix* is a great piece of movie-making, and it's very Christian. And it's very un-Christian. It's neither and it's both. That's the perfect kind of art. Labels only detract from the artist's intention. Unless the artist's intention is to perpetuate Christian culture. A lot of writers want that. I don't understand that. I don't get it. I don't like it."

"Is this something you've talked with Frank about?" I asked.

"Frank understands exactly how I feel about this, and so does my publisher. I talk about this every time I go on the radio, every chance I get."

Peretti ambled over. "I'll go ahead and be the other guy." He grinned.

"I'm happier being identified as a Christian author. I want literary excellence, I want to be a good writer, but I'd like to reflect the gospel."

Dekker folded his arms as Peretti sat down and kept talking. "Most of my books are blatantly Christian. *This Present Darkness* is just blatantly evangelical in tone. It's no holds barred. I don't write that way anymore, though. I find it a little heavy-handed. It's singing to the choir."

"Other than wanting to reach a broader audience," I asked, "is there something in you that's changed when you say you don't write that way anymore?"

Peretti nodded. "There's a lot of Christian material out there that's just so blatantly Christian, it's just *bad*. It's as if the gospel itself was sufficient to comprise a quality piece of work—*If I put enough scripture in it, it will be good.* Conversations like: 'Well, Joe, you seem so happy! What's happened to you?' 'Well, I found Jesus Christ as my savior. Let me show you in the Bible. Now if you go down to this verse, and this verse . . .' 'Wow, I never read it that way before!'" Peretti laughed. "I try to go a little more deep than that."

"What about limitations?" I showed them the list of taboos for Christian romance novels.

Peretti shook his head at the prohibitions against dancing, nudity, and words like *whore*. "They'd never publish the Bible!" He recalled a complaint he'd heard from another Christian writer: "You can kill and stab and shoot as long as you have all your clothes on when you do it, and don't swear."

I brought up Dekker's warning to the people who were reading him for the first time, that it might be too edgy for them. "Yet your characters still don't curse," I pointed out. "Is that your own personal thing or is that a constraint of the market?"

"That's a constraint of the publisher," he admitted. "My rough drafts aren't like that. In a novel, you want to use language that's true to a character. Every single author I know is much more real about this in their personal lives than they are in their books, you know what I'm saying? Because language changes too. Let's take the word *sucks*. I use the word *sucks* constantly. *Pissed off*. I use that all the time. Some publishers wouldn't allow either of those words. My publisher does."

Peretti raised an eyebrow. "I think there would be a pretty measurable outrage if I put profanity in my books." Peretti pointed out that he's already taken heat for *Monster,* his antievolution book. "He doesn't mention Jesus or God in it," Peretti said, in the voice of a hard-line reader. "Is he backsliding?"

"I think because you almost singlehandedly built that market," Dekker said, "you are more in the box."

Peretti mimed being trapped in a claustrophobic space. "Where are the air holes?" he gasped.

"It's important to understand your market," Dekker continued. "My newer books are not written to the church, yet at the same time, I don't want to disenfranchise that market—piss them off, so to speak. It's less of an issue for the emerging generation, Christians who are eighteen to twenty-four. They have less problems with language because they've done a better job of delineating between their faith and the culture, and they recognize that a lot of the stuff that we call Christian is just cultural. It's the rest of the world that needs to catch up, because it still tries to marry the two."

"Like we're all little Pat Robertsons," muttered Peretti.

Have we talked about how Christians have come up with a Christian version of everything?" asked Peretti. "We have Christian aerobics, Christian peanut butter. Have you been on the floor of the CBA convention?"

"Oh yeah."

Dekker scowled. "All that stuff is quite offensive. We look at it kind of like buying and selling at the temple."

"Each year there's like an unspoken prize for the most outrageous Jesus junk," said Peretti.

I was confused again. "But you write pop Christian thrillers. Isn't that part of it?"

"To think that my fiction would be put in that category, that just horrifies me," said Dekker. "I haven't read a Christian fiction book"—he glanced at Peretti—"well maybe two or three, since I started writing."

"Then let me ask you about something I noticed when I was browsing out there," I said. "There are sections for thrillers, romance, science fiction, mystery. It seemed like the one section they didn't have was 'literature' or even 'general fiction.' Why is it that almost all Christian fiction is genre fiction? It seems like you have to go back to Graham Greene or Flannery O'Connor to talk about Christian literary fiction."

"My initial answer is: It sells," said Peretti.

"Literary fiction sits there," echoed Dekker. "It's interesting to a few elites in different corners of the literary establishment, but it's not popular."

"That's certainly true in the mainstream market too," I said, "and yet there continues to be literary fiction that gets published, even if it's read by far fewer people than genre fiction."

"But for a lot of Christians who are agenda-driven," Dekker said, "literary fiction doesn't influence culture nearly as much as popular fiction does, so it's not useful for proselytizing or whatever. That's not where I come from, but that's where they would come from. Literary fiction is simply something that's written for yourself."

Clearly, Dekker was totally rejecting Wallington's depiction of his books as a spoonful of sugar to help the medicine go down. So I wondered how he would respond to the criticism about blending Christianity and pop culture. I flipped through my notebook to find a quote I'd written down from *World*, a far-right culture magazine that had tried to make a case for a return to literary fiction in the Christian market: "Christianity can compete with high culture on its own terms, but in embracing the pop culture, evangelicals have opened themselves up to what is shallow, fake, and empty in contemporary life. Instead of filling those voids, pop Christianity falls into them."

Dekker seethed. "The presupposition is so asinine, so far off, that you need go no further than recognizing that pop culture isn't shallow. I'll tell you something. That same person who wrote that would go to the natives that I grew up with, watch some kind of ritual *lap-lap* dance, which is a very sexual ritual, and think, *Oh, how fascinating. It's so deep.* They'd love it, they'd study it, it would be in *National Geographic*. You know what? It's pop culture in that culture."

Dekker went on. "Jews have always excelled at using common stories to transmit ideas. Jesus, a Jew, adopted storytelling as his primary paradigm for communicating his message. Because at the time, everyone did it. It wasn't just him. But maybe he did it better. Whether or not you think Jesus was the son of God, or whatever you think of him, everyone agrees that he is a brilliant communicator. So how could you say that using pop culture today is somehow less brilliant?"

"Look at it this way," added Peretti. "Here's the rabbi in the synagogue, and he reads from the Torah, and it's very formal and it's according to religious ritual. Then here's Jesus out on the mountainside telling stories."

The publicist was making wrap-it-up motions, but I wanted to ask Peretti about his books, especially the early ones, which seemed to me so not Christ-like. "You seem like a warm, friendly guy," I said, in utter honesty. "But in your books, I sense a lot of anger. Is that true? Do you know where that comes from?"

"Let's see. We're going to have to get to the specifics. Who am I mad at?"

I had written down one quote, more or less at random, from *Piercing the Darkness*. I read it back to Peretti, a description of a social worker as "this invader, this cancer, this vicious imposing enemy."

Peretti suddenly looked quite sad, and when he spoke again, it was more quietly than before. "I was very angry when I wrote that." He haltingly tried to explain the circumstances that that book had grown out of, then stopped and said simply, "I lashed out a lot at people in the early days."

"Do you think you wouldn't do it in the same way now?"

"No. I'll tell you why. It's not fair. A good writer will try to fill out his villain and see that villain from all sides. You don't just have totally good guys and totally bad guys."

"The thing that bothered me about it is that if I were in your world, I'd be one of the villains. A lot of talk among liberals now is about how to find common ground with conservatives, and how to build bridges so that we can move forward together, but your books quite literally demonize liberals. They worship demons. They are demons."

"I think in my earlier books there is a definite polarization there, and a demonization of the left. I think actually that was a measure of immaturity on my part, and a shallow outlook on things."

"You said you're writing another *Darkness* book. How do you think it will be coming back to that world from a different perspective?"

"That will be interesting. It's eighteen years later and I've had a lot of . . . It's going to be a different kind of book. You're going to have a lot more . . ."

He trailed off and Dekker threw in a suggestion: "You can have right-wing guys be the demons this time. Balance it out."

If it was supposed to be a joke, Peretti responded somberly. "That might not be so far from the truth in a lot of cases." He went on, "I'm past the polarization thing. The other day I was thinking of someone on the left who's always smearing us, and I thought, well, we don't say very nice things about them either."

"I'm toying with a book about reconciliation," Dekker said. "It's more about Islam and Christianity. It's going to be a very delicate subject, but . . . A thriller that has very strong themes of reconciliation, that would be a fascinating thing."

As Wallington walked me out to my car I tried to figure out what had just happened. I certainly wasn't one of those people who thought all evangelicals are little Pat Robertsons, but I *had* thought Frank Peretti was. If he'd put that hostility behind him, did it represent some broader cultural shift? The *Darkness* books had set the tone for twenty years of Christian pop fiction. Would a radically different sequel mark a break with that past?

Obviously I considered the possibility that Peretti was snowing me, but in a way, that was nearly as hopeful. Sure, there was a worst-case scenario: Maybe he thought lying to me was justified because if I learned to like him I'd be more open to his message and eventually accept Christ—and then someday we would sit around and have a good laugh about how I'd once been so far gone that he had to lie to me in order to save my immortal soul. But if his reason for soft-pedaling his message was that he couldn't bear to say what he really thought to my face, that would be a pretty good sign. It meant that even if he still believed everything he'd written in *This Present Darkness*, he was now placing at least as much value on, as his brainwashed New Agers put it, *getting along like a civilized family on this earth, and respecting the other man's right to his own views.*

On my way out of the store, I ran into Jack and his son. Not eager to get into another conversation about humanism versus existentialism, I made my small talk with the boy instead. He told me his name was Josh, and that Frank Peretti had inspired him to start writing a novel himself.

"That's terrific," I said. "What's it about?"

"It's about an archeologist, like Indiana Jones, only Christian, because I want to spread the word." But Josh told me he was actually writing a second novel, too. Something more serious. "It takes place during World War Two. It's about this guy in a concentration camp, and how he becomes Christian and stuff."

7

Children will see it and be joyful

Now I *had* to find the little Pat Robertsons. If Frank Peretti—a man who should have been thumping a Bible with one hand, casting off demons with the other, and throttling a gay abortionist with his feet—had made such an effort to distinguish himself from *those other, really crazy, Christians,* would anyone take a stand for extremism? To fully explore this parallel universe, I would obviously need to go deeper inland, away from the border zones where people speak both languages and feel obliged, if not always eager, to accept my foreign currency.

That's how I ended up in Montgomery, Alabama, looking for the littlest Pat Robertsons—the twelve-and-under demographic that Jesus suffered to come unto him. The children's market is one of the most heavily targeted in Christian pop culture. There's a financial motivation for this, obviously, just as there is for the bombardment of merchandising that all kids face. But there are other reasons this market is particularly important for Christians. "Families are concerned about the values being foisted on their kids," *Christian Retailing* editor Andy Butcher told me at the CBA trade show. Even moderate and liberal Christians, who may not particularly want their kids preached to, and who may be perfectly happy consuming only secular media as adults, will seek out "soft Christian" kid culture because they know it won't be offensive or "blatantly irreligious."

That's the mindset that has made *VeggieTales* one of the most popular children's video series—Christian or secular—of the past 15 years, having sold well over 50 million copies. The show's digitally animated anthropomorphic vegetables make only the mildest references to God, but the stories, often retellings of Bible chestnuts, promote basic Christian morals. This God-lite approach is now being mimicked by a host of new cartoons. The bestselling Christian video of 2006, ahead of both *VeggieTales* and *The Chronicles of Narnia*, was the latest in a series called *Hermie and Friends*, distributed by Tommy Nelson, the children's division of Thomas Nelson. Tommy Nelson's chief rival, the Zondervan division Zonderkidz, sells *Boz*, created by one of the originators of *Barney*. Other soft Christian kidvids—all with book, toy, and game ancillaries—include *Horned Avenger*, *Bug Rangers*, *Bugtime Adventures*, and *Gigi, God's Little Princess*. Those wanting more explicitly religious content can look to Psalty the Singing Songbook and the God Rocks!, the Christian Wiggles, whose "cool, catchy, and contagious" tunes could get Richard Dawkins tapping his toes.

The creators of these more overtly evangelical products have an additional motivation for targeting children. According to a 2004 poll by The Barna Group, nearly half of all adult born-again Christians made their "commitment to Christ" before the age of thirteen; two-thirds did so before eighteen. Wait until they're grown, and they're much harder to win over. What's more, kids who come to Christ before their teen years are more likely than any other group to remain "absolutely committed" throughout their lives. "What you believe at age thirteen is pretty much what you're going to die believing," pollster George Barna explained to *Christianity Today*. Or, as the owner of Kidz on Earth—one of the CBA's only dedicated children's stores—put it, "Kids are like wet cement: You need to imprint them at an early age."

And so I flew to Montgomery to experience the hardest of hard sells in Christian kid culture: a live appearance by Bibleman, the evangelical superhero.

The Caped Christian made his direct-to-video debut in 1996, at the tail end of the first wave of *Batman* films and hard on the heels of *Power Rangers*—his most obvious inspirations. To say *Bibleman* is low-budget is like saying Jim Caviezel got an ouchie in *The Passion of the Christ*. This is a show where reflective surfaces are added to the heroes' costumes so that lights shined at them become "special effects." Aimed at an audience of six-to ten-year-old children, mostly boys, *Bibleman* actually reaches fans as young as three. Although the show's appeal is limited by its in-your-face preaching—Bibleman quotes scripture while battling villains—each video regularly sells more than 250,000 copies, and in 2001 *Bibleman* captured 11 percent of the Christian video market. There are Bibleman toys, CDs, a board game, and even a computer game, one of the few Christian entries into that market.

Bibleman's powers derive from his "full armor of God," a line of accessories described in Ephesians 6. That's the same chapter of the Bible that inspired Frank Peretti to write his first novels, and in effect, *Bibleman* is spiritual warfare for tots.

> Therefore put on the full armor of God, so that when the day of evil comes, you may be able to stand your ground, and after you have done everything, to stand. Stand firm then, with the belt of truth buckled around your waist, with the breastplate of righteousness in place, and with your feet fitted with the readiness that comes from the gospel of peace. In addition to all this, take up the shield of faith, with which you can extinguish all the flaming arrows of the evil one. Take the helmet of salvation and the sword of the Spirit, which is the word of God.

The imagery is perfect for getting kids riled up for God, and a number of entrepreneurs have cashed in on it before and since Bibleman. At Christian Supply I saw a plastic armor of God playset and armor of God pajamas, with a shield of faith pillow. For babies there are armored teddy bears, as well as armor of God bibs, which, as the father of messy two-year-old twins, I had to admit were kind of appealing. But while most interpreters render the armor in ancient Roman or medieval style, Bibleman's version is pure comic-book superhero, an explosion of purple spandex with yellow plastic accents. The sword of the spirit, which is the word of God, closely resembles a lightsaber. The Bible does not mention a cape, but as a super-hero, Bibleman is obliged to have one.

If non-Christians have heard of Bibleman at all, it's probably because for the first seven years he was played by Willie Aames. In the 1970s and '80s, Aames was the shaggy-haired costar of *Eight Is Enough* and *Charles in*

Charge, and his only superpower was snorting three grams of coke a day. Eventually he cleaned up, was born again, and took a new job as Bibleman. His episodes are now in perpetual reruns on TBN, and I sat down to watch one.

The show opens with the backstory of our hero, Miles Peterson, "a man who had it all: wealth, status, success. Still, something was missing." I don't know about you, but when I feel that something is missing I usually mope around the house or browse YouTube for videos of cats falling off stuff. Miles, however, goes tearing out into a rainstorm and collapses into a sobbing heap. "Then, in his darkest hour," Miles finds something half buried in the mud: a Bible. Not just any Bible—a *radioactive* Bible. No, actually it is just any Bible. But apparently that's enough to turn him into Bibleman.

In this episode, Bibleman and his sidekicks, Cypher (the black guy) and Biblegirl (the girl), go up against a villain called Primordius Drool, a mincing green-skinned fop with a lisp and a fondness for show tunes. Subtlety is not *Bibleman*'s strong suit. The same actor also plays a talk show host named Sammy Davey, who is a classic stereotype of a New York Jew, complete with nerdy glasses and a giant Jew-fro. Slouching and cringing, Sammy Davey needles and browbeats poor Bibleman in an accent so thick that he pronounces Bibleman with the same inflection as names like Silverman or Lieberman.

The heart of the show is the fight sequences, typically involving a darkened warehouse (all the better to obscure the lackluster choreography) and Bibleman swatting away CGI fireballs with his lightsaber while announcing, "Isaiah 54:17 says 'no weapon forged against me will prosper!'" Every now and then, Bibleman shares a lesson with his sidekicks, as when he laments that people "allow their minds to cover up what God has placed on their hearts"—a near perfect pitch for the common evangelical notion that feelings are to be trusted above rational discernment, a belief that many nonevangelicals would be distressed to hear is being passed on to eight-year-olds.

The best thing that can be said for the show is that nobody seems to be taking it very seriously. The performances are wildly campy, and the script, written by Aames, is stuffed with corny meta jokes. At one point, Biblegirl asks Bibleman how he knew something would happen and he replies, "I wrote it that way." If not the sort of comedy that actually makes you laugh, it at least affirms that the people involved have a sense of humor.

Shortly after this episode was filmed, in 2003, Willie Aames left the program. No one wants to explain the exact circumstances, but Aames has said it was not his decision, and the fact that he was replaced with a younger, hunkier actor is probably not a coincidence. At one point in the episode I watched, someone jokes about whether Bibleman can still fit into his costume. "I've been watching my points for weeks!" Bibleman objects. Maybe, but Aames's first post-*Bibleman* appearance was on VH1's *Celebrity Fit Club*, a weight-loss reality show, and one *Bibleman* insider told me that the crew had taken to calling Aames "the grape in the cape." So it wouldn't be surprising if the producers had wanted to "take the show in another direction."

The new Bibleman was twenty-eight-year-old Robert T. Schlipp, a trim, clean-cut, apple-scrubbed children's pastor. With him, the show took a strange turn. In the Willie Aames era, Bibleman's nemeses usually had names like the Prince of Pride, the Gossip Queen, or the Fibbler, and their evil schemes involved puffing people up with pride, spreading malicious gossip, and causing kids to lie. You know, typical human sins that can be overcome by a guy with a lightsaber. But the first adventure with the new Bibleman features a very different kind of villain: the Wacky Protestor. His scheme is to "convert the kiddies to atheism," which he defines as "the belief that there is no God, no faith, no hope, and no future." Somebody needs to work on his sales pitch.

We never find out exactly what the Protestor is protesting—"under God" in the Pledge of Allegiance, no doubt—but it's easy to see why he's called wacky. Played again by the actor behind Primordius Drool and Sammy Davey, the Wacky Protestor is an obvious rip-off of Jerry Lewis who manages to be both queeny *and* Jewy in one package. His MO is to zap decent churchgoing kids with a device called the neuroiconoclasticskeptisizer, which causes them to go glassy-eyed and say horrible things like, "I don't wanna go to Vacation Bible School." Because there's *no way* a child would say that unless he was under some evil influence. Then he promises to show them a world with "no God," "no rules," and "no chores." It's true: At my house, we just throw the dishes away after we eat.

In 2006, the *Bibleman* franchise was purchased by Tommy Nelson and relaunched with a higher budget and a new commitment to earnestness, making it both more watchable and less worth watching. The current incarnation strikes a balance between midcentury values lessons and cultural warfare. One episode is about a sports drink that turns children disrespectful. The villain coaches them in the fine art of rolling their eyes and saying "Whatever." As if that's something kids need help with. The next episode is about an evil TV executive who makes sure that only celebrities who are bad influences get airtime—all part of "his life's passion: blocking the gospel of Jesus Christ from reaching kids." Yes, that's the only reason *Bibleman* isn't on NBC in prime time.

From the beginning, the *Bibleman Live* tour has been an essential element of the franchise: part traveling ministry, part promotional campaign. Phil Vischer, the creator of *VeggieTales,* has observed that the success of the *Bibleman* videos seems "due primarily to the relentless church touring schedule of the accompanying live shows." I wanted to see one for myself.

The drive from Montgomery Regional Airport to Evangel Temple, the homey brown-brick church where the *Bibleman Live* crew was setting up for the evening's performance, is a gentle arc through pleasant if familiar suburbs. The radio in my rental car was set to a news station, which I turned on just in time to catch an urgent-sounding announcement to "stand by for news coming out of Jerusalem." There had been tensions between Israel and Lebanon recently, so I stood by. "The biblical book of Genesis is being read in synagogues in Israel and around the world to confirm the Jewish claim for the land of Israel," said a reporter. "I'll have more details on this story in a moment." There was a music sting redolent of hard news to come, and then an upbeat announcer. "It's time now for *Prophecy Today,* a look at current events in light of biblical prophecy. Now with the latest . . ." I switched over to the local NPR station: "A former Christian bookstore owner has been indicted on one hundred and forty-one counts of securities fraud and eleven counts of property theft. Authorities say Sybil Watkins of Dothan owes more than seven hundred and fifty thousand dollars to fifty creditors, some who were church friends." I pressed the presets until I found music.

I pulled into the church parking lot behind an unmarked forty-foot tour bus. Inside the church I found Steven, the liaison between the church and the *Bibleman* team, who also happened to be Robert T. Schlipp's former roommate at Evangel University in Missouri. That explained why Bibleman would be performing here, for an audience of maybe a hundred seventy-five instead of the six hundred he sometimes plays to. The tech crew was having some trouble adjusting the set for the smaller stage. It was not all that elaborate—two raised platforms, canvas backdrops. The main concern was where to place several large spinning floor lights and the Bible Cave's futuristic computer consoles—four-foot Lucite boxes stuffed with random bits of machinery, plastic tubing, Christmas lights, and holographic paper. Everything was crowded together and there wouldn't be any time for the performers to rehearse before the show. Schlipp, hands in the pockets of his blue jeans, didn't look thrilled.

And then, noticing that I'd noticed, he shrugged it off. "It's not about the blocking, it's not about the staging," he said to me by way of introduction. "It's about what God can do through us. We try to achieve excellence in ministry, but part of it is God's responsibility, because it's really his show." He pulled on a black baseball cap and smiled a bright, Colgate grin. "I'm Robert T."

I suppose that Peter Parker, in person, would also be shorter and more ordinary than you'd imagined him. Robert T. turned out to be the kind of guy people never call *Mr. Schlipp*. They never call him just *Robert,* either; it's either Robert T. or, mostly, R.T., which suits his mellow, Northern California demeanor. R.T. invited me to tag along for an appearance he'd be doing before the show at the local LifeWay, a major Christian bookstore chain, so I helped him shove an important-looking metal case into Steven's hatchback, and then slid into the backseat so we could talk while Steven drove.

"So, how did you get to be Bibleman?" I asked as Steven lowered the volume on a Beatles CD.

"I was a children's pastor at a church in Rocklin, California. My friend called who had previously been the children's pastor there and said, 'You need to have Bibleman in.' And I immediately confused it with another ministry called the Bible Answer Man"—an apologetics radio show. "I'm like, 'I'm sure it's really cool, but we have elementary aged kids here,' and she just starts laughing. She's like, 'No, *Bibleman!* He's like *Batman for Jesus.*' And I'm like, 'I'm not sure *that's* such a good idea either.'

"So I went to my senior pastor and he said, 'Well you know when Corey was here she brought in Psalty the Singing Songbook, and it was *amazing*. It was *fantastic*. Everybody *loved it.*' I said, okay, we'll do it." The night before *Bibleman Live* was to play Rocklin, a nervous R.T. drove a few hours to catch the performance in the next town over. "I wanted to see how bad this thing really was, because it sounded, like, not cool. I really didn't get it. I love kids and I thought I had a really good bead on the kind of stuff kids like, and this didn't sound like it to me. It sounded kind of cheesy and lame. A grown man running around in spandex for the purpose of teaching kids about Jesus? So I went out to see this event and I was blown away."

R.T.'s story picked up speed as he recalled that night. "The lights come up, Bibleman runs out in the full armor of God, sword of the spirit in his hand, and he begins battling evil in the name of God, shouting scriptures, and this villain's just writhing, just getting pummeled. *Oh no!* The villain takes off running and Bibleman stands strong and . . . Five minutes into the show, I realized: *This is what God created me to do.*"

R.T. brought *Bibleman Live* to his church repeatedly over the next few years, making friends with Willie Aames and dreaming about how he could do something similar. "This wasn't hokey. It was *cheesy*, it was *campy*, it was *goofy*—but in a good way." During this time, R.T. met a fellow children's pastor, a woman who would later become his wife. One day he said to her, "Honey, someday I'd like to go into full-time children's pastoring. I'd love to produce videos like *Bibleman*."

"*Bibleman*?" she replied. "That's pathetic. You know *Bibleman's* a joke, right?"

She came around eventually, and when R.T. got a call asking if he wanted to step into the shoes of peace, his answer was yes.

We arrived at the LifeWay and a manager showed us into a back office. R.T. opened his metal case. Folded neatly inside was the full armor of God. R.T. lowered his voice. "I'll just warn you I have to get really . . . disrobed."

"Do you want me out of the room?"

"I'm okay if you're okay. I just didn't want to surprise you, bro."

While R.T. stripped down to his tighty whiteys, I asked him what he brings to *Bibleman* that's different from Willie Aames. He said that since he couldn't compete with his predecessor as an actor, he focused on improving the message. "In all honesty, my personal experience in the past is that sometimes the entertainment factor held this big lure that conflicted with the scriptural impact. And I don't believe that's the case anymore—and that's a great thing." In the old days, *Bibleman Live* was a commercial venture; today it's run as a nonprofit ministry, though there's clearly some cross-pollination with the highly profitable Thomas Nelson.

"So, thinking about how you once reacted to the idea of *Batman for Jesus*," I said, "when people ask you who Bibleman is, what do you say?"

"The same thing," he said, and laughed. R.T. zipped up his costume. Up close, the neoprene gloves and belt showed some wear, but the logo on the breastplate—a combination of a cross and an open Bible inside a flared oval—was impressively professional, if strangely corporate. R.T. was just Velcroing on his purple ribbed codpiece when—before I could fully process the idea of *Bibleman's codpiece*—Steven came in to say that a Christian radio host wanted to do a quick interview. R.T. picked up the phone and whispered quickly, "God, give me wisdom in answering these questions tonight." Then an on-air sign must have lit up somewhere, because Robert T. suddenly became Bibleman.

"*Fantastic,* Bob, how are things?" he exuded. "Amen! Well, tonight is going to be an *exciting* night at Evangel Temple. Not only will we have stage illusions and live music, but we are going to have something absolutely incredible tonight. We are going to have a *message*. A message that will hopefully inspire a boy or girl to make the most important decision of their life: the decision to follow Jesus. And you know, Bob, I've heard that there are evil villains lurking around Montgomery. And if one of those evil villains should rear his ugly head tonight, there *will* be battles."

Wedged behind a small folding table near the cash register with his helmet resting beside him, Bibleman looked less than heroic. A sales clerk asked why he removed the helmet. "I think it's important to show I'm a real person," R.T. told him. "Bibleman doesn't have any powers that aren't available to anyone, so when I talk to kids face-to-face, they can see that. Also, it hurts like heck."

Ten or twelve children, hands clasped shyly behind their khaki shorts and plaid school uniforms, lined up for autographs while their parents studied a rack of DVDs. Earlier, R.T. had asked the LifeWay manager if there was anything in particular he could do. "Just sell some videos," the man had replied. But selling videos did not appear to be R.T.'s goal. I wasn't sure what he was trying to accomplish. Not when the question he asked almost every child who came up was "What's your favorite verse in the Bible?"

Having had this gig for a few years, he had to know what the response would be: in almost every case, a look of anxiety and dismay that said unmistakably "I've just been busted by Bibleman." And he wouldn't let them off the hook. He'd just smile at them until they were forced to mumble something like "I don't know" or "I don't have one." One very young boy finally said, "Uh . . . *two?*"

"Two?" said R.T. pleasantly. "You like verse two? That's great."

Sometimes he'd alternate his opener with "Do you love God?" That was at least easier, although some celebrity-shocked tykes had trouble stammering out an assent even to that. A five-year-old boy came up, and R.T. leaned forward with a grin and asked, "Who was Jesus?"

"Uh . . . The son of God."

"And did Jesus pay the price for your sins?"

The boy squirmed and nodded uncertainly.

"How did he do that?"

He squeaked a reply, but I couldn't make it out.

When we got back to Evangel Temple, the lobby had been transformed into a *Bibleman* showcase. Four long merchandise tables had been set up in front of a shiny green *Bibleman* banner. In addition to DVDs there were *Bibleman* action figures for $12.99, cape and mask sets for the same, and a telescoping "light sword" for two dollars more. I pressed a red button on the sword's handle and it lit up, vibrated, and made swooshing sounds. I pressed again and it quoted scripture: "The sword of the spirit is the word of God." On another table were the new *Bibleman* BibleZines, Thomas Nelson's corporate synergy at work.

Against the far wall was a smaller table inviting people to sponsor a third-world child through World Vision, a major Christian charity that often partners with evangelical entertainment ventures. The group was offering new sponsors free "*Bibleman:* Hope changes everything" T-shirts.

Inside the sanctuary, families were sliding into pews. Blond boys ran down the aisles in their capes and masks. Giant video screens on either side of the stage played a loop of ads for Tommy Nelson products, scenes of Robert T. visiting the Dominican Republic with World Vision, and the stars of *Bibleman* giving their testimonies—those endlessly retold stories of coming to Christ that are at the very heart of the evangelical experience. One in particular struck me, though not for the reasons it was supposed to: The actor who plays Bibleman's sidekick, Cypher, talked about the moment he first realized that "either you're an accident and nothing matters, or you're not, God created you, and your life has meaning."

I was thinking about how to explain to R.T. why this got under my skin, when the lights dimmed. An announcer came out and told the kids Bibleman needed their help and they should boo really loud when the villain came out. Then the show began. I had certainly not expected to be blown away, the way R.T. was when he first saw *Bibleman Live,* but I was still surprised to be actively disappointed. Surprised, because I didn't realize that I had any expectations for the show to not live up to. I had seen several of the videos and it simply hadn't occurred to me that the live version could be worse.

The first sign of trouble came when Bibleman made his entrance and began lip-synching his dialogue. It was the same technique used in *The Great Passion Play,* only this audience was in the same room as the stage. Were the costumes too hard to mike? Were the actors, with all their jumping around, breathing too hard to deliver their lines? Then there was the plot. For some reason, Bibleman had decided to host a *Family Feud*–style game show for Cypher and Biblegirl. Only, Cypher and Biblegirl weren't on the stage with him. Their scenes were prerecorded and shown on the video screens, so that Bibleman could "call" them back at headquarters. So, to recap, Bibleman stands onstage at a church in Montgomery while his prerecorded voice holds a conversation with entirely prerecorded footage of two other characters. And what he's asking them is how five hundred people surveyed answered the question "What did Jesus do?" ("Miracles!" people in the audience shout. "Die on the cross!")

In the middle of this, Bibleman catches someone sneaking into the Bible Cave. The audience boos as instructed, which turns out to be a mistake, since the new character is not a villain, but a friend of Bibleman's named Gilbert, a nerdy klutz who wants a job as Bibleman's new sidekick. Judging from the perplexed looks of the kids who had just been jeering him, Gilbert has never appeared in the videos, despite his apparent chumminess with Bibleman. Perhaps it's an attempt to confuse the audience into submission. Then another unfamiliar character appears, wearing a cowboy hat and Western shirt. It is an awkward moment for the audience. Should we boo? He sneers, and the kids catch on and begin to boo, though with a notable lack of enthusiasm. This isn't always a problem, though. R.T. told me that on his first tour, when the bad guy was a character kids already knew and hated from the videos, one boy stood up and yelled, "I will find you in the parking lot, and I got a stick!"

At least the kids come alive for the fight scenes. During one melee, the bad guy attempts to outsmart Bibleman by pointing out, "You talk about peace, but you swing a sword. Where's that in the Bible?" To which Bibleman replies, "Hebrews chapter four, verse twelve. 'The word of God is sharper than a sword sharpened on both sides.'" And then he whacks the villain before you can say the word *metaphor*. But R.T.'s preshow fear about the cramped stage comes true when somebody leaps without looking and knocks one of the floor spotlights off a platform and sends it crashing to the ground. Later R.T. told me that kind of thing can't always be prevented, because it was no simple accident. "I believe in spiritual warfare. I believe there is an enemy out there, as sure as there's a God. And he will do anything he can to distract people from God's message."

When the show was over, R.T. came back out with his helmet off for an "altar call." For many Christian entertainers, the whole purpose of any event is the altar call at the end, when people are invited to come forward and publicly accept Jesus for the first time. About twenty children, some apparently as young as three, advanced to the stage. One of the boys tried to reach up and touch Bibleman's boot. "Can everyone repeat after me?" R.T. asked the kids. "Dear Jesus." (*Dear Jesus.*) "I know you're really great." (*I know you're really great.*) "And I want to follow you." (*And I want to follow you.*) "I want you to be my very best friend." (*I want you to be my very best friend.*) "That's awesome." R.T. grinned. "Give them a round of applause. These are the real superheroes."

Finally, the announcer came back to make a plea for the World Vision children. "Think about how much you have in your lives, and then think about these kids. These kids don't have enough clothes. They don't have any real toys." He choked up a little. "These kids will never get to sit at a *Bibleman Live* show."

Back in his street clothes after the show, Robert T. signed autographs for little Biblemaniacs. "What was your favorite part?" he asked each one, and each one answered "the fights." "You like the fights, huh? Well, remember to fight the good fight of faith. Not with your brothers and sisters!"

Later, I asked R.T. if he ever worries that kids are too attracted to the violence of *Bibleman*.

"It's really tough," he said. "If you read the entire Bible cover to cover, it would be really hard to put it down and say there was no violence in this book. There is violence in the Bible. There are times that God calls people to do things that are aggressive. It's how we *use* that aggression. It's not anger toward other people. We really try to encourage kids toward Ephesians 6, which tells us that our battle is not against people on earth but against spiritual forces. The spiritual forces of pride and anger and rage."

"Personally, I wouldn't call *Bibleman* a violent show," I said, "But the element of shouting Bible verses during fights does disturb me. I understand that it's a way of helping kids learn the words of the Bible and its message, but at the same time, they're using that message as a weapon."

"But they're not really fighting," said R.T. "Maybe I'm being simpleminded in this respect, but if two kids are gonna pick up toy swords, or Lucasfilm Ltd. lightsabers from *Star Wars* or the sword of the spirit, and they're gonna swing them at each other and *play a game,* isn't it nice that they're quoting scripture while they play a game? If they're really beating each other up, we have a problem, but that's not what happens. If it gets to that point, usually they're not shouting scriptures anymore."

I wasn't sure, but I let it pass, and asked R.T. how he thought tonight's show went. "Sometimes things come off fabulously well, and sometimes they don't come off as well as I would like for them to," he admitted. "But I really have the philosophy that it has less to do with production elements than it does with the message. At some point you've just got to decide which is most important—is the production most important or is the message most important? And if the message is most important, great. Do everything you can for the production, but at some point decide, *we've done everything we can.*" It sounded to me like the opposite of bookstore owner Chuck Wallington's philosophy, that Christian art can't settle for *good enough* precisely because of the message it represents. But R.T.—and the parents of Bibleman's many fans—argue that the results are on their side. "At the end of the day, it is really about will God use this? *Does* God use this? The answer is, *yes, hands down.* God shows up, God does what only he can do. About ten percent of the people who attend a *Bibleman Live* event will make a decision to follow Christ at that event."

R.T. anticipated my next question. "I grew up in the church and I accepted Christ when I was *really* young," he said. "So I believe that a child can make that decision because that was my life experience. There are people who say, 'Do you think a kid really understands?' Well, I have a one-year-old daughter, and I know she knows her dada. She knows her mama. Abigail knows us and she loves us. Now does she really know what it means to fully love? No, but I've met a lot of adults who don't know what it means to fully love either. So if you tell a child, 'There is a heavenly father who loves you and he has a plan for you,' a lot of kids are going to be very responsive to that. They will know God at their level, and as they mature and grow, their relationship with God will mature and grow."

R.T. asked about my faith, and I explained a little bit about being a secular Jew and a humanist. He seemed extremely interested and asked searching but not obnoxious questions, so after talking for a while, I raised the subject of how many Christians insist on defining "nonbelievers" on Christian terms (beginning, for instance, with the notion that we don't believe in anything), and how in doing so, they come off as ignorant and offensive. I mentioned Cypher's video testimony about how the only alternative to faith in God is believing that everything is an accident and nothing matters. "I certainly believe life has meaning, I just locate that somewhere other than God or gods."

R.T. put his hands on the table. "Most Christians would find it extremely hard to find meaning outside of God."

"I understand that, and I have no problem with anyone saying that. It's making negative claims about what non-Christians believe that I have trouble with. Why couldn't that testimony have been just, 'God created me and my life has meaning,' without the stuff about how people who disagree have empty and miserable lives?

"And, yeah, it's not only Christians who do this," I went on. "Every now and then in my secular elitist circles I'll meet someone who says, 'Religion is just a crutch for the weak.'" R.T. laughed, and I continued. "That bothers me just as much, and I'll say, 'I've met a lot of Christians, and they're not weak.'"

"I can do all things through Christ who strengthens me," R.T. interjected.

"Right. So that guy sounds ignorant to you, and if you were going to have a conversation with him, I'm sure you'd prefer it if he stuck to—what do therapists call it?—'I' statements: 'I believe that being responsible for my own decisions gives me strength,' not, 'You're weak because when things go wrong you take comfort in a fantasy.'"

R.T. asked if he could pray for me, which didn't surprise me. And then he prayed that my book would help Christians see some hard truths about themselves, even if it hurt. Which I hadn't expected at all.

8

How awesome is the Lord

I f it is important to get people on the hook when they are children, it is equally important, and far more difficult, to keep them wriggling there as teenagers and young adults.

According to The Barna Group, one-third of American teens identify themselves as born-again Christians. Its research into teenagers has found that while most are active in the church, this commitment slips as they age; 61 percent of today's twentysomethings say they were "spiritually active" as teens but no longer are. A less reliable statistic—but one that has galvanized pastors who believe it reflects what they see in the pews—is that if current trends continue, only 4 percent of today's Christian teens will be "Bible-believing Christians" as adults.

This concern has spawned a massive effort to make Christianity relevant to today's teens. Entwined in this is the recognition that teenagers are particularly vulnerable to the enticement of secular culture's fleshpots. As young people become more independent of their parents, more concerned for the approval of their peers, more addled by their hormones, and more curious about the world around them, it becomes harder to keep them down on the evangelical farm. A robust Christian youth culture that is every bit as cool as what the world has to offer is considered vital to their protection. At the same time, teenage believers themselves seek to express their genuine faith using the cultural forms of their generation.

Accomplishing these twin goals with any semblance of creative integrity is not easy. Leaving aside music for now, most of the Christian teen product that I saw reeked of desperation—"Xtreme worship" T-shirts, hyperactive devotional books (sorry, *devos*) with titles like *Instant Messages from God* or Rapture manuals like *How Awesome Will It Be? A Teenager's Guide to Understanding and Preparing for the Second Coming.* And most kids know it. There's a reason MySpace is still far more popular with young evangelicals than any of the Christian alternatives that have sprung up—MyPraize, YourChristianSpace, HisHolySpace, HolyPal, PeopleFisher, etc.

The real problem, though, is the disconnect between how adults want teenagers to perceive life under the authority of God—in a word, glorious— and how Christian teenagers actually perceive it—occasionally glorious, but also confusing, complicated, and distressing. Evangelical publisher Michael DiMarco, whose wife, Haley, is the former Thomas Nelson brand manager who created BibleZines, has pointed out on his blog that while young adult fiction is big business in the mainstream market, Christian YA books tend to gather dust on the shelves. The raw secular stuff, he writes, "sounds like their world around them, while sugary sweet, no-question-left-unanswered Christian fiction and nonfiction sounds, well, fictitious." Indeed, I doubt anyone has ever had a conversation like this one from *Going Crazy Till Wednesday*, a typical Christian YA novel that is part of Focus on the Family's *Brio Girls* series:

> "Jake was really cool about it, don't you think? He made me think of my life verse: 'I can do all things through Christ who gives me strength.'"
>
> "That's a good verse," Hannah said. "It sounds like you."
>
> "Thanks!" Becca couldn't think of a better compliment than that. And hearing it from Hannah, who took Scripture as seriously as anyone Becca knew, made it even more meaningful. "I hope it describes senior year for me," she confided.

In his book *Eyes Wide Open,* William D. Romanowski agrees that Christian art fails if it doesn't reflect life's uncertainties. He quotes authors Hilary Brand and Adrienne Chaplin who, in the book *Art and Soul,* declare, "God does not need us as his spin-doctors."

But this is a minority view, especially when it comes to products for teenagers, who are presumed to need more guidance than adults. To make matters worse, God's self-appointed spin doctors rarely bring their A game. The most ubiquitous form of Christian teen culture is the message T-shirt, and for every semiclever concept—"body piercing saved my life," with a close-up of a nail in Jesus's hand—there are dozens that can only make nonbelievers cringe: "1 cross + 3 nails = 4 given"; "No high like the Most High"; "Jesus beat Satan with an ugly stick," with a picture of the cross. One shirt has a graphic of a video game controller and the text, "A crowd looks on, a man is pounded, the ground thunders, blood is spilled, this is not a game—Jesus died so you could live." If this is intended to tell kids that Christianity can be just as violent and fun as Mortal Kombat, I can't decide if it's inappropriate or unpersuasive.

To be sure, not every message is objectionable. One Christian company sells a shirt that says "Can't we just love one another?" with half of the letters represented by symbols of twelve world religions. (I do wonder, however, what happens when a kid wearing it runs into one sporting another shirt I saw, "My God can kick your god's butt.") There is even some witness wear that is subtle and legitimately fashionable. One popular brand is Not of This World, and the initials NOTW, artfully silk-screened onto hoodies and ribbed tank tops, have become the hipsters' WWJD. Less attractive, but inarguably trendy (as of this writing), are countless Livestrong-inspired gel bracelets imprinted with phrases such as "live4ever" and "Godstrong."

If you talk to the kids who wear this gear, or the people who sell it, they'll tell you that their purpose is to win souls for Jesus. Not that they expect the unsaved to fall down on their knees and pray as a result of seeing the Cingular logo stretched out to look like a cross, but they do believe that a humorous shirt can be an icebreaker. At a minimum, they hold that merely seeing a scripture-based shirt is enough to *plant a seed* in the nonbeliever's heart.

In *Shaking the World for Jesus,* Heather Hendershot argues that the stated evangelistic intent of witness wear, and much other Jesus junk, is not what really makes it popular. Rather, its true meaning is found in its manifold effects on the wearer himself. It is important to remember that many Christian teens love God with a uniquely teenage passion. Writing in *The New York Times Magazine,* Mark Lilla, author of *The Stillborn God,* observed, "All teenagers are dogmatists; a teenager with a Bible is simply a more intense teenager." When teens latch onto an idea or an identity, they often throw themselves into it with fervor and want everyone to know about it. The problem is, many teenagers are also by nature socially awkward and inarticulate. They are constitutionally incapable of stopping a friend in the hall to talk about how totally awesome Jesus is. Wearing a shirt that speaks for them satisfies their need.

At the same time, that "Capture the Rapture" button or Jesus fish Hacky Sack serves as a totem that reinforces the wearer's own faith each time he sees it. And it signifies his membership in a larger tribe of Christians. In this respect, witness wear serves the same function for evangelical teens that Ozzfest shirts do for high school metalheads—it makes them feel that they *belong*. This function, says Hendershot, is precisely why the consumerist aspect of evangelical culture is integral to its nature, rather than, as many critics have it, a sad irony or hypocrisy. "To purchase Christian products is to declare one's *respectability* in a country in which people are most often addressed by mass culture not as citizens but as consumers." To be a market in America is to *matter*. This is especially important to the nation's misfit youth.

> Teenagers tend to be alienated, rebellious and horny. Secular teen culture cashes in on these feelings by providing music and music videos that portray teens as alienated, rebellious and horny. [Christian culture] acknowledges the problems that teenagers face, but it offers up Jesus as a solution. It also implicitly offers up itself, as a commodity, as a purchasable solution. If many Christian teens already feel like geeks, imagine how much worse it would be if they didn't have their own [pop culture].

Twenty years ago, the pop Christian "solution" to rebelliousness was usually to quash it. James Dobson rose to prominence on his authoritarian parenting manuals.* Today, however, evangelical teens are more often

---

*In *The Strong-Willed Child,* Dobson describes how he beat his pet dachshund with a belt because it wanted to sleep next to an electric heater instead of in its dog bed. "Just as surely as a dog will occasionally challenge the authority of his leaders," Dobson explains, "a child is inclined to do the same thing, only more so."

encouraged to embrace rebelliousness as an expression of their faith. Ardent secularists who see the church only as an oppressive institution will roll their eyes, but the Jesus-as-rebel trope is easily supported by the Bible. Romans 12, as any Christian teenager can tell you, says, "Do not conform any longer to the pattern of this world," and what is more appealing to adolescents than nonconformity?

Remember Krystal Meyers, the Christian Avril Lavigne who played at that festival I went to in Kansas with my sister-in-law and her friends? I mentioned being baffled by her hit song "Anticonformity," but later I looked up the lyrics and I could kind of see her point.

> *Pressure from my so-called friends . . .*
> *I'm measured by some stupid trend . . .*
> *Everyone is just like them . . .*
> *So I'm anticonformity*

That's not to say there's no—let's call it *paradox*—in a rebellion based on obedience to the Bible. A few months after that first concert I got to see Meyers play again at a larger festival. When she got to her big hit, she announced, "Now I want everybody to scream as loud as you can: *Anticonformity! Anticonformity!*" And without the slightest hint of irony, eight thousand arm-waving fans chanted *anticonformity* in perfect unison.*

And yet, it's not like secular teenage rebellion is any more genuine. Sex, drugs, and pierced tongues may shock Mom and Dad, but Meyers is right that they're just another mode of conformism. The paradox of simultaneous rebellion and obedience helps explain the enduring popularity of those parody shirts that Chuck Wallington of Christian Supply found so tacky, in which corporate logos are given a Christian makeover. On the one hand, they subvert the mainstream culture, turning an icon of fleeting cool into one of eternal truth (not too different from how pothead parodies of the same logos transform their meaning from *buy in* to *drop out*). On the other hand, they allow Christians to plant a flag in mainstream society, since

---

*"One of the dirty little secrets about adolescence is that the young fear the very freedom they crave," writes Lilla in the *Times Magazine*. "They intuit the burden of autonomy and want, quite literally, to be 'saved' from it."

mocking a cultural touchstone is the privilege of an insider. Almost anything is fair game in this genre. There's an NBC peacock proclaiming "Nothing But Christ." A beer can that reads "Bloodweiser. His blood's for you," and even a strained *Brokeback Mountain* gag, "The original 10 Commandments BROKE BACK on the MOUNTAIN." Perhaps the most outrageous is an emulation of Mountain Dew's "Do the Dew" logo that says "Do the Jew." The Jew being Jesus and *do,* in this context, meaning accept as your Lord and savior.

At the retail show in Denver, I had a chance to shake hands with one of the country's leading voices for Christian teen rebellion, Stephen Baldwin. Baldwin, the youngest of the acting brothers, became a born-again Christian in 2001 and quickly fell in with the evangelical skateboard and BMX bike crowd. "You've heard of Jesus freaks?" he now tells skater crowds. "Well, I'm the first Jesus psycho!"

Baldwin is not only *Xtreme!* about his Christianity, he's plain old extreme about it too. An avatar of Ryan Dobson *Be Intolerant* evangelicalism, Baldwin espouses a facile arch-conservatism that is the parallel universe version of his brother Alec's facile liberalism. His ministry's motto is "There's no democracy in a Kingdom." He spoke at the 2004 Republican National Convention and has partnered with Teen Mania, a youth ministry that is controversial among evangelicals for its militaristic trappings.* Stephen Baldwin puts the *fun* in *fundamentalist.*

Baldwin took the Christian bubble by storm in 2004 with a skate-and-sermon video called *Livin It* that sold more than 150,000 copies. The next year, he began taking the Livin It team on tour, selling out stadiums around the country. It helped that there was already a well-established Christian niche in the skating scene, so Baldwin could count on the participation of several nationally known pros, including Christian Hosoi, a genuine legend. Baldwin was in Denver to promote his memoir, *The Unusual Suspect,* and I joined the long line for autographs. From the whispers that trickled

---

*Teen Mania founder Ron Luce describes his manifesto, *Battle Cry for My Generation,* as "a rocket-propelled grenade disguised as a book." He likes to say that the "virtue terrorists" of MTV are "just as bad as al Qaida," even as he gleefully appropriates MTV style.

back, I gathered that something about Baldwin's appearance was taking people by surprise. His tattoos maybe?

Or maybe that he'd been packing on the pounds. I almost didn't recognize the puffy guy with the soul patch and Jesus cap as the handsome young actor from *The Usual Suspects*. Also, he was a little . . . orange. Had he been using some off-brand tanning cream? As Baldwin signed my book—"GOD Bless"—I asked him if we could talk a little bit at a Livin It event he'd be hosting a few months later in Pennsylvania. He nodded vigorously. "Holler at me there, dude."

Bensalem, Pennsylvania, is a suburb of Philadelphia about an hour and a half's drive through sporadic summer rain from my home in Brooklyn. I arrived at the Commerce Bank Amphitheater a little before one in the afternoon; plenty of time to mill around before the skate and BMX demos would begin. The overcast sky hung low above the damp lawn, but at least it was warm. Girls wore shorts and tank tops, guys wore Philadelphia Eagles T-shirts. Roadies were wiping down the powder-coated steel ramps and rails from American Ramp Company, a Christian manufacturer of modular skatepark equipment. Red and black Livin It banners snapped fiercely in the wet breeze, lending a touch of Soviet-style pomp to the proceedings.

Next to the skate area, a rectangular ring of vendors had set up under a white canvas tent. At one end, a local motorcycle ministry sold popcorn and cotton candy under a banner of a biker shouldering a cross on top of his Harley. The other end was dominated by the stars of the show, the King of Kings Skate Ministry. Each of the crew's athletes had a custom skateboard deck on sale for $49.99. I've ridden a skateboard exactly once in my life, when I was about nine (and ended up in the emergency room with five stitches), so I can't speak to the construction of the KKSM decks. I can, however, say they looked great, having none of the cheesy, dated design of so much Jesus junk. Mason Cornwall's graffiti-inspired deck showed an arm with a cross tattoo handling a mean-looking yellow-eyed snake. Joshua Kasper's depicted him as a cute manga warrior kneeling in front of Calvary Hill. Tim Byrne's had a retro Jesus wearing a "Tim is my homeboy" T-shirt.

The tented patio was crowded with kids keeping out of the drizzle, which seemed to be tapering off. Doing a circuit of the tables, I picked up a copy of *Breakaway*, Focus on the Family's teen guy magazine. Christian Hosoi was on the cover; articles inside explained how DNA proved the existence of God, how football can turn guys into "champions for Christ," and why the prosocial message of *Mean Girls* is outweighed by the "profanity, immodesty, sexual situations and alcohol use." Moving on, I stopped to take some literature from supporters of Rick Santorum, the right-wing senator then in the middle of his ultimately failed reelection campaign. I noticed that his Democratic rival wasn't represented—but then how would his staff have known, as Santorum's did, that a Christian skate and BMX demo would draw thousands of potential voters? The volunteer told me that it had been his idea to contact Livin It about setting up here, and I asked him why he'd thought of it. "Billy Baldwin has been a big supporter in the past," he replied. Yes, he said *Billy*.

An understandable mistake, and in any case, he was far from the most confused person here. Other than a few church groups, most of the kids had come strictly for the skating and clearly had no idea what else was in store. "Why is there all this Christian stuff?" I heard a fourteen-year-old boy ask. Several older teens, toting their own boards, had been invited by members of the King of Kings crew themselves; the pros had spent the day before the event trolling Philly skate parks. Not that I met any kids who were bothered by the evangelizing. They may not have been *Bible-believing* Christians, but they were all Christian nonetheless (or as one kid put it when I asked if he was Christian: "Yeah, but . . . nah"). At a table promoting a "bold & beautiful girl's conference" I caught the eye of a dark-eyed blonde wearing a tiny pair of handcuffs on a chain around her neck. "So have you heard of Livin It?" I asked.

"Who?"

"The skate team."

"No."

"Are you a Christian?"

A pause to think about it. "Yeah."

"But that's not why you came."

"No."

I began to feel a certain respect for youth pastors who know how to get teenagers talking. "Did you know that there was a Christian skate crew?"

"There is?"

"Um, yeah. Livin It. They're a Christian skate crew."

"Half the skaters I know are Christian."

"Do you know who Stephen Baldwin is?"

"Yeah."

"What do you think of him?"

"He's cool."

She'd never heard of him. "What do you know him from?"

"Skateboarding?" I didn't think so.

I moved on. A middle-aged pastor was handing out miniature beach balls stamped with his church's web address. I took one for my twins. They like balls and can't read. I talked with the pastor a little bit about the skateboarding phenomenon. It's a major sport today, even losing much of its outsider edge, but he'd never heard of it growing up. After a while he asked me if I had any "spiritual leanings."

"I'm Jewish."

"Well!" He beamed. "You're one of God's chosen people!" I smiled politely, but he wanted me to know he was serious. "We're only adopted into the family, but you are the family." Once again I marveled at the genuinely friendly reaction this information (the limited version) always seems to bring out in evangelicals. But I'd begun to understand why I couldn't enjoy the enthusiasm. After all, my answer didn't tell him anything about me as an individual, so what if I had said I was Buddhist or Muslim or *nothing in particular*? I'm sure he'd be friendly, but it wouldn't be the same gushing response, and that doesn't seem fair. When I meet somebody whose view of the world is so starkly divided between Us and Them, it doesn't exactly make me feel better to be thought of as Us. He leaned in closer. "You know, Jesus was Jewish and he came to fulfill all the Deuteronomic prophecies."

I excused myself. The demo was getting ready to start and I hadn't seen Stephen Baldwin yet. I went back to the King of Kings Skate Ministry table and found a beefy security guy wearing a KKSM ball cap. I introduced myself and asked where I could find Baldwin.

"He's not coming, dude."

"He's not coming?"

"Nope."

"You're serious? He told me—he told me to holler at him here."

"He's shooting a movie in Bulgaria."

"Bulgaria?" I was under the impression that Livin It was all about Stephen Baldwin. "Will he be on the rest of the tour?"

The beefy guy shrugged. "He comes and goes."

I guess my impression was wrong.

A DJ flipped on a digital turntable and began playing a mix of punk, hip hop, and hard rock. I didn't recognize any of the songs, so I assumed they were Christian. An MC hopped onto the central platform holding a wireless microphone. After a few words of welcome to the spectators—about four hundred lined up behind yellow caution tape—he pointed to the sky. "You noticed it stopped raining? That's because *God is good!*"

The five skaters began their warm-up, drifting back and forth from quarter pipe to rail to quarter pipe. Only this wasn't warm-up, it was the event. I'd never watched skateboarding on TV or anything, but I'd always assumed that I would enjoy it. In fact, it's really slow and boring—not at all like those Tony Hawk video games. Yes, it's probably more interesting if you know what's happening. The MC called out names of moves with each skater's run, but it all looked the same to me. Every time a skater got from one side of the park to the other, the MC said, "Good job!" If they tumbled, which they did as often as not, he said, "Nice try!"

So I wasn't disappointed when the demo ended after only half an hour. Unfortunately this was followed by twenty minutes of preaching. First each of the five skaters had their turn, taking the stage in their torn jeans and baggy T-shirts. "I just want to share with you guys that Jesus is real," said Luke Braddock. "You can be punk rock, but be punk rock for the Lord. You can be hip hop, but be hip hop for the Lord." A few people began wandering off. Then a guy named Andrew Palau came out. He's the son of a well-known West Coast evangelist who was one of the first to embrace extreme sports at his church. Palau invited people to come pray with the skate pros. A dozen or so people came forward, a fair number of them girls in tight jeans. Palau wanted more. "Turn to the person next to you and say, I'll go forward with you if you're ready to go," he said. As a psychological tactic it was shrewd, and seemed to work on a few people, but if the point of the altar call is for people to publicly announce that they've given their life over to Christ, what kind of followers is such quasi coercion going to get him?

When the praying was done, the focus moved to a set of taller ramps for the BMX demo. Now *that* was cool. These guys did do tricks like I'd seen in video games, twirling and somersaulting twenty feet up in the air. I could have watched it for hours. Except that twenty minutes in, it started to rain and the event had to be cut short. The MC made no comment on this, but I could only surmise that either God was now bad, or that he prefers skating to BMX—in which case we're just going to have to agree to disagree.

A few weeks later I called Stephen Baldwin's publicist to reschedule our conversation, only to be told that he couldn't talk to me because he was "busy doing publicity for his book." This seemed like a strange reason to turn down an interview request, but it did give me an idea. Since the memoir probably addressed everything I wanted to talk to him about anyway, I could construct an interview myself, using passages from the book as his answers. I could even take stuff out of context to make him look stupid! But no, that wouldn't be right.

Or necessary. All Baldwin's "responses" below are his exact words from *The Unusual Suspect.*

Stephen, I've read that you call yourself a Jesus psycho. You're not actually psychotic, are you?
Stephen Baldwin's lost his freaking mind.

So . . . that's a yes?
I lost my mind a few years ago, literally. But don't worry. I got a new one.

Oh, you mean when you were born again. That happened after 9/11, right?

Even the way I came to my faith probably makes you question my sanity. After all, the whole country watched 9/11 come down. Very few people took it as a sign from heaven that they needed to turn their lives over to God. But I did, because that's exactly what God wanted me to do. *That's a bit of a reach there, Stevie B.* Yeah, maybe, except I know it's not. God spoke to me. He first spoke through our housekeeper, then he spoke through my wife's conversion, and finally he spoke through the events of 9/11.

Well thanks for anticipating my reaction, though I don't think I would have called you Stevie B. Your housekeeper was a Brazilian woman who had a prophetic vision that she'd been sent to you by God to convert your family, starting with your wife. That makes total sense, but I didn't realize that God also engineered 9/11 as part of the same plan. This whole time I was blaming Osama.

Further and perhaps more surprising is I've come to this faith in a more intense and hard-core way than I could have possibly imagined.

How so?

I feel like I've gone skydiving and I'm falling from the sky toward earth at 120 miles per hour. The wind is howling in my ears and whipping across my face. But somehow I feel calm and at peace.

Wow! Totally freaking awesome. Are there any other hard-core extreme sports that faith is like?

I believe that faith in Jesus Christ is shooting par golf or better every day. Walking with Jesus beats the thrill of the greatest shot you've ever hit.

More thrilling than golf, you say? That's hard to believe. What is it about Jesus that's so cool?

I'd always imagined Jesus was the sweet, cuddly, loving dude, and suddenly I find out he makes Conan the Barbarian look like Conan the wimp. He didn't come with a guitar singing "Kum By Yah." Jesus brought a sword to the earth and he's still swinging it.

That's in the Bible?

"Don't imagine that I came to bring peace to the earth! No, I came to bring a sword. I have come to set a man against his father, and a daughter against her mother, and a daughter-in-law against her mother-in-law. Your enemies will be right in your own household!" (Matthew 10:34–35 NLT)

So when you hear, "What would Jesus do?" you think, "Kick ass"?

God has called me to go and make disciples of the youth of America. That is what I am going to try to do, and if you try to stop me I am going to break your face.

Gotcha. Sorry about saying ass, by the way.

An ass is a donkey. Jesus rode one.

True that. So what if the youth of America don't want to be disciples? What if some of them are Jews or Muslims or Hindus?

If eternity doesn't matter to you, stick with whatever else is working for you. All those people are praying to something, but it ain't the one true God and it isn't the truth.

But like you said, maybe it's working for them.

You can take that chance if you want. But keep this in mind: A day of judgment is coming. Don't blame me when that lever is pulled and you start falling toward hell.

What about the positive aspects of Christianity? Are there any concrete benefits, other than the par golf stuff?

I like to ask friends of mine, happy couples who seem to have a pretty good marriage, I will ask them, "How's your sex life?"

I remember thinking that was funny when I was, like, sixteen. What does that have to do with Jesus?

Here's what I tell them: Imagine taking a healthy sex life and inviting the power of God into that exchange.

Well, I'm willing to experiment, but I'd want to set ground rules first. Speaking of sex, I gather you think infidelity is a pretty big problem in today's marriages.

Men want to think having a little action on the side is normal, natural, perfectly acceptable behavior.

Yeah, men are pigs, but isn't there some way we could shift the blame to women?

Wives feed the monster by letting their husbands read magazines that, even if they aren't pornography, they might as well be. All of this opens the door to lust and enables the spiritual forces of darkness to have a field day.

Yes! Bitches get what they deserve, letting us read Maxim! *You don't mind if I say bitches, do you?*

Why the hang up on words, anyway? The word *bitch* refers to a female dog.

Fuck yeah!

Now I'm not saying I should be allowed to walk around dropping F-bombs.

Oh, sorry. Let's talk about your career. Why don't you have one anymore?

The buzz and critical acclaim surrounding *The Usual Suspects* placed me and the other guys in the film in a position to become very, very big. It worked for Kevin Spacey and it worked for Benicio Del Toro. And if I had played the game according to the rules it would have worked for me as well. I could have gone on to become an A-list actor.

So why didn't you?

God had other plans. I just didn't know it at the time.

So you passed on the A-list career and instead got everlasting life in heaven. On the other hand, Benicio got to bang Scarlett Johansson in an elevator. Let's call it a draw. You followed The Usual Suspects *with* Bio-Dome. *Why?*

God wanted me to make the film.

No, I said Bio-Dome. *The Pauly Shore movie.*

One of the reasons kids will listen to me today is because they recognize me from the movies. But not just any movie. One movie: *Bio-Dome.* God had me make this film to give me the platform that would later become my life's work.

Wait, God was behind Bio-Dome? *9/11 wasn't bad enough?*

God called me before I was born to take the message of Jesus Christ to the part of the youth culture in America most people overlook. That's why he opened a door to that very culture through a movie many of my advisors told me not to make.

When you put it that way, it makes perfect sense. Except I'll bet Pauly Shore gets recognized by, like, twice as many kids. I wonder why God didn't call him instead?

You know what I hear coming from you? Everything coming out of your mouth is motivated by hate and anger.

Sorry, I didn't think you could detect sarcasm in a fake interview. By the way, does it bother you that I'm manipulating this whole conversation?

Hey, man, I walked around for thirty-five years thinking I called the shots in my life. That's what we all want to think. *I am in control of my life. I have a choice. I have free will. I can do whatever I want whenever I want to do it and drop dead if you don't like it.* I used to think this. And I was wrong. My experience in Jesus has shown me that the free will you think you have outside of God is a lie from Satan.

In that case, you won't mind if I bring up some of your really crazy beliefs, like how a person who gets a heart transplant can absorb the memories of the donor, and this proves that the Bible is true because of all the times it says people's actions are determined by their hearts.

Solid science backs this up.

I'm glad to hear it, because it sounds a little nutty.

Maybe. But I'd rather be a nut whose eyes are opened to the true nature of reality, than go through life oh so smart, but oh so blind.

Let's talk about your hard-core lifestyle. Tell me about the first time you went into a Christian bookstore looking for something cool and exciting.

I walked out of the store disappointed and a little disillusioned. Rather than complain to the store clerk I decided to take it up with God. "Yo, God, what's the deal here?" I said. This was sort of my own Ebonics version of the Lord's Prayer.

Ha! You should have said "What the dilly-o." That would have cracked him up.

That's my message to the body of Christ in America. LIGHTEN UP!

In that case, maybe you should stop shouting. And ease up on the swords and "day of judgment" stuff.

We cannot ignore God's wrath. It is coming. And it may arrive sooner than we think.

As long as you're keeping it light. Anyway, I know all the blood and gore in the Bible is what gets the kids hooked. You're big on that story from 2 Kings where the angel slays 185,000 Assyrians in their sleep.

Dude, that ain't no wussie stuff. That's the power of God!

What about the power of God today? Has God ever answered your prayers?

Yeah, God has answered my prayers. And no, I'm not confusing a coincidence with divine intervention. A coincidence cannot explain how four days after Hurricane Katrina I went before God for three days of very serious prayer. I wanted to do something that would make a genuine difference in the lives of the evacuees sitting around the Astrodome, and I wanted whatever I did to involve the Livin It skate team.

I'll bet that threw him a curve. Most people probably would have wanted it to involve medical care or permanent shelter or reuniting families.

For three days I bombarded heaven with the same prayer, asking God to open a door for us to do something in Houston. Then my cell phone rang. Ron Weigele, the director of the Livin It skate tour, a division of the Luis Palau ministry in Portland, Oregon, had just received a call from the head guy of the Astrodome. He asked if it would be possible for the Livin It team to relocate to Houston! Anyone who just read that and said to themselves that this was just an odd coincidence is a dumb-dumb. There is no way something like this would just happen in the natural.

I'm convinced. It's too bad none of the 1,330 people who died or the 770,000 who were left homeless thought to pray also. But whatever. As long as God got your skate club a gig. Did Katrina upset you a lot?

When things happen, instead of looking at the surface events like the wind and the flooding of Katrina, I need to ask what God could be up to through these events. For Stephen Baldwin, being the kook that I am, in this new realm of possibility, I'm having an awesome time. Weather patterns are changing. The unimaginable is pretty much the lead story on the news every day. Just about everybody I know is wondering where this whole deal called life is going. Me, I'm not worried. Why? I no longer rely on myself for the outcome.

Can't we still worry about the world a little bit? If nothing else it'll keep us giving to charity and helping the poor and stuff.

Go ahead and delude yourselves thinking you can cure all of society's ills along with fixing the environment. People have been trying for two thousand years to get it right, and they've only screwed things up more.

You're right. Fuck the poor. But shouldn't we do anything to help our fellow Americans?

I believe a lot of what is wrong in America today is a result of the fact that we are not evangelizing the youth culture of America. We can build camps, we can do this, we can do that, we can do whatever we think is good for them and will better their lives and yada, yada, yada ya! But if they don't know about Jesus, then none of that other stuff matters.

Less bettering of lives, more talking about Jesus. Got it. Hey, you might want to tell Bono. He calls himself a Christian, but then he does all this trivial work on third-world debt or whatever.

Look, Bono, I am a huge fan of yours. You've got great talent. I just think in my opinion, and it's only my opinion, that you would do far more good if you preached the gospel of Jesus rather than trying to get third world debt relief. If you asked me, and you didn't but here it is anyway, I would tell you to preach the gospel on MTV. God will take care of that third world country.

While we're on the subject of people who are going to hell, how's Alec?

The love we have as a family is stronger than any of our personal views about God or politics or anything else. My brothers and sisters have been very supportive of the change in my life. Very supportive. We have mutual respect for one another, and I will not violate that by throwing Jesus in their faces.

That's smart. After all, it's not like Jesus would want to set brother against brother and create enemies within one's own household. But can't you at least drop a few hints?

I believe it was Saint Francis of Assisi who said we should preach the word at all times and when necessary, use words. What's he saying? Shut up and live it. That's the key part of how we are supposed to go and tell people about Jesus.

Oops, I'd better call Bono and have him cancel that sermon he was planning for MTV tomorrow night. Somehow he'd gotten the idea that talking about the gospel was a more effective witness than trying to get third-world debt relief. I mean, shut up and live it, right? Anyway, I notice that your book ends with a "sinner's prayer." What's that?

That's a prayer that acknowledges all the crap you've done and asks God to forgive you and take control of your life.

Careful, I don't think you're supposed to say **crap.**

Hey man, where does it say in the Bible that I can't use the word crap?

Um, same places that it says you can't drop the F-bomb, I guess. Colossians 3:8, Colossians 4:6, Matthew 12:36, Titus 2:7–8, Ephesians 4:29 . . .

Hey, guess what, I don't believe using the word crap is a sin. What do you have to say to me now?

I say, I don't believe gay marriage is a sin. Let's call the whole thing off. So why do you think the church has such a hard time reaching today's teenagers?

Too many churches and Christian organizations don't try, or if they do they end up producing some cheesy pile of dung that is about as relevant as a Pat Boone song to a hip-hop rapper.

I'm sorry, did you just say "a hip-hop rapper"?

The other day I was sitting in church and a promo video for a very popular men's ministry came on. I've gotta tell you, it was the biggest pile of stinking cheese I've seen. Apparently these people want to reach out to a younger audience. So they had some fifty-something guy read a script where he comes on the screen and starts saying, "Yo, man, what's up, how ya doing dawg, yeah, how you doing." I guess they figured if he talked like that young men would immediately connect with him. If I was a kid in church and I saw that thing I would fall over laughing.

Ha ha ha! That's hilarious. Obviously they should have gone with a pudgy forty-two-year-old guy saying dude and gnarly and saying the Lord's Prayer in Ebonics.

You are an idiot.

Okay, that was out of context.

9

For their rock is not like our rock

S ince 1830, the institution now known as Trinity Lutheran Seminary, in Columbus, Ohio, has trained scholars and pastors of the
American Lutheran Church. In some ways, the hushed brick halls
of this bastion of mainline Protestantism are as culturally distant from conservative evangelicalism as my own world of the New York media. But
here, too, there are attempts to bridge the gap.

In a lower-level classroom, fifteen graduate students listened attentively,
pens poised over notepads, as a bearded theology professor in a dark wool
suit jacket drew their attention to an important primary source. Striding
over to a CD player, he cued up the unmistakable chime of '80s pop.

Love will find a way (How do you know?)
Love will find a way (How can you see?)

"Amy Grant was often compared to Madonna," Professor Mark Allan
Powell picked up his lecture as the last synthesizer chords faded out. "She
was Christian music's first and maybe last overtly sexy singer. That was the
first thing she got in trouble for." Powell chuckled. "We'll probably talk
about Amy Grant a little more later. We won't get through this class without
talking about her a number of times."

"This class" is HTS 2204: Contemporary Christian Music, "a theological
and pastoral analysis of popular genres of contemporary Christian music

152

and their impact on Church and society." It is, as far as Powell knows, the nation's only academic course on the subject.

Powell paced the front of the room, speaking in a precise and engaging manner. He explained that "Find a Way" is notable for being the first Christian rock song to land on the *Billboard* Top 40.* Back in 1986, he reminded the class, that was nearly unthinkable. "In this period, there was a real divide between Christian and general market music. Amy Grant is the exception that proves the rule." Today, Powell added, "It's a divide that is eroding."

Indeed. Contemporary Christian music—commonly known as CCM— is a powerhouse that Amy Grant's early fans could only have dreamed of. There is now a Christian parallel for every genre of mainstream music: rock, punk, reggae, folk, dance pop, rap. According to the Gospel Music Association (whose name dates from an era when Christian music *was* gospel music), Americans spent more than $720 million on Christian recordings in 2006, making CCM a bigger niche than jazz and classical combined (and that's not counting illegal downloading; a 2004 Barna survey found that young Christians are "just as likely as other teens to engage in music piracy.") Throw in concert tickets and merchandise, and the industry's revenue soars to well over $1 billion. While the music industry as a whole has been struggling, CCM sales have increased more than 80 percent since 1995. More to Powell's point, in 2006, 64 percent of CCM albums were sold through mainstream retail outlets, rather than Christian bookstores. The pace of Christian music's crossover into the mainstream is accelerating rapidly. Ten years ago, there were probably fewer than a dozen CCM artists who had registered in the mass consciousness—and there always seemed to be a healthy space between the time when one dropped off MTV and the next one arrived. Stryper in the 1980s, dc Talk and Jars of Clay in the 1990s, P.O.D. in 2000. But lately Christian artists have been taking over the mainstream: Switchfoot, Relient K, Casting Crowns, Underoath, Flyleaf. Where had these bands come from?

Ever since attending SHOUTfest with my sister-in-law and her friends,

---

*Debbie Boone's "You Light Up My Life," the most popular song of the 1970s, owed its allegiance and success to a prerock aesthetic.

I'd been trying to get a grasp on Christian rock and pop—finding the Christian stations on my road trips, sampling whatever caught my attention on iTunes. But with no context for what I was hearing, my random explorations only made me feel more lost.

When I contacted Powell for advice, he understood. A few years ago, he was in a similar position—an outsider to evangelical culture who developed an itch to understand why every time he wandered into a Christian bookstore, the music section had taken over more floor space. Powell, who had a previous life as a rock critic for the *Houston Post*, went looking for a comprehensive book on CCM. Not finding one, he set out to write it himself. The result was the *Encyclopedia of Contemporary Christian Music*, with entries on 1,900 artists.*

Powell invited me to sit in on one of his seminars, where he would present a brief history of CCM—"thirty-five years in two and a half hours." HTS 2204 may not be the most taxing course Trinity has to offer, but it is not a lark either. It has two chief purposes. The first is cultural. "In many respects," Powell has written, "Christian rock stars and music celebrities have replaced television evangelists as a primary media connection between pop culture and pop religion. Not knowing about Rebecca St. James or Steven Curtis Chapman may be this decade's equivalent of not knowing about Robert Schuller or Jimmy Swaggart in the 1980s." The second is theological. Powell believes that CCM offers "a window on American piety."

"It becomes a way of understanding American Christianity," he told me before the class began. "Just a quick example: Probably the biggest Christian rock band of the eighties was named Petra. *Petra* means *rock*. It's a pun, of course, because they play rock music. Rock solid. The biggest Christian band of the nineties was called Jars of Clay, which is something fragile and breakable. What was popular in Christian music in the eighties was triumphal music." At the time—Stryper time—there were at least three Christian songs titled "Armed and Dangerous." On the other hand, "what was popular in the

---

*Following Powell, I'll use the term *CCM* to mean all Christian music, even though it has taken on negative connotations for many Christians, who now apply it only to the corporate music released out of Nashville.

nineties was vulnerability, brokenness, fragility. That reveals something about our culture and about the culture's connection to religion."

Powell began his lecture with the late 1960s emergence of the Jesus people—the tribe of Christian hippies also called Jesus freaks. "Jesus people were rejected by mainline Christian churches," he said, "primarily because of appearance. Back then you did not go to a Lutheran church if you did not wear a suit and tie. You did not go to a Lutheran church in a T-shirt and blue-jean cutoffs with long hair and beads. The Baptists, Nazarenes, C&MA, Pentecostal churches welcomed these people with open arms, and it flooded their ranks. And I think a lot of the strength of conservative evangelicalism today is in some way tied to this."

Evangelical churches, as well as influential leaders such as Billy Graham and Bill Bright of Campus Crusade for Christ, also embraced the music of the Jesus people (although there were, and still are, fundamentalists who could never reconcile Christianity with rock 'n' roll). There wasn't much of this "Jesus music" at the time—a handful of artists given to bluesy jams or Beatles-inspired harmonies—but it was enough to spark a revolution. "The music was characterized by a passion and a purity of motives," Powell told his students. "These artists weren't doing it to make money, and they did not make money. It was somewhat evangelistic, but that wasn't even the primary motive. It was more just, the joy of being born again welled up within them, and if you were a musician it spilled out into your music. It was also characterized by low production values and what I'll charitably call moderate talent. Most of these artists simply did not have the chops or the voices or the same level of talent that would now be in contemporary Christian music today. Nevertheless a lot of critics, especially those who were there at the time, will say this is the best Christian music there ever was, because of the passion and the purity."

The father of Christian rock was Larry Norman, who wrote the Rapture theme song "I Wish We'd All Been Ready." "The term *Jesus freak* was first coined to refer to him," writes Powell in his encyclopedia, "and no other person in history has ever been more deserving of the appellation." He looked the part, certainly, with his blond hair down to his waist, but more than that, he was plain weird—a mercurial crank with a reed-thin voice and a talent for dark, visionary poetry. Powell played a Norman song called "Why Don't You Look Into Jesus?" a foot-stomping rocker allegedly written for Janis Joplin.

> *Gonorrhea on Valentine's Day*
> *And you're still looking for the perfect lay.*
> *You think rock 'n' roll will set you free,*
> *You'll be deaf before you're thirty-three.*

A murmur rose through the class. Many of the students had heard more contemporary Christian music than I had, but nothing like this. "I don't think any Christian music now would touch sex and drugs the way this guy does," one man observed.

Powell agreed. "One would not say *gonorrhea* in drive time. That would not make it on Christian radio."

Artists like Norman, Love Song, and the All Saved Freak Band never intended to start a Christian music industry, but one grew up around them after secular labels and performance venues shut them out. The Southern gospel label Word created a rock 'n' roll spin-off to accommodate these strange new acts, and similar ventures soon followed. By the late '70s, however, the hippie era came to an end and the welling up of joy that inspired Jesus music went flat. To meet demand, record labels turned to artists with more professionalism but decidedly less purity and passion, and retained a coterie of studio musicians and producers to help churn out albums. "We created a monster," the former head of Word has said.

This was the era when the industry began to actively promote artists as *safe* equivalents to mainstream acts. Whitecross was the Christian Aerosmith, DeGarmo & Key were the Christian Hall & Oates. This solidified the barrier between Christian and mainstream music. The more Christian rock tried to mimic secular hitmakers, the less reason there was for non-Christians to pay any attention to it. At the same time, Christians became emotionally and financially invested in their musical ghetto.

"Two events that I take as pivotal for inaugurating this parallel universe phase are the conversion of B. J. Thomas and of Bob Dylan," Powell told the class. First, Thomas outraged Christian audiences when he tried to perform his innocuous pre-Christian hits. "In the middle of one of his concerts he did, like, four or five Christian songs and then he sings 'Raindrops Keep Falling on My Head,' and about two lines into it, somebody stands up and screams at him that he's possessed by the devil." Then Dylan was booed and picketed by his former fans when he refused to play any of his pre-born-again songs. Society's rules were clear, said Powell. "If you are a Christian artist you sing Christian songs for Christian audiences. If you are a secular artist you sing secular songs for secular audiences." CCM's rapid growth allowed it to adhere to this rule. By the end of the '80s, top Christian artists could earn gold and platinum albums without any attention from the general market.

The 1980s and early '90s gave Christian rock its poor reputation among outsiders. There were some hidden gems—alternative artists writing creative and challenging music—but the Christian industry largely ignored these. CCM was a serious business now—most of the major Christian record labels were, by this time, wholly owned subsidiaries of secular conglomerates—and the demand for profits meant chasing the lowest common denominator.

Gradually, however, CCM began to undergo a transformation. Emblematic of this was Sixpence None the Richer, who had an inescapable mainstream hit in 1999 with the jangly pop ballad "Kiss Me." Christian artists had crossed over before, but this was different. For one thing, most people who heard the song had no idea that it was "Christian." How could they? It was a simple, romantic love song—a real love song, not a covert, Jesus-is-my-boyfriend one. What's more, Sixpence may have sounded like other popular bands—10,000 Maniacs and the Sundays were the usual comparisons—but only in the way that, well, the Sundays sounded like 10,000 Maniacs; they were an authentic band sharing a musical idiom with other authentic bands, not a knock-off.

Sixpence's success forced the CCM community to finally address a question that had been rumbling in the background since at least the Amy Grant era: What makes music Christian? Tellingly, industry insiders answered wrong, and fans rebelled. The Gospel Music Association—apparently concerned that its annual Dove Awards were going to be dominated by Sixpence and other artists who refused to pump their songs full of explicit references to Jesus—hastily adopted a clunky definition to keep these bands out. Christian music, declared the GMA, is "music in any style whose lyric is substantially based upon historically orthodox Christian truth contained in or derived from the Holy Bible; and/or an expression of worship of God or praise for his works; and/or testimony of relationship with God through Christ; and/or obviously prompted and informed by a Christian worldview."

This formula, Powell noted, reflected the industry's heritage of fundamentalism, which cherishes firm distinctions between the spirit and the world—distinctions that most evangelicals now view with disdain. "We don't experience faith as a compartmentalized, religious aspect of life," Sixpence's lead singer, Leigh Nash, has said. "I don't feel like I'm more of a Christian when I'm saying my prayers than when I'm kissing my husband." The backlash against the GMA, which retreated two years later, indicated that many evangelicals had developed a listener-centric definition of contemporary Christian music more like the one Powell used in compiling his encyclopedia: "music that appeals to self-identified fans of contemporary Christian music on account of a perceived connection to what they regard as Christianity."

And yet, I couldn't help but think of my sister-in-law's friend Dustin, counting the number of times a band prayed during its set and sneering at "crossover" artists. As I would soon find out, the debate hadn't been settled, it had just caused divisions to harden.

In the 2006 book *Body Piercing Saved My Life,* a lively and indispensable survey of the contemporary Christian music scene, author Andrew Beaujon observes that many CCM songs "tend to evince an adolescent theology, one that just can't get over how darn *cool* it is that Jesus sacrificed himself for the world." Beaujon is drawn up short by the music's shallowness. "It's self-centered in a way that reflects evangelicalism's near-obsession with having a personal relationship with Christ," he writes. "It's *me* Jesus died for. *I* just gotta praise the Lord." I thought about how Powell singled out Petra and Jars of Clay as the quintessential band names of the 1980s and 1990s, and it occurred to me that one of the biggest Christian bands of this decade is Mercy Me.

"People often ask me, 'As a trained theologian, what do you think of the music theologically?'" Powell told me when we first met in his office. "My short answer is: Heresy is rare and so is profundity. Rarely do these songs make theological errors, but they don't usually have a lot to say."

"Are the two connected?" I asked. "Maybe they just don't get adventurous enough to make errors?"

"That could be. It's also somewhat the medium," he said. "Just as one does not usually listen to Top 40 radio to learn to navigate the complexities of romantic relationships, the complexities of a spiritual life are not usually the topic of Christian radio."

I started to speak, but Powell was ahead of me. "What I think you were about to say is, 'There are those poetic artists who have some pretty profound things to say about romantic love.' And there are, I think, Christian artists who have some pretty profound things to say about spirituality. They don't dominate the Christian radio charts. Nor would the other be true in secular radio. I think that's a fair analogy, to say that Christian music deals with spirituality in a way that's equivalent to how secular music deals with romance."

"What about political or social issues?" I asked. I told Powell about a conversation that Dustin had had with another kid at SHOUTfest. The boy had remarked that Dustin looked like the singer from Green Day (it was the eye shadow, I think) and Dustin replied that he used to like the band before they started cursing so much. "Also," he said, "a lot of their stuff is very political." The other guy nodded. "They're hard-core Democrats. You can tell."

Like Dustin, a number of Christian teenagers had told me they don't like any politics in music, but I wondered if that was just because the politics of mainstream musicians tended to be liberal. "Does Christian music reinforce conservative politics?" I asked Powell.

"The claim would be that they try to avoid it," he answered. "But in fact, what they avoid is very selective." He listed some of the two dozen antiabortion songs that have been major hits. "Some of them I think have actually been quite good and quite effective. Many I think have been disastrous." The better ones, he says, tap into the regret or mixed feelings that some people have after ending a pregnancy. By contrast, there are several CCM songs written from the point of view of a fetus that becomes aware of its mother's plan to abort it—and in some cases prays for God to forgive her. "The attempt to ascribe adult intelligence and reasoning to an unborn child sensationalizes the rhetoric surrounding the abortion debate in an irresponsible way, and ultimately makes the position of those who are opposed to abortion appear untenable and ridiculous," said Powell.

Worse still, he said, is a singer named Carman, who is one of the best-selling Christian artists of all time. Carman is a musical chameleon who has recorded in styles ranging from lounge lizard to country to rap, never with any credibility. His popularity stems from his aggressive preaching, which often incorporates political themes. "Carman videos occasionally voice opposition to gays, advocate the restitution of school prayer and ask for the distribution of Bibles instead of condoms in public schools," writes Heather Hendershot. One of his antiabortion songs, said Powell, "likens abortion doctors, and even people who would vote pro-choice, to blood-thirsty, neo-Nazi baby-killers. I actually think it would be an embarrassment to most of the antiabortion people I know." And yet, it sells extremely well. "But if a Christian artist were to write a pro-choice song, they would have *no* chance of *ever* being considered" by Christian retailers or radio stations. "Even if they quoted scripture and prayed to God, did all the right Christian things. No way."

Still, it would be incorrect to claim that CCM as a whole has a strong political agenda. The subject matter of Christian music is as broad as the interests of Christians. Part of the Gospel Music Association's abandoned criteria for CCM was that it be "obviously prompted and informed by a Christian worldview." Remove the word *obviously*—to whom, after all?—and you actually have a definition broad enough to encompass U2 and Sufjan Stevens, artists who have been enthusiastically embraced by many CCM fans, even if they operate entirely outside the CCM industry (and even if the gatekeepers are less accepting; Christian radio stations will generally not play U2 songs, though they will play covers of those same songs by approved CCM artists).

"The world at large has missed out on a lot of very fine music," Powell insisted. "Almost whatever style you like, I can show you music that you would probably think, *This is really good stuff,* but you've never given it a chance." And that quality is no longer relegated to the underground. In 1997, said Powell, *Rolling Stone* reviewed thirty Christian rock songs and declared them "no more insipid or derivative than thirty songs randomly selected from the *Billboard* Hot 100." Put that way, I had to agree.

"So why is it that it doesn't get played on mainstream radio?" I asked. "Personally, it doesn't bother me to hear somebody singing about his faith, even if I don't share that. There are a lot of great rock songs from points of view I don't share."

Powell agreed. "I love George Thorogood, but I don't actually think that I am bad to the bone, nor do I ever want to be bad to the bone."

"So is it simply bias? Even Christian songs that aren't explicitly about Jesus or being Christian get shut out."

"There has been anti-Christian bias, but I do not think that is usually what is going on. Most people are not anti-Christian, they just don't like music that is a means to an end. Imagine that the Good Rubber Tire Company puts together a band, and it happens to be a really crack-good rock band, and they write a bunch of really good rock-pop songs, and only one of them is about how wonderful Good Rubber Tires are. They put out an album, thinking that people will buy their album for the nontire songs, and once they get the album, every time they play it, they hear the tire song. I think that if the tire company did that, radio stations would not play the album, there would be a backlash against it—they would think, *we're being used.*" Powell pointed out that there are increasing numbers of CCM artists who don't have this utilitarian view of their music, but they're usually deemed guilty by association, which is one reason so many of them now resist the "Christian" label.

"When I ask my non-Christian friends about this," I said, "a lot of times they'll say, 'You know what? I don't want to hear *Jesus, Jesus, Jesus* in a song. I don't have a problem with other people listening to that, but it just doesn't appeal to me.' Then I go to their CD case and I say, 'You have all these Bob Marley CDs. You replace every reference to Jah with Jesus and you've got exactly what you say you don't like.'"

"Or they'll listen to Johnny Cash, who is *Jesus, Jesus* an awful lot of the time," said Powell. "It has to do with artistic integrity, it just seems authentic. The worst thing that can happen to music is, I listen to it and I do not feel this is the music the artist *had* to make, or maybe even *wanted* to make. I feel like the artist is trying to do what they think is going to sell. Britney Spears is an example, or the Spice Girls."

I cut him off, groaning. I was about to say something I knew one should never say to a rock critic. "I like Britney Spears!" I protested. "I'm perfectly happy to listen to contrived, disposable pop music, to enjoy it on that level, knowing full well that it was made so that I would enjoy it on that level."

"I think I would get that," said Powell magnanimously.

I thought some more. "But I don't think I'd defend the same music if it was about Jesus," I said. "Even as a non-Christian, I feel like it's okay to sell pop music as pop music, and maybe it's not okay to sell Jesus as pop music."

"With spiritual themes, the expectation is higher."

"Britney Spears just wants me to dance to her songs, not base my entire life around them."

"You want an example?" Powell pulled out a CD with a long-forgotten new-wave pop song from 1982, a ridiculously chirpy tune with the chorus, "You'll have to excuse us / We're in love with Jesus." Powell registered the look on my face and grinned. "It's the equivalent of a black velvet painting of Elvis, only this actually offends me at a level that a velvet Elvis doesn't."

Powell stopped the CD and reminded me that CCM is generally far more sophisticated today, and partly for that reason, it's reaching a broader audience. One thing I'd already learned is that, while today's nonevangelical teenagers and young adults are gradually getting exposed to Christian artists, it's still something they tend to take notice of. The next generation of pop fans, however, is being groomed on "family friendly" radio stations that frequently play Christian artists alongside Hilary Duff and Good Charlotte without comment. Radio Disney, the definitive arbiter of tween taste, keeps dozens of CCM performers in its regular rotation: Aly & A. J., the Jonas Brothers, Everlife, Jessie Daniels. One young singer, Cali, even has a kind of bubblegum update of "I Wish We'd All Been Ready" called "Toodaloo Earth." One of Radio Disney's breakout artists is the squeaky clean Jump5. I saw them perform an energetic set at SHOUTfest. My two-year-old twins danced their diapers off.

And Powell clued me in to another trend that might be equally significant. "Back in 1999 I did a test with some of the seminary students. I wrote the names of three bands on the blackboard—Third Day, Newsboys, Skillet—and said, 'How many of you know what I've written?' In a class of forty-five, there were maybe four hands. Now when I do it, forty-four hands go up. Contemporary Christian music is making inroads into mainstream, mainline Christianity. One reason is the change in the music since the nineties. Vulnerability appeals to mainline Christians, triumphalism does not. The theological infrastructure has become more acceptable to mainline Christianity."

If CCM's inroads into mainline Christianity and mainstream America is partly a result of its less dogmatic message, it seems possible that as a simple function of capitalism, the need to continue conquering these new markets will strengthen that trend toward moderation. And as culture is influenced by art, that trend could reinforce the continued moderation of evangelicalism as a whole.

But there was still the matter of Dustin and the many other kids like him who are convinced that *real* Christian music means spreading the word—aggressively, if possible. I'd talked to a lot of people who had very different opinions about Christian rock, but while most could explain what they liked and didn't like in the music, I hadn't found anyone who could articulate an overarching theory that would put all these varying approaches into perspective.

And then I picked up a book called *Apostles of Rock: The Splintered World of Contemporary Christian Music,* by Jay Howard and John Streck. I hadn't read far past the subtitle when answers began to click into place. Howard is a professor of sociology at Indiana University–Purdue University Indianapolis and a former Christian radio DJ. When I contacted him about his research, he invited me to join him at a five-day Christian music festival called Cornerstone in Illinois. Imagining a supersized SHOUTfest, I shuddered, but agreed. As it turned out, Cornerstone would transform my perception of Christian pop culture like nothing else.

I tracked Howard down at his family campsite in Sherwood Forest, one of the dozen official campgrounds on the six hundred acres of Cornerstone Farms, where more than three hundred bands would be performing over the next five days. There would be time to explore the scene later. For now, I wanted to talk to Howard about CCM. We walked down a dirt track to the midway, and sat at a picnic table near a funnel cake stand.

Howard has been to every Cornerstone Festival since the annual event was inaugurated in 1984. His trim beard is now flecked with gray and his hairline is receding, but he looked youthful in his faded jeans and plain white T-shirt, and his shining blue eyes radiated good humor and intelligence. His two kids, the older one in her teens, have been coming to Cornerstone every year since they were born, and they appeared unembarrassed to be seen with him. I pegged him as the cool, but not too cool, dad.

I told Howard about my first exposure to Christian music and the lecture I'd gotten from Dustin, the sixteen-year-old authority. "There's another side to the story, isn't there?" I asked.

"CCM has always had this navel-gazing complex, debating, *Well, what is authentic Christian music?*" he replied. "I had this conversation with teenagers who were camping with us last year. 'What do you think about Switchfoot? They only said *Jesus* once on that album. Are they really Christian music?' Trust me, we had this debate twenty-five years ago. This is nothing new." As Howard sees it, there are really three different genres of CCM, and three different types of CCM fans. He calls them *separational, integrational,* and *transformational.* The breakdown is not along aesthetic lines, and any of the CCM camps can accommodate pretty much any musical style. Instead, said Howard, "people choose their sides based largely on theological differences about what is the proper relationship for Christians to have to the surrounding culture."

Historically, CCM has been dominated by the separational camp. "Separational contemporary Christian music takes the viewpoint that the surrounding culture is evil. So therefore, what Christians are called on to do is to come out and be separate, and then to convert other people so they can come out and be separate." Separational CCM is music with an agenda. Most people, said Howard, will tell you that the agenda is to win nonbelievers to Christ, but that's hard to justify since the more religious the lyrics are, the less likely non-Christians are to listen to them in the first place. In fact, the real purpose of separational CCM, and some artists now embrace this, is to encourage or instruct people who are already believers. Either way, Howard pointed out, the most effective strategy for accomplishing these goals is to create music that mimics whatever styles are most popular in the mainstream. There have always been some separational artists with their own, authentic sounds. Bob Dylan was one,* and a new generation is

---

* "I Believe in You," from Dylan's *Slow Train Coming* album, contains the quintessential separational lyric, "Don't let me change my heart / Keep me set apart."

well represented at Cornerstone. But in general, separational artists are imitative, because they either want to trick non-Christians into listening, or persuade Christians that they don't have to leave the fold to have music that sounds like what their friends are listening to.

Lyrically, separational artists favor "straightforward, propositional claims about God and humankind," Howard and Streck write in their book. They see themselves as ministers who just happen to use music as a tool. Integrational artists hate being called ministers; they are entertainers. "Integrational CCM," said Howard, "sees surrounding culture as not completely evil. At least, surrounding culture, when it lives up to its highest ideals, can be seen as consistent with Christianity. It's at least acceptable. So rather than writing this *come out, you must be converted* music, you simply present a wholesome alternative to the Madonnas and Marilyn Mansons of the world. You don't have to be in-your-face religious, and you might even record a whole CD without a reference to Jesus or God. It's more what's missing that defines it. Christians fall in love and can write love songs. And also, Christians get divorced, and they can write a song about the pain of divorce. But you won't find songs glorifying extramarital sex or glorifying drugs."

Fans of separational music, like Dustin, assume that integrational artists scrub Jesus references from their songs because they want to cross over, or sell out, to a more lucrative audience—and indeed, most CCM artists who do achieve mainstream success are firmly in the integrational camp; Relient K, Switchfoot, and Jump5 are all examples. But integrational artists say they simply don't feel called to preach, and they don't think they have to just because they have a platform. As one singer told me, nobody gets mad at a Christian plumber if he doesn't stop in the middle of fixing your pipes to share his testimony. Why should entertainers be held to a different standard?

On the other hand, Dustin and his friends can rightly ask why, then, integrational music traffics so heavily in God-is-my-girlfriend songs. The artists obviously do want to sing about Jesus—whether out of genuine passion or a desire to sell in the Christian market—so why disguise him as *you* unless it's to pass among nonbelievers? One response is that what separational fans call selling out is really *engagement,* which is what evangelicals are called to do; that in fact one should make sacrifices to be part of the larger culture, because if Christianity is strident but separate, it is essentially sterile.

One of the most influential books of the last two decades of evangelical culture is *Roaring Lambs* by Bob Briner, a *cri de coeur* for crossing over. In his most famous analogy, Briner likens Christian pop culture to the Japanese tennis circuit. He explains that tennis in Japan is hugely popular and big business. As a result, Japanese players have no incentive to leave their country. "I can make a million dollars a year and never leave home," Briner quotes one Japanese star. "Why do I want to fly all over the world to make less money and lose a lot of matches against the Europeans and Americans." Briner adds, "With this kind of attitude, no Japanese player will ever win Wimbledon or the U.S. Open . . . Even more sadly, no Kukis or Kamiwasumis will be out there in the great international mix of players, bringing their own very special flavor, adding their own special perspective to the sport."

So, while integrational artists are not ministers, they are still dedicated to evangelism—they simply have a different idea of what kind of evangelism is most effective. Integrational artists say they may have a more subtle message, but it has a better chance of reaching the target audience of the unsaved. And it has benefits beyond witnessing. One of these is again expressed best by Briner:

> The best way to stop the spread of popular music with its vulgar suggestive lyrics is to record great music that uplifts the human spirit. Christian artist Amy Grant retards the spread of evil every time one of her records plays on a secular radio station. Those who criticize her for "crossing over" into the secular world with music that is not distinctly Christian forget one thing. Her music takes up the air time that could have gone to one of the multitude of recordings offering only degradation and moral rot.

Since I've already admitted to being a fan of Britney Spears, you probably shouldn't trust my opinions on degradation and moral rot, but there is a related argument for Christian rock that I found compelling. While many Christian children and teenagers are only allowed—or only choose—to listen to CCM, more consume both Christian and mainstream music. They are educated, however, to use extreme caution when listening to non-Christian bands. One concept I'd heard from several young CCM fans is best summed up by a kid quoted in a *New York Times* article cited by Heather Hendershot: "If you listen to secular music, you have to think about what they're saying. Here the message is simple. It's put in simple terms. You can understand it and you don't have to worry about the influences you get in secular music."

When I first read this, I scoffed. Great lyrics are supposed to be complex. Who wants to turn off their brain just to be entertained?

And then I remembered what it was like to be a teenager. Escape from the hard work of thinking about everything was, in fact, one of the main reasons I listened to music. Not only is it all right for Christian kids to want that same avenue of retreat, but more non-Christian kids would do well to develop the kind of critical listening skills that Christians bring to secular rock. It is to the great credit of evangelical teens that they aren't as thoughtless as the rest of us about such things. And I suspect that once that critical habit is developed, it becomes hard to turn off when listening to Christian music, which might, after all, be less "safe" than advertised. When I was in the back office of the Montgomery LifeWay store with Bibleman, I happened to notice on the manager's desk a copy of a CD by the Christian metal-core band Demon Hunter. A Post-it note stuck to it said, "David— We had a customer complaint on this CD. Her daughter bought it and she says it bashes non-Christians." Not only did the girl *notice*, she felt empowered to protest. You can't argue with that.

Howard's third genre of CCM is *transformational*. In *Apostles of Rock*, Howard and Streck describe transformational CCM as "music stripped of its utilitarian purposes and rendered valuable only through its ability to manifest both truth and quality. Art no longer serves religion but is drawn inextricably into it." This is the music that Howard himself has a strong preference for, and it is what brings him each year to Cornerstone, one of the few Christian festivals that embraces it. "Transformational is much more about getting people to ask the right questions, rather than trying to provide all the right answers," he said. Lyrically, it forgoes clear, propositional statements in favor of poetic ambiguity. "It is much more about exploring brokenness and failure. It's the most honest of the three types, I think. In separational songs, particularly, there's this real tendency to try to have everything wrapped up and happy by the end of the third verse, that God made it all better again. Transformational songs are much more willing to admit that things don't always get better."

"Because it's not a sales pitch," I said.

"Right. Separational artists want you to think everything comes together and you'll be perfectly happy when you become a Christian. That's really kind of baby Christianity."

And when transformational Christian artists sing songs that are not explicitly religious, it is not because they are trying to fit in with the world—as integrational artists are—but because all songs are religious to them. Howard repeated a quote from one of the most influential transformational songwriters, T-Bone Burnett: "If Jesus is the light of the world, there are two kinds of songs you can write. You can write songs about the light, or you can write songs about what you can see from the light." Transformational music, said Howard, "expresses a worldview."

"But if you can't hear it, is that still true?" I asked.

"I would say absolutely. The Christian worldview is more than just evangelism. There's a Christian view on love, or a Christian view on war or a Christian view on whatever the topic happens to be. I think if you listen to a whole body of work of a band like Over the Rhine, their Christianity will be hard to miss. A single CD or a single song, sure, you can miss it. But to somebody who really absorbs their entire catalog, those messages become consistent and themes become more clear over time. Besides, if you go to the other end of the argument, you're saying that in order for something to be Christian, you've got to have the four spiritual laws in a three-minute pop song."*

But the artist's expression of their worldview, Howard reminded me, is only a by-product of their art, not the purpose of it. What really makes transformational music authentically Christian is the artistry itself. "The best articulation of that I've heard comes from Genesis, Chapter One,

---

*Formulated by Bill Bright in 1956, the Four Spiritual Laws are: (1) God loves you and offers a wonderful plan for your life. (2) Man is sinful and separated from God. Therefore, he cannot know and experience God's love and plan for his life. (3) Jesus Christ is God's only provision for man's sin. Through Him you can know and experience God's love and plan for your life. (4) We must individually receive Jesus Christ as Savior and Lord; then we can know and experience God's love and plan for our lives.

which says human beings are made in the image of God. Well, what is God doing in Genesis, Chapter One? He's creating. So the argument is that part of what it means to be created in the image of God is to be creative. The act of creation and creativity is in itself an inherently Christian act." Non-Christians who listen to transformational music often don't even recognize it as Christian—or try to say that it's not *really* Christian—largely because we have been conditioned by three decades of CCM to define Christian music as only the bad stuff. Pedro the Lion, Victoria Williams—that's *real* music, not CCM.

For Howard and other fans of transformational CCM, its special appeal is in its potential to be, as the name suggests, transformative. "I think if there's a legitimate indictment of the church today, it's that we're subcultural rather than countercultural. A subculture, sociologically speaking, buys into the vast majority of the values of the surrounding society but tacks on its own things. We buy into the same materialism, we say, 'Nope, money won't make me happy,' and then we go out and work sixty hours a week to buy stuff, because we *act* like stuff *is* going to make us happy, and we go out pursuing stuff—just like the rest of the world does.

"Sociologists contend the number-one value in American society is self-actualization or self-fulfillment. Everybody thinks, *I have a right to do whatever it takes to make me happy*. Christians aren't really a whole lot different from mainstream society in that regard. I mean, we divorce at nearly the same rate as mainstream society. That's because we've bought into this idea that happiness is the ultimate American right. We don't challenge the materialism of our culture. We don't challenge the self-indulgence in our culture. We don't challenge the American superpower *we have a right to tell the rest of the world what to do* kind of thinking. A counterculture rejects some of the key dominant values of the surrounding society. The only values that we're worried about are abortion and gay rights. That's it." His voice took on a sardonic tone. "Because those are sins we don't commit; those are sins other people commit." He paused, and added, "The Bible has more than two thousand verses about poverty and maybe five or ten that you can interpret as being about abortion, but we're all about abortion. Those two thousand verses about Christians' responsibility to widows and orphans and aliens and strangers and the poor? We manage to be blind to all of that, but we can find those five verses about abortion."

All of this, Howard laughed, explains why non-Christians who have never heard transformational CCM tend to hate Christian music. The explicit message of separational CCM is removed from any genuine Christian context. "I think it feels tacked on to non-Christians. It feels artificial." He added, "I think that is a reflection of the state of the church as much as it is a reflection of the state of separational music."

Howard pulled on a light jacket. A band called the Lost Dogs would be starting soon, and he urged me to join him for the set. Before we got up, I asked him how Christian music has changed American Christianity.

"I don't know that I'd give it that much credit," he said. "Despite all the pretentiousness of rock 'n' roll, rock 'n' roll really hasn't changed the world very much." He thought for a second and then said, "Well, it's altered the church to some extent—making it more open perhaps, less 'anything different from the way we've always done it is evil.' It's helped knock those doors down."

"That's not nothing," I pointed out.

He smiled. "But it's also taken twenty-five years."

10

Celebrate a festival to the Lord

An hour west of Peoria, Illinois, the two-lane highways become little more than asphalt shortcuts through the surrounding cornfields. On the long, straight roads, it is easy to push your speedometer to eighty-five and hard to find anything worth slowing down to look at. But hidden down one of the gravel driveways that snakes off Route 15 is the front gate of the Cornerstone Festival. The change of scenery is surreal, like ascending a sand dune in the Sahara and finding a three-ring circus.

Cornerstone, which began in 1984 and now attracts some twenty-five thousand people each year, is neither the oldest Christian rock festival nor the largest. But it holds a special place in the pantheon as "the granddaddy of the alternative fest," as Jay Howard put it. Recently other festivals have started introducing "fringe stages," where fans of hard-core or indie music can find relief from the smooth pop-rock that dominates CCM. "At Cornerstone," Howard said, "they're *all* fringe stages."

This commitment to musical adventurism stems from Cornerstone's roots in the early Jesus movement. The festival is run by Jesus People USA, a commune founded in 1972 as a traveling rock 'n' roll ministry. JPUSA (pronounced *ja-poo-za*) purchased Cornerstone Farm in 1991 and uses it sporadically for retreats and other events throughout the year, but the group is based in inner-city Chicago, where it operates several charities and small businesses. Members live meagerly (but only by first-world standards, they point out) and pool their incomes and resources. While JPUSA is careful not to push its somewhat controversial lifestyle on other Christians, its broadly countercultural ethos pervades Cornerstone.

As a result, Cornerstone has always been something more than merely an extended concert. The music is the main draw—twelve straight hours a day from one in the afternoon to one in the morning, on eight stages simultaneously—but there are also workshops, sports, films, and art exhibits. Most people camp out—pitching tents in the woods, along the lake shore, or next to their vans in the parking lot—and the shared experience of late nights and early mornings, of dust and heat, of dancing and worship fulfills the overused Christianese promise of *fellowship*.

Howard's wife had saved us a couple of seats inside the red and white striped tent where the Lost Dogs, the band he liked, was about to go on. I figured out pretty quickly—from the fact that there were seats, for one thing—that the Gallery Stage was Cornerstone's holding pen for grown-ups, a haven for fans of singer-songwriters and roots rock. It seemed a good way to ease into the festival, where most stages were dominated by bands with amps that go to eleven.

The Lost Dogs turned out to be an alt-country band, and a decent one at that. As much as the music, I enjoyed their sense of fun—of irony, even, which my sister-in-law's friend Dustin had assured me has no place in Christian music. At one point, a member of the band recounted a time he'd gone to a concert by Barry McGuire, the "Eve of Destruction" singer who later became a major force in early Christian rock. "The couple in front of me, they were keeping careful score," he said. "Every time Barry did a Christian song, the husband would lean over and whisper, 'He's really in the spirit now.' But if he did one of his earlier numbers, the man would shake his head and say, 'He's in the flesh.'" Then the guitarist bent down and picked up a large piece of cardboard from the stage. "We don't want you folks to work that hard," he said, "so we made this here meter." He held it up and began swinging a movable arrow from "In the flesh," at one end to "Anointed" at the other.

I also noticed that the band seemed to have some liberal politics, or at least skepticism about conservative politics. I asked Howard about it. "Separationals are much more likely to be your right-wing Republicans," he said. "The transformational artists are much more likely either to be more liberal in their orientation or to be more cynical about politics completely.

Integrationists will tend to keep their politics to themselves." With Cornerstone being heavy on both separational and transformational music, I wondered how the political dynamic would play out.

The heart of Cornerstone is a rolling tangle of dirt roads and patchy fields known as the Midway. Here, two dozen rectangular tents housed the smaller concert stages, as well as workshops and merchandise booths. In among these were volleyball nets, skate ramps, prayer stations, and other enticements to diversion or reflection. Barefoot pilgrims made a slow, meditative walk through a delicate stone labyrinth. Women in peasant skirts and bandanas skipped a circle dance to Irish folk tunes. Tattooed girls in vintage dresses and combat boots lined up for cherry snow cones.

Heading south, a dust-choked road led to a series of larger stages and finally, up a painfully long and steep hill, to a natural amphitheater and the main stage, where the festival's headliners played nightly to crowds of ten thousand or more. All along this road, amateur bands set up their own "generator stages," performing for tips and adding to the joyful noise regardless of their usually limited talent. It was common to suddenly come across three guys with shaved heads playing their metal hearts out on a seven-foot patch of grass while five other guys stood around them nodding to the beat. One generator band drew a larger crowd by employing a backup dancer dressed in a robot suit made of cardboard boxes and aluminum foil. Meanwhile, campsites everywhere afforded glimpses of the spirit of Cornerstone. A sign on a tent housing the First Church of the Living Dead declared the inhabitants "gother than thou." Several groups put out begging bowls to cover their travel expenses. One tent had a sign offering free lessons in Esperanto.

When I first arrived at Cornerstone I had been given a pink wristband, a program, and a map of the grounds. But a more essential map—of what I came to think of as the Cornerstone psyche—was the constantly changing quilt of fliers that covered, from top to bottom, the Port-A-Potties. The diversity of musical styles represented was impressive and at times ridiculous. The bill for Norma Jean described them as "a blend of screamo, hardcore and math metal." Apparently, people here took their subgenres of noise almost as seriously as their faith. One kid was even wearing a shirt that said "Music is my religion." That sounded a touch idolatrous, so I questioned him and he mumbled something about Jimi Hendrix. Later, I looked it up. "The word *church* is too identified with religion, and music is my religion," Hendrix once said. "Jesus shouldn't have died so early . . . They killed him and then twisted so many of the best things he said. Human hands started messing it all up and now so much of religion is hogwash."

That seemed to describe the Cornerstone philosophy well. A lot of people here identified as *red-letter Christians,* who believe the words of Jesus have been hijacked by worldly authorities. One popular shirt commanded: "Don't go to church"—and on the back: "Be the church."

I brought up the music-versus-church issue that afternoon with a twenty-one-year-old guy named Evan who offered to share his Pizza Hut. He took a more conciliatory position. "The church helps me with my Christianity on Sundays and my music helps me with it on other days," he said. As Evan listed the punk bands he had come to see, I questioned the idea of Christian punk, given the genre's historical connection to rebellion and anarchism. "Christian punk has more of a heart," insisted Evan, "because they can sing about pressure to conform to the world. Secular punk bands don't have anything to whine about other than girls and the government. Not that the government is so bad."

Though I'm not especially a fan of punishingly loud music, I felt comfortable at Cornerstone in a way that I hadn't at any previous Christian event. The fest had what can only be called a *nice vibe.* I don't think I've ever been in such a large group of people with so few assholes. Maybe it was the sense of brotherhood or the lack of alcohol, but rarely did I witness any petulance or hostility, which was especially remarkable given the blend of potentially antagonistic subcultures. Even the hipster one-upmanship was largely tongue-in-cheek. A sign at one campsite declared its occupants "scener than you." Truthfully, genuine scenesters would probably sneer at these corn-fed rebels in their fauxhawks and bullet belts, but most Americans, even on the coasts, wouldn't hesitate to call this a hip crowd. Scarification is still outré, even if the scar is a Jesus fish. When the singer of a world-beat folk ensemble called Madison Green told the audience that he had recently cut off his dreadlocks to help him "dialogue with Muslims" in his hometown of Dearborn, Michigan, I was struck by how much evangelical culture has changed in the last thirty years. Once pastors donned ratty jeans and grew their hair out to relate to the youth; now Christian hipsters put on square drag to reach an unsaved public that's more conservative than them.

If there is a quintessential Cornerstone artist, it is probably David Bazan, who played the festival for the better part of the decade with the band Pedro the Lion.* Among the qualities that made Bazan such an important figure here was not only the depth of his talent, but the fact that he actually had more credibility in the secular world than the Christian one. Bazan had been raised in a strict Pentecostal household, but had grown into the kind of Christian who treasures the Jesus who freed his followers from religious rules. In the book *Body Piercing Saved My Life,* Bazan describes his Cornerstone gigs—one of his last remaining attachments to the Christian culture industry—as missionary work: efforts, in writer Andrew Beaujon's paraphrase, to lead "his listeners out of the desert of certainty, preaching the gospel of doubt."

But Bazan was not at the festival this year, and everyone had a theory about why. Some said JPUSA had finally gotten fed up with him for drinking beer and cursing during his sets. Others claimed it was Bazan who had gotten fed up with his fellow Christians for hassling him about the same. Either way, the Pedro the Lion fan base had apparently found a worthy replacement in a strange and wonderful band called mewithoutYou. They had first played Cornerstone at a generator stage, and had been invited back to play officially the next year. MewithoutYou is less emo than Pedro the Lion, but has an equal facility for meandering melodies and allusive poetry. Lead singer Aaron Weiss has a wild, pleading voice reminiscent of early Neil Young. One afternoon I was talking with someone about the band, and he said I should make sure to catch Weiss when he gave a talk the next day. "You want to see different?" he said. "This guy is different."

Back at the Port-A-Potties I was surprised to see a flier for a band I actually knew: MxPx. I went through a pop-punk phase a few years back, and had

---

*Or, more accurately, *as* Pedro the Lion, since Bazan was the group's creative force and only permanent member.

accumulated a few of their MP3s without knowing anything about them, certainly not that they were Christian. I caught up with lead singer and songwriter Mike Herrera at the press tent, where most of the artists show up eventually. Herrera is tall and rock-star handsome, with a thick head of black hair and a double-pierced lower lip. Since MxPx has recorded for both Christian and secular labels in its ten years, I asked him about the pros and cons of being in the Christian market. "I guess the pros are it's a smaller swimming pool," he said. "It's easier to get big and you don't have to be as good."

"That's not really a pro for the fans, is it?" I pointed out.

Herrera peered at me over his black sunglasses. The fans, he returned, are often their own worst enemies for refusing to listen to non-Christian rock. "If they paid more attention, I think it would change how much a lot of these bands could get away with not being original." He added that when fans do put pressure on Christian bands it's not to improve as artists, but to be saintly. "If other Christians like you just because you're Christian, you have to do what's right in their eyes. Which I totally don't agree with, because I think people are people, and just because you're in a band doesn't mean you're any different really."

Cornerstone is the only Christian festival MxPx plays, and that's partly because it's one of the few that does not require performers to sign a contract affirming that they have not done anything "unbiblical" in the recent past. To be a top CCM artist—which MxPx, P.O.D., and other crossover stars really are not—is to be under constant scrutiny. Most of the major CCM labels in Nashville have morals clauses in their contracts, and some artists have "accountability boards" or tour pastors to help keep them on the right path. Artists who have been caught in extramarital affairs have been exiled from the business for years.

To some extent, all of this reflects a lingering suspicion of rock 'n' roll among evangelicals. The younger generation may have totally embraced the form, but older Christians, especially those in positions of influence, often feel that while it's possible to "redeem" rock for God, constant vigilance is a must. They're comfortable with the light rock tunes that the radio plays, but anything else has to be proven innocent. No rock song won the top prize at the Gospel Music Association's Dove Awards until 1996. At SHOUTfest, white rapper KJ-52 closed the show not with a one-for-the-road party anthem but by leading the audience in a worship song, something typical of Christian festivals. "We just wanted to end this on the right note," he said, implying that rap music couldn't really be spiritual. Evangelicals often say that it is the content of the message that matters, not the look or style of the messenger, but outside of Cornerstone or the emerging churches, few seem to believe that. Tacking Christian lyrics onto "carnal" music, one minister told me, "is like a rose in a prostitute's hair; somehow it ruins the rose."

While alternative fests like Cornerstone give fans a way around the gatekeepers, most people who listen to Christian music hear it on the radio, and the rules there are especially tight. Many of the bands that are popular at Cornerstone are simply not convincingly religious enough for radio programmers.

"You have to have your JPMs to get on the radio—your Jesus Per Minutes in a song," Lori Lenz told me. Lori is a freelance publicist who represents the kind of indie rockers who seethe when their CDs are relegated to the Christian bin. I met her in the press tent one afternoon and she invited me to join her and her friend Doug Van Pelt for a soda in his RV. Lori's bands almost never get played on the major Christian radio stations, which play exclusively adult contemporary or pop, but she does sometimes try to get them onto a few specialty rock shows. "Every time," she said, "our radio promoter requires the bands to write up a paragraph of why they wrote the song and why it's appropriate for Christian radio. And every time, the bands just shake their heads and go, 'I don't understand why people can't seek out their own salvation. Why can't they read it and chew on it and work it out themselves?' And I think it goes to this motto all the radio stations have: *Safe for the whole family*. They want there to be no risk, nothing that you could ever possibly question in their programming."

"It's a dumbing down for the masses," chimed in Doug. Doug is the editor of *HM*, the Christian "hard music" magazine that he founded in 1985 as *Heaven's Metal*. "Christian radio programmers go after the demographic that supports them, which is the soccer moms" who just want something innocuous they can listen to when they're ferrying the kids around.

"It's a milk-not-meat mentality," said Lori. "One band I worked with has a single right now—and I know the guys, I know why they wrote it. It's an insanely spiritual song, but never mentions Jesus in it, and they are having the worst time getting played. We hear flak about it all the time because people just do not get it. But they don't want to take the time to get it either."

Doug brought up a singer-songwriter named Derek Webb. His band, Caedmon's Call, is an eclectic but easily digestible folk-blues ensemble that has had six number-one hits on Christian radio. But as a solo artist, Webb has been almost completely shut out of Christian radio and bookstores for his challenging lyrics on faith and politics. In 2007, Webb told *Christianity Today* that for Christian radio, "*Safe for the family* is a terrible and counter-productive slogan. If anything, artists are called to radical truth-telling, which can be very subversive, very dangerous. Artists should challenge what we believe. We can't be safe any more than Jesus was safe." For the new generation of Christian rock musicians, the principles of the Christian culture industry often violate of the principles of Christianity.

Some of them have even come to see the small-mindedness of the gate-keepers as a blessing in disguise. Getting shut out of the Christian bubble forces artists to compete in the general market. Not only is this good for the artists, it's good for Christianity, which stagnates when it separates itself from the culture at large. And it's also good for the mainstream, which benefits, both spiritually and aesthetically, from the "salt and light" of these Christian artists. By trying to protect itself, the official Christian culture industry is both consigning itself to irrelevance and allowing a more interesting alternative Christian culture to become more relevant than it would otherwise.

I told Doug and Lori that I liked the idea of more interplay between the Christian and secular music scenes. It seemed like each could benefit from the other. But I said I was still concerned by those people, especially teenagers, who think they need to burn all their secular albums once they find Jesus. In the documentary *Why Should the Devil Have All the Good Music*, which was filmed at Cornerstone, one singer grimaces as he recalls throwing away all his old albums. "I remember the day I was like, 'This is an idol. This is an idol in my life,' and I took all these records—it was so hard, I had to not think about it; I had to turn my mind off—and I walked out to the Dumpster and that was that." A few years later, he adds, "I tried to start buying them back, but I couldn't find some of them."

"I think a lot of people coming to the radical, revolutionary idea of

Christianity," said Doug, "there is like a honeymoon phase. You are reading the Bible and the words are jumping out of the page at you and you're very conscious of leaving your old life behind. And many people equate the messages of Steve Miller or Green Day with their old lifestyle—they lost their virginity to this Green Day song, so they don't want to hear that again. It's reinforcing your old worldview. Like, if you and I went shopping and I was just saying, 'Let's rip some stuff off' over and over again, I was just pressing you with that *let's steal* mentality, you would want to shut me off."

But, Doug said, most people get beyond this phase eventually. "Most Christians are intelligent, and they get to the point where they realize, 'I don't have to worry about hearing an errant idea. The truth can stand on its own. It doesn't need to be protected.'" He continued, "*Bible good, secular bad* is very close-minded and very small-minded. There are a lot of teachers that encourage people to think, use their brains that God gave you and engage the culture, learn things from a nonbelieving person. You know, it's kind of a radical idea for some people."

Lori wanted to catch Anberlin at the Main Stage, and she offered me a ride up the hill in her golf cart. Golf carts are the only kind of vehicle allowed at Cornerstone, and having one makes you very popular. As we putted through the Midway, Lori kept stopping to pick up friends, and there were soon five of us stuffed into the little vehicle. I ended up perched precariously on the back bumper alongside a friendly round-faced guy named Jon Young who plays guitar in a band called the Myriad. He was wearing a Guster T-shirt—they're a hip, non-Christian band from New York—and I mentioned that a friend of mine had recently married the singer from that group. "They're the best," said Jon.

When the bumpy trip had reached its end, Lori, Jon, and the others went backstage to watch the performances from the wings. I said good-bye and joined the audience spread out in the field and up the steep hillside that faced the stage. The band wasn't on yet, and a giant video screen played promos for an interfaith AIDS charity and a Christian YA novel called *Dark Star: Confessions of a Rock Idol*. Kids threw Frisbees and beach balls and lined up for food. A girl in a Kurt Cobain T-shirt sat cross-legged, weaving together strands of grass to make what looked like a crown of thorns. A teenage boy with a "Free Hugs" sign was totally undercutting another boy whose sign read, "Hugs $1." I snapped a picture of a guy with a Hebrew tattoo on his bicep. "It means 'hope, faith, and God's desirous love,'" he told me.*

Anberlin was competent but nothing special. Although I hadn't actually developed a taste for screamo music, I'd apparently been pummeled into a state where ordinary rock 'n' roll felt a little boring, and I ended up slogging back toward the smaller stages to catch the final performances from some of the more edgy bands. A concussive machine-gun beat and roaring vocals drew me toward one of the roadside tents. Standing on my tiptoes to see over the wall of sweat and flying limbs that filled the space, I could make out the band Zao tearing up the stage. In *Why Should the Devil Have All the Good Music,* one singer half-jokingly likens the intensity of the punk and hard-core tents to a neo-Nazi rally. My own sense was that the frenzy was directed more internally—that the Cornerstone mosh pits functioned less as a motivation to action than a kind of shamanistic meditation (though of course no Christian would use those words). The song ended and the audience erupted into cheers. "How you doing, Cornerstone?!" screamed the singer. "We want to thank you guys for coming out so late. We should be in bed now." I looked at my watch. It was eighteen minutes after midnight. So not metal.

Another warm, hazy day. The cars in the parking lot had acquired a thick layer of grime and the air swarmed with dusty particulate. "Just be glad it hasn't rained," more than one person told me. Apparently, Cornerstone is usually plagued with rainstorms that turn the roads into rivers of mud.

Burned out on music, I decided to investigate some of the festival's other offerings. There were workshops and seminars on a fascinating array of topics: global poverty, songwriting, Celtic monasticism, Nietzsche, *Doctor Who.* As I passed a mock Day of the Dead service, I'm sure I heard the instructor say, "Let's go ahead and pass out those skulls."

---

*Later I showed the photo to my rabbi, who burst into giggles. "Well, it's completely illiterate," he said, but what tickled him was not the poor spelling and grammar but the word supposedly indicating godly desire, which he said the Bible uses only in reference to physical lust.

I stepped inside a tent to hear a speaker from Christians for Biblical Equality, a group that believes "the Bible, properly interpreted, teaches the fundamental equality of men and women." There was a good crowd. One dude was obviously there to pick a fight, but overall there was a palpable hunger in the atmosphere, as if the young women here—and many young men too—had been waiting for years to hear explained what they must have known in their hearts all along: that God does not want women to be subservient to their husbands and that he does want them to share leadership in the church. I was pleased to see it, but soon became disheartened that such a rudimentary form of feminism was still necessary in 2007.

However, the fact that Cornerstone embraced Christians for Biblical Equality—which despite its modest agenda is authentically controversial in its circles—made me curious about how the festival would address the topic of homosexuality. The seminar on the subject had a title that held out a promise of tolerance: "Don't be afraid to ask . . . or tell!" As a slogan, at least, it seemed an improvement over some of the T-shirts I'd seen around. These had, on the front, a rainbow design with the words "I'm in love with a man." And on the back: "His name is Jesus."

I took a seat in the packed tent where John Smid had already begun speaking. A pale and squishy-looking man with a soft voice, Smid was explaining the psychological basis for homosexuality. "A woman's primary need is for safety and security, so when a woman is wounded enough by men, she's likely to go *anywhere* to find safety," he said. "A man's greatest need is to feel respected, and if a man doesn't feel respected, *he'll* go anywhere." My jaw dropped. This is what turns people gay? Because before I met my wife, I often felt disrespected by women, and it never occurred to me to remedy that by sucking cock.

I picked up the literature that had been left on my chair and saw that Smid was the director of Love In Action, one of those ministries that promises to turn gays straight—and that Smid himself is an "ex-gay." And yet the more I listened to him, the harder I found it to believe that he'd ever even met a gay person, much less been one. "Don't make the mistake of pitying them," Smid told the audience. "People that are broken and narcissistic love people to feel sorry for them." I looked around. There were a lot of families here. Mothers and fathers. Brothers and sisters. No doubt many people who were themselves struggling with their sexuality. Some were already in tears.

Smid went on to say we should not be misled by the phony science in "the mainstream media." Mocking articles about gay penguins and sheep, he declared, "I'm insulted when people trot out some animal as proof that homosexuality is natural. We are not animals." Now, one reason these stories get so much attention is that evangelicals used to argue that the *absence* of gay animals was proof that homosexuality *wasn't* natural. But I was hardly surprised that Smid would use the evidence against this old argument to redefine the debate in his favor. After all, he'd already accomplished a much trickier redefinition when he got married in 1988.

"*Homosexual* is not a noun," he continued. "There is no such thing as a homosexual. There are only homosexual acts. Satan contrived a plan to make people believe that men and women were born intrinsically homosexual, because if he could sell that lie, there is no God big enough to change it." Interestingly, Smid acknowledged that not every gay person— sorry, every person who commits homosexual acts—could actually learn to become attracted to the opposite sex, or even to eliminate their homosexual urges. These people, he said, could be happy and please God simply by committing to a life of celibacy. "Don't tell me it can't be done," he said. "We resist sexual urges all the time. If we didn't, we'd all be having a big orgy right now."

Maybe we would, maybe we wouldn't, but either way, it was irrelevant. The gay people I know have, or want, relationships that are much more like the one I have with my wife than they are like simultaneous sex with dozens of strangers. We can, and usually should, resist our fleeting sexual urges. But resisting the desire to form an intimate, lifelong bond? The longing to have and to hold, to love and to cherish, for better or for worse? Yeah, I suppose you could repress that, but it would probably cost you your soul.

I thought about objecting publicly, but decided not to bother. In the short term, it would be pointless. I knew I wasn't going to persuade anybody. But I also knew that in the long term, my objection would be unnecessary. After all, John Smid's ridiculous fallacies were so evident to me simply because I know lots of happy, healthy, and normal gay people— Christians among them. And someday, inevitably, so would everybody else in this tent. For that reason alone, Smid had already lost. What was harder to shake was the thought of the many people who would suffer needlessly in the years or decades until he realized that. Against Smid's direct orders, I felt sorry for them.

You walk through the merch tents, you see all that stop abortion and political stuff, which I just try to avoid." That's what one man told me, and no doubt there were others like him, but I was actually impressed with how many people at Cornerstone seemed engaged with political stuff. I mean, really engaged, not just swallowing what they were spoon-fed by the religious right. To be sure, I found a lot to disagree with in terms of individual issues, but as I walked through those tents what I saw in the aggregate was a commitment to a vigorous and open discussion.

Perhaps out of mischief, someone had placed the pacifists a few feet away from the army recruiters. I asked Sam Smith of the Christian Peace Fellowship if there'd been any tension, but he shook his head. A scruffy, plump man in a tie-dye shirt, Smith said he was more worried about the kids walking around. "You seen the imagery a lot of these bands use? Have you looked at the T-shirts? I see a lot of death, bullets, war. It disturbs me. I have two kids. I don't want them mesmerized by that." Over his shoulder, his teenage daughter mimed a hypnotized look. I guess when your dad's a professional pacifist, you learn to cope.

"I think they would say that's spiritual warfare," I noted.

Smith rolled his eyes. "Once you have that mindset, it's too easy to think you have the right to use real violence. I even had one kid come up to me and say, 'How can you be a Christian and be against war?'"

Smith wasn't even the most radical pacifist here. There was also a large contingent from Christian Peacekeeper Teams, a group that made headlines the year before when several of its members were kidnapped in Baghdad, where they had been protesting the U.S. occupation. At a presentation they gave one afternoon, one member explained that authentic pacifism meant opposing not only war but the entire "demonic" system. "We live a lifestyle that needs to be defended by war," he said. "In a world where there is this kind of divide between the haves and the have-nots, the only way to maintain that level of injustice is to have the world's strongest military."

Most of the causes being promoted at Cornerstone were far less radical, but intriguing in their own way. A cryptic series of postcards and T-shirts bearing the message "To write love on her arms" turned out to be a campaign to help compulsive self-cutters. I was already aware that this is a major issue among young Christians—Krystal Meyers played a song about it here, and another band played one at SHOUTfest. I wasn't able to find any evidence that cutting is actually more pervasive among evangelicals than other young Americans, but it would make a grim kind of sense. The creator of one self-injury support group told *Christianity Today* that the most important message to give a cutter is that "Jesus loves her as she is, and that his atonement is sufficient for her sins." Perhaps only someone who has never taken a step back from her religion could overlook how the concept of atonement through bloodshed just might be what gets a confused kid into trouble in the first place.

There was also a lot of emphasis on third-world poverty and AIDS—hardly controversial issues, but notable nonetheless, given that these are not usually campaigns the media associates with evangelicals.

As I said, there were more than enough disagreeable organizations to go around. One outfit was collecting signatures on an "abstinence from MTV" pledge. "MTV has gone from being a music channel to being a sex channel for youth," said the flier. A ministry called Live Offensively was selling T-shirts that said "Abortion is not a crime . . . But it should be," and Testimony Time had a line of bumper stickers so outrageous I couldn't imagine anyone purchasing them except ironically:

Any Sex that can Put You in Hell ISN'T SAFE

On Judgment Day You'll Meet FATHER GOD, not mother earth!

In case of Nuclear Attack,
Prayer will be restored to public schools

Stop Abortion America!
GOD punishes National Sins By Natural Disasters

There are no atheist [*sic*] in hell.
Now they believe, but too late

Fairy Tales Say A Frog Became A Prince.
"Scientists" call it Evolution

The BIBLE says MARY was with CHILD,
NOT A BLOB OF TISSUE

How Sad—Kids run wild & Dogs go to Obedience School

Repent—It's not "cool" to be in Hell!

And then there was Rock for Life, Cornerstone's semiofficial pro-life organization, with its own dedicated concert stage and adorable logo of a fetus playing an electric guitar. Rock for Life is a project of the American Life League, which is probably the country's most extreme antiabortion group that is not blowing up clinics. It was formed in response to what its founders saw as deadly compromises by other organizations—the willingness, for instance, to back antiabortion laws that made exceptions for victims of rape or incest. One flier on the Rock for Life table was called *Conceived in Rape: A Story of Hope.* "When [people] hear of a situation such as mine," the writer says, "instead of saying, 'Oh how awful! You mean to tell me this woman was raped and was actually forced to carry that baby?'—people could say, 'You mean to tell me that God rewarded this woman with the gift of this child's life for the suffering she endured? How good is God!'"

The flier then goes on to assert that, in any case, "the effects of abortion are similar to the effects of rape," so allowing it is really just punishing the victim twice. These people are not kidding around. That much is obvious even before you get to the brochure comparing women walking into an abortion clinic to the cattle cars that brought Jews to Auschwitz. Rock for Life has a significant amount of support from Christian artists, though as with any organization that courts celebrities, it's not clear how aware the artists are of everything Rock for Life stands for.

At one end of the Rock for Life table was a large sign on fluorescent green cardboard announcing that South Dakota had passed a law banning virtually all abortions and soliciting messages of encouragement to the state's pro-life movement. Around it, dozens of people had taped up index cards with words of gratitude and blessing (one woman signed herself

"Bride to one, mother of eleven"). I contemplated the women who would be forced to turn to dangerous back-alley abortions, or to give birth to their rapists' children. I thought about the doctors who would be sent to jail for trying to save their patients from serious injury. I picked up a Sharpie, thinking about the best message to send the people who were trying to force this on their state.* A few choice words came to mind. And then I thought about the many admirable Christians I'd met so far, the ones who were genuinely trying to live up to Jesus's example, and what message they would write down. I didn't focus on their opinions about abortion, which almost certainly did not line up with my own. Rather, I imagined them feeling the same anger and fear that I felt at that moment. What would they do with these emotions? I wrote and taped up my message to South Dakota's pro-life leaders: "I forgive you."

One of Professor Mark Powell's criticisms of the Christian music world is that it has very little sense of its own past. Mainstream rock is built on the foundations of history. Whatever a band's influences or an audience's reference points, they are likely to go back decades. Christian artists and fans, however, almost never listen to anything that's not currently on the radio—and there are no Christian oldies or classic rock stations.

"The contemporary Christian music scene is thirty-five years old," Powell told me. "It's understandable that early on it would have been imitative of the general market, but if you had said that people who have a certain ideology are going to have a separate genre of music, and they're going to have their own magazines and their own awards shows and their own festivals and their own radio stations—what will it look like thirty-five years from now? I would have guessed that it would have evolved into having its own sound. No one could tell what it would be. But that didn't happen. I think it largely didn't happen because there isn't any history."

For that reason, the used and rare CD and cassette racks at the far end of the Cornerstone merch tent weren't just a business, they were a rebuke to the CCM powers-that-be in Nashville, and a testament to the rebellious streak of RadRockers owner Mike Delaney. A lanky man with the long hair

---

*The law was later repealed by popular referendum.

and John Lennon glasses of an aging hippie, Mike took some time to show me the music he'd rescued from oblivion.

I mentioned that I'd heard a lot of good music at Cornerstone, and I was starting to feel that mainstream radio and music stores were doing a disservice to their customers by almost arbitrarily shutting out Christian rock. Mike gave me a lopsided smile. "To the extent that the worldview has been identified with fundamentalism, I can't fault the mainstream for not wanting to embrace it," he said.

"Maybe some of these bands could help the mainstream understand that there's more to Christianity than fundamentalism," I proposed.

"We need that more now than ever," Mike agreed. In and of itself, he said, a pop music divide is trivial. But it's a manifestation of a larger cultural gap that's led to a destructive political polarization. "That's what the Democrats don't get. Back in the Kennedy era they had a whole range of issues they could appeal to Christians on, saying, 'We're doing God's work': race relations, the Vietnam war. But ever since *God is dead* was declared in the late sixties, and the mainstream denominations have gone down the tubes," the Christian left has had nowhere to turn. "And now we"—evangelicals—"mostly have doofuses and fools that represent the fundies—like James Dobson."

"I thought you were going to say Pat Roberston," I said. "My experience has been that when Christians want to prove they're not fanatics, they distance themselves from Pat Robertson."

"That's easy. That don't cost you. But try to distance yourself from the hit man James Dobson." Mike asked me if I'd been to Creation, the country's largest Christian festival, which draws four times Cornerstone's numbers. I said I hadn't. "It would confirm all your worst fears," he said, "I went there in 2004 as a vendor. I'd already signed all my contracts and gave them all my money, so they had me by the balls, and they made me sign an addendum to the contract that specified that only Creation Festival could approve anybody to do voter registration. And my heart sunk with the fear that what would happen did happen: They had a forty-foot Republican trailer where you could climb up the steps and get the spiel from the right-wing extreme machine about why you should not vote for Kerry. And I just wanted to freakin' throw up and hit somebody. But I've got a livelihood to protect and I couldn't very well throw a tantrum and complain. They'd just kick my ass out for being a liberal."

Mike seemed like the right guy to ask about something I'd been mulling over. The open-minded, intellectually adventurous spirit of Cornerstone may still be a small force in evangelical culture, but it seems poised to become influential beyond its size. The younger demographic that's drawn here will soon grow into positions of leadership in the church and society. The bands and speakers are thriving by reaching audiences outside the traditional, conservative Christian bubble. The people here and others like them, I asked, can they transform the church from within? If not actually liberalize it, at least yank it away from fundamentalism?

"They can," said Mike carefully, "but only the right way. The way the New Testament uses the imagery of leavened bread. The yeast in the dough will rise slowly over time, organically." He adjusted his weathered baseball cap. "The problem is that mainstream liberal and moderate churches stagnated and lost their cultural relevance. The Lutherans, Anglicans, and Methodists, they were never the driving force behind the growth of the Christian music industry in Nash-hell. The moderate voices never expressed themselves in a commercial way, so their voices are muted today. You don't hear them unless you're part of their flock."

He went on, "But we're never gonna be rid of fundamentalism." That's a natural part of the human condition, he said, and one that's on the rise right now for a reason. "There is some kind of link that hasn't been fully explored yet between the rise of fundamentalist evangelical Protestantism in America and the rise of militant Islam," he said. "It may have to do with the threatening nature of modernity, it may have to do with the rapid advance of secularism, it may be because of the gross excesses of corporate globalism and the lessening power of nation-states and the rising power of the corporate world—but whatever those forces are, it's not an accident."

I tried to bring the conversation back to ground level. "But then there's a couple of issues where the entire Christian culture, from the fundamentalists to the folks at Cornerstone and progressives, are kind of in lockstep," I said, "and that's abortion and homosexuality."

"No they're not. They may seem to you that way on the surface, but that's just because those of us who have such shitty choices at the voting booth, what are we going to do?"

"Here's what I'm thinking of," I explained. "Certainly I'd expect a lot of antiabortion sentiment at a Christian festival, but Rock for Life? Having them being the primary representative of that—it seems to me there's a way of coming from that side of the issue that's also about engaging in a discussion, as opposed to Rock for Life, which is really the most extreme of the antiabortion groups."

"You're absolutely right," Mike conceded. "I know the guy behind that, and he's a douche."

"So why doesn't Cornerstone find somebody other than Rock for Life to represent a more thoughtful antiabortion position?"

"I don't think they feel that they have some overarching responsibility to steer the political or theological underpinnings of the event heavy-handedly in an ideological direction. That impulse is a fascist impulse, to control the conversation. Besides, you have to credit them for what they have accomplished in twenty-five years, which is insanely amazing stuff. Of all these events, this one represents best the center, or not-so-far-right, so let's give them credit. You mentioned homosexuality. I happen to know they struggle with it internally. I'm one of those who would say, if you're so concerned about gay marriage, and what it's going to do, why don't you spend a little more time fixing Protestant fundamentalist marriages, because you're divorcing at the same rate as the general culture. Don't worry about abortion. How about helping unwed mothers take care of their babies? If you're going to be pro-life, be pro-life consistently. Worry about nuclear proliferation and a whole range of issues that affect life."

"So where are the fliers saying that?"

He shrugged. "Come back next year."

On my way out of the tent, I passed the Rock for Life table again and noticed that my index card was gone. Big surprise. I was walking out when I saw a pile of literature I hadn't noticed before, promoting Rock for Life's argument that birth control pills are, in fact, chemical abortions. There was a drawing of an frowny-face embryo wearing a baby bonnet. And then I saw another flier: "IVF Violates Human Dignity."

I sighed as I walked away reading the flier. I know something about in vitro fertilization. It's how my kids were born. My wife and I had tried for a year to have children naturally before we found out it wouldn't be possible. Thirty years ago, that's how it would have ended, with us childless. But now doctors are able to bring a sperm and egg together in a laboratory, and then insert the resulting embryos into the woman's body. Gina and I were lucky. The procedure worked the first time, and she gave birth to two healthy babies, a boy and a girl.

Some conservative Christians object to IVF because doctors have to create more embryos than they actually use—and often the ones that do get used don't successfully implant in the womb. These three-day-old embryos, the argument goes, are actually children, cruelly sentenced to death.

Obviously, I don't see it that way. An embryo created in a lab is no more a child than an individual sperm or egg, since it has no potential to grow unless it is implanted in a womb—just as the sperm and egg have no potential to grow on their own. Besides, embryos fail to implant all the time as part of the natural reproductive process. Any married couple that regularly has unprotected sex creates embryos and then loses them. An infertile couple could easily "kill" far more embryos trying to get pregnant naturally than during the process of IVF.

So I figured I knew what to expect from the Rock for Life flier, and that it wouldn't bother me. But as I walked into the sunlight, I saw that it made a different argument, one that stopped me in my tracks.

I felt liked I'd been punched in the stomach.

I looked away from the paper in my hand, squinting into the sun. Then I reread the sentence that had upset me. It was worse the second time. I could feel my throat constricting. I began to feel enraged. And this time I did not feel forgiving.

In a second, I was back at the Rock for Life table. A young man saw me and came over. He was in his early twenties, with a black cap that set off his pale face. I held up the flier. "Have you read this?"

"Have I read it?" he answered warily.

"Have you read it? Do you *agree* with it?"

"Well, yeah. That's why it's out there."

I reached into my bag and pulled out the photo of my children that I carry with me on all my trips. On this trip alone, I'd been away nearly five days already, and was missing them more than usual. The picture, taken in my backyard, showed them in their new spring wardrobes, holding hands, with big natural smiles. It was creased from overhandling.

"Do me a favor," I said. "Look at this picture"—he looked down at it— "then look me in the eyes and tell me that I think of them as *objects*."

He kept his eyes down. "I don't know what you . . ."

"'IVF turns children into commodities,'" I read out loud. "'When a couple undergoes IVF, they are saying, "We want a child no matter what," and the child becomes an object.'" I waited until he looked up at me again. "I love these children more than anything in the world. If you honestly believe that I think they're objects, you'd better be able to say it to my face."

The kid's eyes darted left and right. At the other end of the display, his colleague kept her face down and slid farther away. "The main point," he said, "is just about all the embryos that get killed . . ."

"No it's not." I showed him the section that began "If IVF did not bring death or harm to human embryos, would it be okay?" The answer was no: assisted reproduction violates "marital integrity."

He looked at me again. "I'm just a volunteer."

I almost reached over the table and ripped out his stupid lip ring. "Take some responsibility, man," I yelled. "You said you agreed with this. Or did it never occur to you that these are real people's lives you're talking about?" I held the picture up once more. "Do you want to think about it again? Do you want to tell me the world would be better off if they'd never been born?"

"I want every child to be born," he said quickly. "That's the whole reason I'm doing this."

"Then don't hand out fliers saying that my children violate human dignity. Do you get how offensive that is?"

"All I'm saying is you don't need to kill embryos to have children. If I were in that position, I'd make a different choice, like adoption."

My head was swimming. *Like you have a fucking clue what you'd do,* I thought. And, *Choice? Choice is what you're working to outlaw, idiot.* I had to get out of there. "Look," I said, with my last ounce of calm, "I know you didn't write this, so you need to think really hard about what it says. And if you can't say it out loud, then maybe you don't really believe it. And if you don't, you should talk to the people you work for, and tell them that, and tell them why."

He didn't answer, and I felt drained. So I turned around and walked back out to the Midway, gripping my photograph tightly.

"Daniel. *Daniel!*" Someone was calling me. I looked up and saw Jon, Lori's friend from the Myriad. "You okay? You look . . ." He trailed off.

"No, I'm fine," I said. He raised an eyebrow. "Ah, I just got into a fight with some dude."

"Really? What happened?" I handed Jon the picture of my kids. "They're adorable," he said. Then I handed him the flier. He asked, "What's IVF?"

I explained, and began to tell him about my confrontation with the guy from Rock for Life. Jon listened carefully and read the flier. He hadn't even gotten to the part that upset me so much, when he said, "Well, I don't agree with this." He fingered the section that asked, "What about infertile couples who desperately want a child?" and read hurriedly, "'No one has the right to a child. Cooperating with God's plan for human procreation ensures that all children are accepted as gifts.'"

His brow wrinkled. "To me, that's the same as saying that if you have cancer, it's God's will, so just accept it." He handed the flier back to me. "I hope you don't think there's only one opinion about things like this. Because I hear a lot of shit from my brothers in Christ."

I nodded, and Jon went on. "Some things we just have to struggle with, you know? Look at gay marriage. I know what the Bible says, but I have gay friends who adopted a child, and now this little girl that nobody else wanted has a loving . . ." He shrugged.

"Thanks," I said. "I feel better now."

The Jesus Village tent was packed shoulder to shoulder in anticipation of Aaron Weiss, the mewithoutYou front man who would be speaking soon. No one could say exactly what the topic would be, but well over a thousand people were eager to hear it. The canvas flaps bulged, and I squeezed into an overflow crowd spilling out onto the road near the side of the stage.

Since being told that Aaron was "different," I had learned that this reputation was largely based on his passion for environmentalism that bordered on—or crossed the border into—obsession. Everyone seemed to know two things about Aaron: He had transfigured his band's tour bus so that it ran entirely on used cooking oil, and he ate food out of the garbage. Not just sometimes, but exclusively. Aaron believed that with so much food being wasted in America, he would rather go hungry than buy any. Not that he ever went hungry. MewithoutYou's tour manager told me that Aaron kept track of the days that Trader Joe's threw out stock that was past its sell-by date, and made a weekly "shopping" trip to find the food that would clearly still be edible for days or weeks. He saw the look on my face—half disgust, half amusement, half bewilderment—and laughed, "I know! But wait till you meet him. You'll understand."

Aaron sat down on a folding chair on the stage and the tent grew quiet as he adjusted a microphone. Dressed in a ratty T-shirt and jeans, he had a full, dark beard, flyaway hair, and piercing eyes. He looked a lot like the actor Jason Lee in one of his shaggy phases. When he began to speak, it was obvious why no one knew what the topic would be. He barely seemed to know himself. Yet as he jumped from subject to subject—music, the Iraq war, Jesus, charity—he addressed each with an almost stunning conviction and eloquence, as well as impressive doses of insight, self-awareness, and good humor. And it all sounded conversational and completely genuine. Within fifteen minutes, I'd decided that he was one of the most charismatic speakers I'd ever heard.

When he brought up the war, Aaron warned the audience first, saying he knew some people would rather not hear about it. But he told them it was his duty to talk about it—and theirs too. "Christianity in America has one voice in the media—of the religious right, that says our wars are justified by God." As a result, non-Christians have been left with the impression that the mission of Christianity is to fight evil. "We're not called to rid the world of evildoers," he insisted. "There'd be no one left! We're called to ask God for mercy and forgiveness."

Someone asked Aaron how he had found God. "Ooh, testimony time," he joked. The sharing of one's testimony, that moment when a Christian becomes born again, is evangelicalism's most sacred ritual. Usually. "I came to God through an old-fashioned fundamentalist church that said I was going to burn in hell if I didn't accept Jesus. And I didn't want to burn in hell." The crowd laughed, and Aaron smiled with them. "It was very manipulative and cruel." Eventually, Aaron said, he learned the true nature of God, but not before some terrible and emotionally draining fights with his Jewish father and Muslim mother. Now, he said, they treat each other with mutual respect and humility. "I can't pretend to know everything that God knows," he said. "I just have to trust his love. Are there gonna be Muslims in heaven? I don't know. I sure hope so. I'll go farther than that: I think so."

This guy was different, all right. Aaron took a sip of Gatorade. "Someone just left this half full," he said, and the crowd burst into cheers and laughter. Aaron cracked up. "I'm talking about peacemaking and honoring your parents, but when I talk about Dumpster diving everyone applauds! But that's great. And there's biblical basis for it. People ask, 'What does it say in the Bible about Dumpster diving?'" He took a sip. "At least as much as it says about abortion and gay marriage."*

After Aaron finished, he sat on the side of the stage for nearly an hour, talking with people. When the last fans dispersed he pulled a chair up to where I was waiting for him and plopped down wearily. "My throat's really burning," he said. "I had a hundred and two fever yesterday." Then he apologized for being negative. "What did you want to talk about?"

I started with how much I'd enjoyed his band the other day and asked if he made a conscious effort to write in a style—poetic, ambiguous—that was so at odds with the clear, propositional statements of a certain variety of Christian rock.

"I don't like either tendency, actually," he said. "To me, there shouldn't be an attempt either to sell more records in the Christian bookstores by saying the name *Jesus* a certain amount of times or to shy away from clear, declarative lyrics. Because as far from the fundamentalist spirit as the east is from the west, I do believe in truth, and I would want to declare firmly, 'If we follow Jesus, we need to love our enemies, and we do need to care for the poor and visit the sick and stand up for peace in the world.' Somebody else who has a different perspective, and thinks, 'As a follower of Jesus, I need to fly this fighter plane and drop a bomb on this market,' I would definitively declare, 'I think that's wrong.' So I am not a moral relativist."

What he concentrates on, he said, is not saying anything just for the sake of pleasing an audience. "If you say the word *Jesus* and you don't say the word *shit,* everybody's going, 'Okay, he's one of us; he's telling us what we want to hear.' That's a real easy way to get popular in the Christian sphere. Then of course, there will be many nonreligious people who hear the word *Jesus* is in our lyrics, and: 'Oh, Christian band—screw this.' So I've come to a point where I just don't care about it." He thought for a sec-

---

*E.g., Lev. 19:10: "Do not go over your vineyard a second time or pick up the grapes that have fallen. Leave them for the poor and the alien."

ond. "The thing is, I do care. There's part of me that still wrestles with: How do I appeal to the most people? Then I realize it's not a valid concern. I try to keep it at bay, and so I keep my eyes on speaking what my heart says is true. I fall short of that, but that's where I fix my eyes."

"How much of a problem have you found with secular audiences writing you off because of Jesus in your lyrics?"

"Well, it's hard to say, because most of the people who come up to talk to me like my band, and haven't written us off. So I get the unfair impression that everybody likes us." He laughed again. "If we have been written off, most of the time I would assume it's because of the quality of our music. I don't feel particularly persecuted or neglected. Something that's hard to deny is beauty. Not many people look at Michelangelo's Sistine Chapel and say, 'Yeah, but he was a Christian; that's not very beautiful.'"

He continued, "Anyway, it's not my goal to convert people. It's not my duty to convert people. I feel like my duty is to love people. If they convert to the Christian faith—okay. If they don't—okay." In fact, he added, it's in some ways better not to win converts because of the dangers of filling the ranks of the church without actually spreading the true message of the gospel. "I don't want to pat someone on the back and say, 'Go and be Christian now,' whatever that means, and affirm people's strength in it—and then they go and protest abortion clinics with violence in their heart. That brand of fundamentalist Christianity that most Americans have encountered is the most hurtful possible worldview—the most destructive to the soul. To use the name of Jesus in absolute, complete contradiction to the teachings of Jesus—I think we would be much better off just saying, 'Well, we want this oil; we want this power; we want this economic status; we want to feel better about ourselves by saying this about homosexuals,' or whatever it is than to have violence and hatred in the name of God."

"In your talk just now, you mentioned a few times *the majesty of God.* That's language I haven't heard a lot of. Are you aware that it sounds out of synch with at least the pop forms of Christianity?"

"Yeah. I'd say Christian pop culture errs on that side of *Jesus is my best friend.* It's almost become a joke, Christianity's attempt to make Jesus so palatable or attractive. *Whatever you want, Jesus will do for you.* The problem is that when Jesus demands that we sell our possessions and give to the poor—Well, if that were your best friend, I'm guessing you'd say, 'Nah, that's probably bad advice.' If that's the person of God, the spirit of God incarnate telling you to sell your possessions and give to the poor, I think we would take that more seriously." Then he added quickly, "But I'm a hypocrite. 'Quit using your thousand-dollar guitars to play songs about how you don't need material possessions.' Believe me, I think about quitting so often."

"And?"

"This is where the real change happens: art and creativity and beauty. And people are drawn to hear what I have to say more than if I worked in a retail store. Or in politics. I heard where Bono, from U2, was asked, 'Did you ever want to take up politics?' He said, 'Why move into a smaller house?' I could play guitar in my room. If it were just a matter of expressing myself with art or singing to God, I can do that anywhere. I don't need to be on the stage. But when I have the attention of people who otherwise would not pay any attention to me, I'm going to have the ability to be a voice for something."

He shook his head. "My main question is if *I* in particular am having a good influence. I don't know. I suspect that to use CDs to say 'We don't need CDs' is . . . backwards. But then, you have to operate within the system. Or do you? People buy books, so you have to print books. That's going to cost money that could feed people who are hungry. And the books are going to say, 'Feed people who are hungry.' Tricky. That's why more than anything else, I come back to God being merciful, and I say, 'Thank you, that I don't have to be perfect.' I don't have to figure everything out. I can strive to be perfect, and insomuch as I fall short, I just walk humbly and say, 'I'm sorry, please forgive me, please guide me to a better place.'"

"You know, I've been to Christian bookstores. I don't think most Christians agonize quite so much about printing books."

"Or bumper stickers or T-shirts or coffee mugs," Aaron agreed. "It's something I wish didn't go on. Because it's not even necessary. Jesus said how we'll be recognized, how people would know we're Christian, and it wasn't because we'd be wearing a T-shirt. It's our actions that identify us. People ask, are we a Christian band or Christians in a band? Increasingly, lately, I've been saying 'neither.' I hope I'm a Christian. I hope we're all Christians. I hope we all follow Jesus. But look at our lives: I don't see it. I'm not ashamed of Jesus. I'm ashamed of myself.

"It's really a question of what do you do when rebellion becomes the norm, when you're wearing a stylish new shirt with a cross on it, where the cross represents a dying to all things of the world, and a rejection of all the powers and the comforts and luxuries and values of the world? I'm not sure it can be done. At the same time, if you go about two hundred feet that way, you can find our T-shirts for sale for something like twelve dollars, and it's something I wrestle with and something I don't feel content about. Does the world need more T-shirts? Well, maybe somewhere. Not in America. But yet, we print them. When we started five or six years ago, I had no problem with T-shirts. In fact, my main concern was how do we get the biggest profit margin. So we got the cheapest shirts we could and sold them for the most we could respectably and reasonably sell them for, just to make the most money. It wasn't until just a few years ago that I started to think, *Maybe that's not what we should be doing, is trying to make the most money.*"

"The elements of Christianity that you emphasize, at least when you talk, and I think in your music, too, are different from the elements that are often emphasized in mainstream Christian pop culture," I said. "Is that intentional?"

"Sure. Sometimes I see it like a ship that we're all trying to steer together. You set your course for truth, and if you see it going to one side, maybe it's your job to turn right. If you see it going to the other side, it's your job to turn left. I think if there were an overabundance of Christian culture emphasis on giving to the poor, serving the needy, visiting the prisoner and the orphan and the widow, and peacemaking, and so on, and there was never any mention of the need for prayer, the need for meditation, contemplation, fasting, the humility of confessing that ultimately it's not my efforts that are going to bring peace to the world—if the emphasis was flipped, I would probably be preaching more of that, about God's goodness in mysterious and esoteric ways. Whereas what I see is overemphasis on holy talk and I don't see any holy action, so I've got to try and put feet to our prayers, I've got to try to put hands and fingers to language."

"Well there are some things Christian pop culture demands action on," I pointed out. "Premarital sex and abortion and gay marriage."

"Right."

"Why is that so overemphasized?"

"I can only say something to the effect of, most people aren't homosexual. So it's a really easy one to pick out and say, 'That's the problem! That's the degeneration of our moral values, it's them.' Most people probably never had an abortion. So you can look at that sort of murder and say, 'That's the murder that I want to draw attention to.'" He looked uncomfortable. "By *murder*—I even hesitate to use that language without all these disclaimers, because it's so, in my opinion, overemphasized. I'm much, much more prone to say *murder* in regard to the killing in a war, or even state-sanctioned killing in the death penalty, or the death that comes as a result of us failing to share our abundance with those who are starving to death. All this is the same sort of human failure to defend the right of human life."

He continued. "Jesus never mentioned homosexuality once. How has it become such an issue? Strange. Strange how all the things that Jesus actually did talk about fail to become issues. I mean, you start talking about war, and conservative Christians say, 'Oh, I don't want to be political and protest the war.' Or you talk about poverty and the causes of poverty: 'Oh, that's a political issue; Jesus wasn't political.' Why don't these people deal with the issues that Jesus did? It shouldn't surprise me. If you look at the Gospels, the most respected religious people were the furthest from the spirit of what Jesus was saying. It's just the same thing all over again. But I *am* surprised. I really do continually expect Christians to be the most willing to accept pacifism, peacemaking, or redistribution of wealth, and care for the poor, and rethinking our prison systems and all that. But we end up being the most belligerent and hard-hearted and self-righteous and all the rest. Scary."

"So the conservative bent of Christian pop culture comes from people picking out certain pieces of the scripture and ignoring others," I suggested. "There have been studies that show that the majority of evangelical Christians don't actually know what's in the Bible. I guess they get their information from the *Left Behind* books instead. A guy like Tim LaHaye takes what he finds important in the Bible, much in the way that everyone should do for themselves, and puts his version out there in forms that sell sixty-five million copies and become, in a way, more important than the Bible."

"Did you say sixty-five million?" Aaron gasped. "Wow." He drew his legs up under him. "Sometimes it seems to me that what lies deep in all of us is a sleeping—or maybe a caged—giant of fear and of doubt and of isolation. Deep down I think we all have this suspicion that really none of this makes any sense. *I mean, honestly, come on! Nothing matters! There's no God.* But there's also this small point of hope or of faith or of purpose or meaning—I guess *love* is the best way for me to put it. It transcends any of the material or scientific or philosophical doubts about our existence, but those doubts seem so much larger, so we have to keep them confined. My guess is, to actually open the Bible and read what it says is to force yourself to come face-to-face with those doubts. Like: *Do I really believe this?* It's easier to just show up once a week at a building and have somebody tell you what you need to hear. Particularly things like, 'When it all goes down, you're going to be taken in a warp zone or something, lifted out of here; a whole bunch of bad stuff is going to go down, and you'll be in heaven.' Comforting people with something like, as lousy as their life may feel today, *Well, one day I'll be in heaven.*

"Again, an easy way to become popular is telling people what they want to hear. Telling people there's a different side of things—that of giving to the poor—is just asking to be ignored. If Jesus is going to tell you to give to the poor, Tim LaHaye is not, so you might as well go with Tim LaHaye, because he's going to tell me the good stuff without the hard stuff. I know I would sure love to have everybody tell me for the rest of my life things that sound good and feel good, and encourage me and comfort me. But I think we often reach a point where we decide, from whatever forces are compelling us, *No, what I want is not to be comforted; what I want is not to be encouraged in whatever I've already decided or affirmed in my current beliefs—what I want is the truth.* And I'm not going to be afraid, whatever that may be. If the truth is that I go into the ground six feet and rot and get eaten by worms, so be it. The truth is the truth. If the truth is that fundamentalist Christians go to heaven and everybody else goes to hell, that's the truth.

"Personally, I don't believe either one of those. And the unfortunate thing to me is that it almost seems like people are forced to pick one or the other. So what you're seeing here is my best effort at providing a third way, at saying, *No, it's not meaningless, but it ain't this either.*"

11

Let them praise his name with dancing

I f Cornerstone is a mosaic of subcultures, it is a remarkably fluid one. Monochromatic goths lurk at jam band extravaganzas, dreadlocked hippies mosh in the punk tent, and emo kids patiently indulge their parents' attachment to roots rock.

But there was one group that did not mingle. Its members arrived at the festival no earlier than ten o'clock each night and headed directly for a one-thousand-square-foot aluminum shed accessible only by a treacherously muddy track behind the concession stands. There they remained until one in the morning, dancing, swaying, and praying at one hundred and thirty beats per minute. This was Dance Barn, the largest annual event of the tiny Christian rave scene.

Not that Christians often use the word *rave*. The association with the MDMA-fueled secular scene puts off people seeking a different kind of ecstasy. Besides, Christian ravers, like their secular counterparts, are sick of the media-co-opted word and its 1990s connotations. They prefer *events,* or *parties* or, to set themselves apart from secular ravers, *DJ-led worship*.

Not long after my trip to Cornerstone, I was browsing the forums on Tastyfresh.com, the leading web site for "Christ-centered DJ culture," and I noticed an announcement for a day-long seminar in West Reading, Pennsylvania, on "DJ-led worship 101." It would be followed by an *event* featuring "today's hottest club beats, mixed to glorify Jesus Christ."

○   ○   ○

West Reading's Penn Avenue is a restored thoroughfare of Victorian buildings, housing the kind of touristy shops that announce themselves with
decorative swinging signboards. Only the four-lane highway dividing the
street, and the occasional shuttered storefront hinting at darker economic
times in the recent past, prevent it from completely achieving its aspira-
tions to quaintness. This is Pennsylvania Dutch Country: 89 percent white,
lower-middle income, small-town America.

At 603 Penn Avenue is the Olympian Ballroom, a fading relic of the big-
band era now occupied by a Fred Astaire Dance Studios franchise. One
Saturday a month, from the very unravelike hours of seven to midnight,
the five-thousand-square-foot dance floor is turned over to Club Worship,
one of the longest-running institutions on the Christian rave scene.

Jeff Stoltzfus, the founder of Club Worship, is a youth pastor at a nearby
Mennonite church, not a denomination typically associated with techno
music. The church, which Jeff describes as theologically conservative and
politically liberal, doesn't always get what he does, but embraces it
nonetheless. Club Worship is not a proselytizing tool, he told me. It is
meant for people who are already believers—or at least *seekers,* to use the
Christianese. "To me, luring somebody in with music and then preaching
at them would seem almost coercive," said Jeff. "Our entire purpose is *worship.* All of the elements of our event that might seem entertainment-
focused are genuinely there to create an atmosphere where people can
express their love to God." Jeff said I was more than welcome to attend, but
that I wouldn't see what was really going on. "Worship is not a spectator
sport."

At thirty-six, Jeff is an old man on the scene. His gelled hair is gray at
the temples and his baggy jeans seem less a fashion statement than an
attempt to disguise a developing paunch. When I met him, Jeff was wearing a T-shirt that said "Relevant." That's the name of a popular emerging
church magazine, but as something for a youth pastor to wear to a rave, it
struck me as a little overeager.

I got the sense that he saw himself more as a big brother than a peer.
"There's this weird thing that happens to Christian teenagers in American
churchianity," he told me. "They are still trying to sort out what their own
beliefs are gonna be. They are in transition between this place of believing
what they have been taught all their lives, by teachers and parents, and dis-

covering what they are gonna believe for themselves." He wanted me to keep this in mind as I explored Christian rave culture, and teen culture in general. "It might seem shallow to outsiders, because it is shallow. Like a toddler at the edge of the ocean, they are still learning—just taking baby steps of their own in their faith. I agree that it's sometimes silly, but underneath, there is often a deeper thread running through it that deals with eternal values."

The most prominent speaker at the seminar, who would also be the evening's "guest worship leader," was Andy Hunter, a figure held in awe among fans of Christian electronic dance music (EDM). Hunter is the genre's only crossover success,* a thirty-two-year-old Brit whose deliriously propulsive compositions have become a staple of mainstream video games and movie trailers. In 2006, *DJ Magazine* ranked Hunter the world's 117th best DJ. EDM is a bigger deal in Europe than the States. While American churches have rock bands onstage, British ones often have DJs, so it's not surprising that the scene's biggest star would hail from the UK. (According to *Yoga Journal,* the earliest Christian raves may have been Anglican Masses in the 1980s.) Typically, Club Worship draws from the Philadelphia area and perhaps Baltimore and New York. Hunter had attracted kids from as far away as Michigan and Florida.

"Worship is a lifestyle," Hunter told the nineteen men and one woman seated around tables in the ballroom. "When we get together as a group and really worship, that's when we stir the heart of God. And when we stir the heart of God, that's when we can feel his presence. So this"—he gestured around at the DJ equipment behind him and the dance floor in front—"is our way of entering the throne room and meeting Jesus." Hunter plays both church events and mainstream clubs, and he said the basics are pretty similar. "If you're a DJ, whether you're Christian or not, you're taking people on a journey. You listen to the music that's playing, and with your second ear you're listening to the next song that you're going to mix in." The difference between him and secular DJs, he said, is that "with my third ear, I listen for where God wants me to take people."

---

*Moby is a born-again Christian who has recorded music with Christian themes, but he has never participated in the Christian culture industry or been embraced by its fans.

He continued, "I don't just play 'Christian' music. I will play any good tune. It doesn't have to be deep, as long as it's not offensive." That brought up a question that many people ask upon discovering Christian techno music, much of which is entirely instrumental: What makes it Christian? For Hunter, the answer has to do largely with the heart of the composer. He prays before writing or producing and sometimes keeps a brass bowl in his studio to ritually cleanse his hands. And he believes people can sense this in his music. "I don't think every worship song has to have lyrics," he insisted. "God can make a donkey talk, so I feel he can use music to create a feeling. It's amazing how many people come up to me and say, 'You're different from other DJs. You have such passion.' And that's when you can say, 'Well I'm passionate because I'm passionate about Jesus.'" In this sense, said Hunter, there is a spiritual thread from Christian DJing that runs directly back to the earliest days of evangelicalism. "John Wesley was asked why he attracted such crowds, and he answered, 'I'm on fire for the Lord and people come to watch me burn.'"

Jeff called a break and I went up to talk to him and another DJ, Jon Carlson, about this idea of communing with God through music and dance. Non-Christian ravers often describe their experiences in transcendent terms, so integrating God into this makes more intuitive sense than shoehorning him into, say, heavy metal. But it also must raise concerns for people serious about faith, because if a non-Christian at a secular rave can have a religious experience—by definition a counterfeit one, a conservative evangelical would have to affirm—how can anyone know if what Christians experience as the hand of God at Club Worship isn't merely the same superficial emotional response, rather than a genuine spiritual one?

"I understand where you're coming from," said Jeff, "because if you're fake, as a DJ, you can still create an emotional response using tricks."

Carlson added, "I think if all someone does for their spiritual life is go to clubs and never listens to a good sermon or reads their Bible, their life is out of balance. But if all they're doing is careful exegesis, then their life is also out of balance. God talks to us through our emotions as well as our intellect."

"The stuff we do with trance music is like a Pentecostal church, it draws you in emotionally," said Jeff. Then he added, "Hip hop is like a Presbyterian church, it's about the word."

Jeff has been trying to incorporate hip hop into his events.* A session on hip hop DJing was followed by one on "break dancing as worship." The leader of this workshop was a muscular dancer in red sweats who looked alarmingly like Kevin Federline. "I'ma show you some moves, and you tell me what you see," he instructed. I saw 1985, but other people were more impressed. "I think you're fighting the devil with that," marveled one guy. The dancer grinned. "That was a little skit I created about Adam and Eve in the garden."

Someone else asked, "How do you make sure, when you dance, that you're glorifying God rather than yourself?"

"That's something you really gotta watch out for," he agreed. "A lot of break dancing, you'll freeze and get in a pose, almost like someone's taking your picture. And that's Satan. If this is truly worship, it should be something we do without spectators."

I tried to assimilate the idea that when black kids in the Bronx break-dance, it's Satanic, but that white kids in West Reading can reclaim the dance for God. And then I remembered it was the twenty-first century and most black kids in the Bronx have moved on to other things.

◌　◌　◌

---

*And here I will literally relegate Christian hip hop to a footnote, because hip hop is ridiculously underrepresented in Christian pop culture. It's true that the audience for CCM is mostly white, but then so are the people who buy secular hip hop. Rap music has dominated the *Billboard* charts for at least ten years now, and yet CCM, which in other ways is so slavishly imitative, has largely avoided it. There are a fair number of Christian rappers but few are very good and their impact on the industry has been minimal compared with the influence of hip hop in secular music. Evan, the punk fan I'd talked to at Cornerstone, made the interesting point that Christian rap almost inevitably sounds less authentic than Christian rock (i.e., less like the mainstream variety) because "Worldly rap is so different from Christian rap in terms of the themes." A love song can be Christianized by substituting Jesus for your girlfriend, he said, but "God can't be your ho." It was a joke, but Club Worship's hip-hop DJ concurred to an extent. He said that because mainstream rap glamorizes violence, drugs, and materialism, churches and other gatekeepers are understandably, if incorrectly, concerned that the genre can't be made holy. As a result, one of the few rappers at Cornerstone told me, Christian MCs are forced to reassure the gatekeepers by mentioning Jesus in every verse and keeping the message simple—a recipe for mediocrity at best.

The Bible speaks of dancing twenty-seven times and associates it with tambourines, lutes, and harps. There are no specific references to fog machines, lasers, and glowsticks, but these don't seem like unreasonable extrapolations.

By nine o'clock, the sprung maple dance floor was far from full, but not as deserted as it had been for the first two hours of the event. A sweet, musty odor wafted through the room as the billowing chemical vapors reflected and refracted a dizzying array of "intelligent lighting," swirling beams of color that can be perfectly synched with the music. Images of crosses, birds, and praying hands repeated rhythmically on a ten-foot screen to the side of the stage.

Compared to the atmosphere, the actual dancing was subdued. Kids swooped in place, painting the air red, blue, and green with their glow-sticks. Teenagers popped glowsticks in their mouths, sharing illuminated smiles from across the room. Around their necks, a handful of people wore glow crosses. It was mellow enough that several girls felt comfortable kicking off their shoes and dancing barefoot. Others swayed in place, arms raised and palms open, soaking in the Holy Spirit. Techno beats throbbed under electronically distorted chanting. "Holy, holy is our God almighty. Holy, holy is our God almighty."

I stuck to the back wall, along with a few dozen other people who had yet to feel God calling them to the dance floor. A heavyset guy in giant, multipocketed pants and a T-shirt identifying him as a fan of "DJ Yo-yo" caught my eye; he was one of the few people wearing actual raver fashion. Nearby, another guy wore a shirt showing two stick figures locked in an embrace, circled and crossed out; underneath was the command, "Less grinding, more bass."

I scoped the dance floor. The only physical contact was four girls holding hands in a circle, their heads bowed in prayer. Later I asked Jeff if freak dancing was ever a problem at Club Worship. "Oh, it happens," he said. "There are Christians who go to church on Sunday and watch MTV all week long, and how they learn to dance from MTV is not appropriate if you don't want to get turned on sexually." He lowered his voice as if to share confidential information. "It turns on things that would be better turned on in the bedroom with their wife and not turned on before."

○　○　○

At the rear of the ballroom was a large balcony where the VJ crew mixed the video display. The lead VJ invited me up for a look. He had reason to be proud of his setup, an expensive array of laptops, monitors, DVD players, mixing boards, and electronic keyboards, which he had programmed so he could play video clips like notes on a piano. Down below, the DJ spun a slow trance beat and the VJ accompanied him with a loop of rolling storm clouds, yellow tulips, and raindrops on a tranquil pond.

For faster sets, Club Worship sometimes appropriates footage from Hollywood action movies. "We use clips from *The Matrix*, we use clips from *Swordfish*," the VJ said. *The Matrix* I understood. As novelist Ted Dekker had made clear, evangelicals love its crypto-Christian imagery; Stephen Baldwin describes reading the Bible as "taking the red pill." *Swordfish* was a little more baffling. I vaguely remembered it as a second-rate John Travolta thriller with a first-rate, if completely gratuitous, Halle Berry topless scene. But the VJ had already moved on. "Sometimes we use a few clips from *The Passion of the Christ*," he said, adding that such heavy artillery is usually kept in reserve. "If the audience looks like they're falling out of the worship, you want to put in some of your really worshipful images."

Onstage, Jeff was preaching over a mid-tempo groove while Andy Hunter got set up. "Heaven is gonna be great!" Jeff told the crowd. "It's like the ultimate in intelligent lighting." Hunter propped his headphones in the crook of his neck and began spinning. Now the floor filled up, a hundred or more kids twirling, writhing, and weeping with joy. During the breakdowns, more than a few kids simply collapsed onto the ground, arms outstretched. As a breathy female voice sang, "Here I am at the end, I'm in need of resurrection," a girl on the dance floor dramatically shed her six glowstick bracelets and lowered herself into a cross-legged meditation pose.

Feeling overstimulated, I headed out to the lobby and removed my earplugs. A sign pointed the way to The Upper Room: "Pray, dialogue, reflect, learn, chill." I climbed a narrow staircase and found a dimly lit space with some old chairs and a ratty futon. Eight or nine young people sat around dialoguing on a brown shag carpet.

I joined a couple from out of town. The girl, a twenty-one-year-old redhead named Jess, told me she preferred Christian clubs to secular ones because she doesn't have to worry about guys hitting on her. At most clubs, she said, "It doesn't matter who you are or how you're dressed, as soon as you walk in the door, they're staring at you like you're a piece of meat." She took a drink of bottled water. "Even women don't respect women. It's like, we worked so hard to get where we are and now you're wearing *that* and dancing in a cage? That bothered me even before I became a Christian."

Jess and her boyfriend came to Christ a couple of years ago. "When I became a Christian, I got rid of all my secular music," she said.

"All of it?" I asked. "Are you sure that was necessary?"

"It gets inside you." Jess nodded at her boyfriend. "He made me do it," she said. "I tried to save some of my favorites. I really wanted to keep the first Zebrahead album. I'd say, 'This one isn't so bad,' and he'd say, 'But is it *good?*'"

Back downstairs, I ran into the rave kid in the DJ Yo-yo shirt, who turned out to be DJ Yo-yo himself. He had driven six hours, from Canton, Ohio, near Cleveland, to see Andy Hunter and was not disappointed. He said he appreciated the spirit of Club Worship, but admitted that, as a DJ himself, he would have liked more "shredding the decks" and "underground" music. In other words, what he wanted was not DJ-led worship but a *party,* like the kind he throws back home. That sounded good to me too, and I made plans to check out one of his events.

When the dance was over, worshippers filtered onto Penn Avenue to ribbing from the crowd milling around outside a bar across the street. A long-haired dude cranked up a Van Halen tune in his car and shouted, "Jesus is in the house!" Jeff Stoltzfus shrugged it off, joking, "He's got the spirit."

Jess walked past and waved good-bye. I told Jeff about my conversation with her, and my unease about an intelligent and together young woman who felt the need to keep herself so sheltered. "The Amish have this interesting practice that is a different way of navigating faith and teenage life," he said. "It's called *rumspringa*. Once they reach the age when they can think for themselves, they are basically asked to make a decision: Either follow the way of the church, God's way, or follow the way of the world. They are sort of forced to really think hard about it and then take responsibility for their own faith, rather than resting on the faith of their parents."

"It's hard to imagine the evangelical church embracing that," I observed.

"Yep."

DJ Yo-yo belongs to a group of performers who call themselves the Electro-Spirit Crew. When I flew out to Canton, his collaborator Dan Bartow met me at the airport. The event they had organized for a church in the town of Hudson had been dubbed Movement, but Dan warned me right off the bat that the name would probably prove ironic. "This kind of church crowd usually doesn't really know the music or how to dance to it," he said as I threw my bag into the backseat of his car.

A short, stocky twenty-seven-year-old with tousled brown hair and a goatee, Dan is well-known in the Christian EDM scene under the stage name heldbywill. He wore a karate jacket, baggy jeans, and jet-black boots with three-inch soles. As we left short-term parking, Dan told me that though he'd once taken a few classes at Moody Bible Institute with an eye toward becoming a pastor, he'd recently begun to drift away from organized Christianity.

"I started getting soured by people who claimed to be one thing but are really another." He paused to choose his words. "When people show up at church on Sunday morning, they sing a couple of songs, they feel good about themselves—then they leave and live a totally different life the rest of the week. That just started to bug me, because I really felt like I'm trying to be *real* about my faith." Even the music started to annoy him. "I don't like praise and worship music. The first fifteen to twenty minutes of church service are terrible for me. Because sometimes you show up and you don't really want to sing praise songs. I don't go through every day of my life like, 'Yay! Praise God!' I mean, bad things go on, and I'm not in the mood to sing every Sunday morning."

Dan didn't grow up in the Christian culture bubble, and he has little patience for efforts to draw him into it. He'd once gotten an e-mail from a Christian group organizing a protest against NBC for "degrading Christianity"—a reaction to a rumor that Britney Spears was going to appear on *Will & Grace* as the host of a Christian cooking show called *Crucifixins*. To Dan, it was Christians who degraded Christianity by leaving themselves open to such jibes. "What sucks is *Crucifixins* probably is a *real* Christian cooking show somewhere. Because if you can walk into a Christian bookstore and find some breath mints called Testamints, you could probably find a cooking show called *Crucifixins*. That's actually quite funny."

"So do you consider what you do Christian music?"

"When people hear a song and go, 'Man, that's a Christian song,' it's usually a praise-type song."

"Right."

"Praise, praise, praise, praise. My music doesn't sound anything like that. I wouldn't say my music is Christian. I'm a Christian who writes music. We have different approaches in Electro-Spirit. Some of the other guys, they're definitely trying to minister more than I am. I don't feel embarrassed to say that. I don't think I'm a bad Christian for it."

Dan acknowledged that unlike at Club Worship, I would hear very few if any CCM remixes and a lot of original songs and EDM tracks created by secular artists. "But it will all be things that would be appropriate in a church. No booty-shaking, cussing, sexually oriented stuff."

"So do you go to secular raves?"

"Yeah, I do try to go to raves and shows whenever I hear about them. I'm an electronic music fan. I love it. I live for the beats." He laughed.

"Is it more about the music or the scene?"

"Well, you might have heard about PLUR—Peace, Love, Unity, Respect. It's a big raver thing. A lot of people are all about the community. For me, I love to meet people with a mutual interest. I met some guys who happened to be playing some shows in Pennsylvania and getting real big in the techno music scene a couple of years ago. I tried getting together with them to produce stuff, but they were literally smoking weed in the studio. It wasn't working."

"So are there limits to *respect* when it comes to Christians, or do people basically say, 'You can do your thing and we'll do ours?'"

"I think everyone initially is like, 'Oh, that's cool, man.' If you step over the line and try to push something on them, share something with them they don't want to hear, then it gets ugly. But I think initially most ravers are fairly open to it. They'll turn on you if you step out and say something like, 'Hey, man, maybe you shouldn't drop that ecstasy'—but that really isn't a cool thing to do anyway, unless you are approached about it, or you think there's some serious concern. You really shouldn't butt into people's business."

We pulled into the parking lot of a large white church. "I do have positive reasons for playing my kind of music," Dan finished. "I like to be a positive person in places that are often drug-filled and kind of negative. But I don't really do it as a mission from God either. I admit that that's a God-given talent, but I do it mostly because I just like to rock out."

Inside, we hooked up with DJ Yo-yo, who was rigging lights. His real name is Joe Ambrose, but everyone calls him Yo-yo, a name he picked up during his brief career as a professional yo-yoer. "I went around and yo-yoed for people and got paid for it," he shrugged. "I was sponsored by Duncan."

Yo-yo excused himself to say hello to his parents—his mother was wearing a T-shirt that said, "Yo-yo's Ma"—and I went out to the lobby. Dan was right: this was even less of a raver crowd than Club Worship—a bunch of tweens and teens in interchangeable sneakers, jeans, and sweatshirts, probably all members of this church. I confirmed that with the youth pastor, Joe, who was easy to spot: He was the guy in his thirties wearing sneakers, jeans, and a sweatshirt with a walkie-talkie clipped to his belt; a gaggle of girls hung around him giggling and flirting.

"What do you think of the turnout?" I asked him.

He grunted. "Really, in this area they'd do better off with a band. I'm not even sure what type. Grunge? Like, Fall Out Boy? I'm not really familiar with Fall Out Boy's music, but I know they're popular."

It was almost time to start, and Yo-yo called everyone together for a prayer. "Father God, I just ask that you bless this gathering," Yo-yo began. I'd noticed that evangelicals rarely ask for anything unless they *just* ask for it, as if acknowledging the triviality of their desires in the scheme of things. He went on, "I pray that you remove any obstacles that we have tonight including pride or the desire to do a good show."

Another performer, Malex, added, "I pray that you touch people, if it be your will, through us."

And Youth Pastor Joe said, "I know we don't pray for numbers, but tonight we're praying for three-fifty."

○ ○ ○

That prayer would go unanswered. An hour into the show, the dance floor was empty except for two guys in their twenties whipping their glowsticks around with abandon. You couldn't blame the performers for this. As Yo-yo had promised, the DJs did in fact shred the decks, executing complex mixes that showed a genuine feeling for the music. The live performers, like Dan, who sequenced keyboard riffs and digital samples on the fly, were equally adept. It was the church kids—and the church building itself— that seemed to be in the wrong place. But the performers pressed on, and it occurred to me that if they were proselytizing for anything it was EDM— trying to win over Fall Out Boy fans to the one true faith.

I went back out to the lobby where Malex had set up a table to sell CDs while waiting to do his set. Malex is Alex Markley, a nineteen-year-old student and budding digital entrepreneur. He wore a black shirt and a brown tie patterned with crosses. Malex has been into electronic music since he was six, when he figured out how to strip the soundtracks off his computer games. Now he listens only to Christian electronica.

"Is that in solidarity with the scene, or can you actually tell the difference somehow?" I asked. I was still having trouble understanding what distinguished a Christian instrumental track from a non-Christian one.

"Personally, I do sense a difference," he said. "I do feel negative and positive influences coming from the soul of the artist. I know plenty of very great Christian people who listen to all sorts of stuff, and that's fine. For me, I just try to avoid it." Malex said that being part of the Christian rave scene is inherently isolating. Christians think it's "a contradiction in terms," and playing in churches turns off non-Christians. "They're not even going to walk in the doors," he said. "There are definitely very serious spiritual warfare concerns that are preventing secular involvement in this kind of scene. People actually have adverse physical responses to church buildings— documented cases of getting headaches from coming near churches."

If there was anyone who looked like he felt more out of place here than me, it was DJ Yo-yo's father, who was lingering nearby wearing a light blue Yo-yo T-shirt over his sober plaid button-down. Chuck Ambrose was a gruff man with a striking resemblance to the character actor Dan Hedaya, who played Rhea Perlman's first husband on *Cheers* and Alicia Silverstone's father in *Clueless*. I asked him what he thought of this scene, and his brow furrowed. "It's an adjustment for us. We sent our older son to a college where they taught that syncopation is from the devil. They could document it scripturally. But we thought, *Well, that can't be right.*"

"That seems a bit extreme," I agreed.

"We've heard sermons that if it's not the traditional hymns, it's not Christian. We attended a church that believed that." Chuck glanced in the direction of the pounding coming from behind the sanctuary doors. "At our son's college, if you brought a tape that was the most obviously Christian music, lyrically, but they heard a hint of a beat, they'd toss it out."

"So what do you think—is this Christian music?"

"I struggle with that." Chuck tried to conjure up a justification. "Well, it's in a place that honors God," he offered, looking around. Then his mood darkened again. "You look at the people who come in here, they've got metal spikes in their head." I looked around, confused, seeing only Gapped-out American teenagers; maybe some of the girls had pierced ears. Chuck continued, "I understand the idea is you get them in here and they stay," he said, though I wasn't sure whose idea that was. "But they can pull your church in the wrong direction too."

I hadn't expected such an ominous perspective. I was weighing how to respond when Chuck bent closer and said, "Let me ask you this: How did you get saved?"

"Oh, um, I'm not Christian." Chuck's eyes widened, and to win him back, I quickly added, "I'm Jewish."

Chuck staggered back sharply like he'd been shivved. Was it possible the kinship card didn't work here?

He leaned in again. "Why don't you believe Jesus was the messiah?"

"Well," I said, "I guess I don't believe in the idea of a literal human messiah."

"Yes, it is hard to believe that God could become a man, isn't it? But you know, someone once said, Jesus was either a liar, or he was a lunatic, or he was the Lord."

"C. S. Lewis, right?"

Now Chuck looked downright angry. "I don't know if it was C. S. Lewis," he growled, jabbing his finger at my chest, "but you'd better give it some thought."

○   ○   ○

In a hall off to the side of the sanctuary I caught up with the two guys I'd seen dancing wildly earlier in the evening. They introduced themselves as Jesse and Ken-Ken. In the light they stood out even more. For one thing, Ken-Ken was the only black guy in the building. For another, they were both dressed up, sort of, in matching black suit jackets over blue shirts. Ken-Ken wore an Ecko watch cap and Jesse sported an old-fashioned green flat cap. It wasn't raver wear, but at least it showed some flair.

"You guys have been to raves before?" I asked.

"Oh, yeah." Jesse did a few dance moves and Ken-Ken punched him.

"So how does this compare?"

"Well nobody's dancing!" yelped Jesse. "But honestly, the DJs are some of the best I've ever seen. If I didn't know this was Christian, I couldn't tell."

"We're Christians and everything," added Ken-Ken, "but we don't go to church here."

"I didn't even know there was Christian techno," said Jesse. "I'm glad it's so good, though. I went to a Christian rock concert once and left after like ten minutes—too much preaching. I just wish more people would *dance*."

"Part of the problem is everybody knows each other so nobody wants to do anything crazy," said Ken-Ken.

Jesse nodded vigorously. "I've had to hold myself back because I've seen a lot of crazy stuff at raves. I went to this one rave at an anime con . . ." *Japanese animation. Convention.* I quickly reappraised the situation. *Not ravers; geeks.* Jesse went on, talking excitedly, "Do you know what *yaoi* is? It's a kind of anime that's, basically, guy-on-guy action? Well, there were some fans there—you could tell by their outfits; they had the leopard print and the fishnets—and there were some other guys there who were into cosplay—that's costume play—and their thing was, they were dressed as Tetris blocks. So the *yaoi* guys thought it would be funny to start, you know, *humping* the Tetris blocks on the dance floor." Jesse cracked open a bottle of water and looked in the direction of a wall hanging declaring "Lord Jesus, our hope is in you alone." "So this is a little different," he said.

○   ○   ○

After the show I was helping the performers dismantle their equipment when I felt somebody looming over my shoulder. I turned around and Chuck Ambrose was there, finger out again. "Dan, listen to this." He tugged at his forefinger, as if ticking off an item on a list. "In the beginning was the Word, and the Word was with God, and the Word *was* God."

I glanced around. "That, uh, sounds familiar."

His eyes narrowed. "It's not Clive Lewis."

Outside, Dan Bartow was packing up his car. "It's weird," he said. "I haven't been inside a church in a little while. I don't feel that God really requires me to attend a church. It's not biblical. There were no churches in the early days. The *church* was the believers. The definition of *church* is people who believe in God and Jesus. The thing about tonight—I really consider tonight church, not because it's *in a church,* but because the guys I'm playing with are my closest Christian brothers. If I have a concern, or I want to talk to somebody, I go to these guys. Every once in a while, we all get together in my house. We put out turntables and share bread and grape juice. We call it a groove fellowship."

He shut the trunk. "That's like the early church. It was a bunch of people who got together in the first century, shared what they believed, and they helped each other—they did actual Christian things. I think the church is actually encouraging laziness in some respects, just because if you only go every Sunday and you think that's what's required of you, you stop focusing on the things that Jesus said were really important, like 'Love your brother and sister, love your neighbor; cry with them when they cry and be happy with them when they're happy.' Actually, the real important things that Jesus said, you lose sight of them if you get involved in a corporate type of church."

Several months later Dan e-mailed to say he was leaving the Christian EDM scene entirely. "I have a new project now. It's called Research Division and it's totally mainstream. We're not promoting it in the Christian world. I had a great run as heldbywill, but I'm not interested in marketing my music to a small group of Christians anymore. Why should I? This new stuff is awesome. It can compete with anything that's out there."

12

Our mouths were filled with laughter

T he New Testament is not a very funny book. It commends mirth but hardly ever indulges in any. There is no verse that says "Jesus laughed." For two thousand years, this legacy has shackled devout Christians. As a group, Christians have had a reputation as humorless scolds or kindhearted do-gooders or passionate believers, but rarely has anyone said, "You know who's a funny people? The Christians." When they've elicited laughter, it's usually been at their expense.

That may be about to change. In the last ten years, Christian comedians have established an impressive presence in the world of stand-up comedy. With between eighty and one hundred professional Christian comedians, and countless more part-time amateurs, secular clubs are starting to see the value in holding Christian comedy nights, while churches have learned that they can fill pews and coffers by booking the same acts. Some Christian comedians play only clubs—usually on the same bill with secular comics—while others also (or only) play churches and Christian events. These usually pay better than clubs and have been instrumental in the Christian comedy boom. One agency that books comedians for the church market reported handling 500 events in 2006, up from 150 four years earlier. Recently, the producers of the Blue Collar Comedy Tour put out a DVD called *Thou Shalt Laugh,* hosted by Patricia Heaton from *Everybody Loves Raymond.* It was followed by a national tour and a line of greeting cards.

"We're a little behind the mainstream," said Dan Rupple, the president of the Christian Comedy Association, which boasts around three hundred members. "In the eighties, you saw Jerry Seinfeld, Leno, Letterman, and all of them come out of the clubs doing stand-up. That's where we are now." Rupple's goal is to guide Christian comedians along the same path that secular ones paved twenty years earlier—out of the dingy clubs and into the promised land of Hollywood. I met him at the CCA's sixth annual comedy conference, two days of instruction, networking, and performances that drew one hundred fifty comedians of all levels to a megachurch in Anaheim, California. It would be my chance to see some of the country's top Christian comedians in action. "You're going to have the same reaction as everyone else," Rupple promised me: *I was really surprised by the caliber. I just didn't think it would be that good.*

I smiled politely.

A row of ornamental palms marks the front entrance of the Cornerstone Church (no relation to the festival), a twenty-first-century building that shares a highway exit with two shopping malls and the Richard Nixon presidential library. In common with many "seeker-friendly" suburban megachurches, there is little about Cornerstone's sleek blue-glass facade to indicate that it is, in fact, a church, rather than a well-funded community college or the corporate headquarters of a small electronics manufacturer. Inside, the atmosphere is equally modern, tasteful, and sterile; the earth-tone decor and flattering lights could not be more agreeable if they'd been selected by a focus group, which they may well have been. Arriving early, I relaxed in the on-site Starbucks and flipped through a Christian Coalition voter guide—carefully written to avoid technically endorsing Republicans, while *informing* church members of candidates' positions on "family values" issues such as "teaching homosexuality as an acceptable lifestyle in public schools," "raising state or federal taxes," and "driver's licenses for illegal immigrants." The comedy bar was already set high.

At 5:45 p.m., the auditorium doors opened for the first of two performer showcases that would bookend the lectures and workshops. The room quickly filled up with conference attendees and curious locals. The dress code was Orange County casual—middle-aged dads in aloha shirts and moms in pastel blouses; younger women wore short skirts and tank tops. I sat down in a row of teenagers from the Cornerstone youth group.

One wore a T-shirt that said "I would die tonight for my beliefs." "I hope it doesn't come to that," I told him. He looked at me blankly.

I turned to a girl seated nearby and asked her if she'd seen Christian comedy before. She hadn't even known it existed. I asked what she was expecting, and she thought for a bit before answering, "Something your little sister can hear that you don't have to worry about."

As it happens, this is what most people expect and many comedians cater to that by promoting themselves not primarily as Christians but simply as *clean*. Dan Rupple discourages this. "If you make *clean* the defining trait of what we do, then Bill Cosby and Ray Romano are Christian comedians." But he doesn't necessarily think Christian comics need to invoke Jesus or the Bible onstage either. Like Christian rock, Christian comedy can be about any subject at all—as long as it affirms a Christian worldview: that there are moral absolutes, that no one should be degraded, that people can be forgiven for their sins, that life is not meaningless.

Rupple is one of the pioneers of Christian comedy. An L.A. native, he spent his teenage years doing sketch comedy in local clubs before finding God at the tail end of the 1970s Jesus movement. "My whole group became Christians individually," he said. "We showed up at a rehearsal and suddenly we are all Christians. We said, 'Maybe we can keep going in the same style of comedy, but do it from a Christian perspective.'" They named themselves Isaac Air Freight and rapidly established themselves as the Christian *Saturday Night Live*.* A typical skit would be a *Leave It to Beaver* parody in which Beaver goes to church camp and becomes a Christian: "What would make you go and do a goofy thing like that?" asks Wally. "I don't know, Wally. They were just studying the Bible, and they read the part that said if I didn't I'd go to hell but that God loved me and that he didn't want me to go to hell, and that if I didn't want to go to hell all I had to do was repent for all the bad stuff that I did and accept Jesus as my savior and live my life for him, and then I could go to heaven."

"In hindsight, we weren't always very funny," Rupple admitted. "We felt this self-imposed pressure to sum up the entire gospel story in every routine, and so each routine was steeped in so much theological or biblical

---

*Isaac Air Freight was an intentionally nonsensical name—like Monty Python's Flying Circus with biblical overtones.

information that the jokes got squeezed out. But it worked. It was such a breath of fresh air to the church. The church had grown very stuffy in the fifties and sixties, and when Isaac Air Freight came with comedy, they wanted to laugh so badly, the body of Christ, that you could say anything and they would laugh. One time we were doing a show in San Diego—they were laughing so hard, I cut three routines. I said, 'If they're laughing this hard at this one, I don't want to do these, because they'll die.'"

At least, that's how it was on the good nights. On one bad night, the troupe cut sketches because *no one* was laughing. Afterward, they were packing up miserably when a man came up and told them how hilarious the show was. Rupple grumbled that usually when something is funny, people laugh. "Oh, you're not allowed to laugh in church," the man explained.

At the Cornerstone megachurch, that attitude has been relegated to the dustbin. A warm orange glow lit the stage as a small, older woman trotted out to the microphone standing in the center, and the audience was as eager to laugh as if they were in a comedy club. Like Rupple, Chondra Pierce was a Christian comedy pioneer. One reason the church eventually warmed up to comedy is that Pierce eased them into it, with routines that are less stand-up than humorous storytelling. Pierce is a Tennessee gal with a winning Southern charm and masterful sense of timing. The night I saw her, she told a story about her relationship with her mother. "I grew up in a very conservative church," she began. "*Hair up, skirt down,* that was our motto." Then she described her first exposure to worldly influences. "We turned on the radio and heard 'Jeremiah was a bullfrog.' And I knew we were going to burn." After that she distanced herself from the church and her embarrassingly devout mother. Pierce told all this with just the right touch of self-deprecating humor. In fact, she was about two-thirds of the way through her story when I suddenly realized: *She's giving her testimony.* And I actually wanted to hear how it ended. No wonder churches had embraced comedy.

As a series of other comedians took the stage, I realized that there are varying philosophical approaches to Christian comedy roughly parallel to Jay Howard's categories of Christian music. Pierce represented one type of separational comedy, though other separational comics have a more conventional stand-up style. One of these is Nazareth (one name only), who injected some social commentary into his routine.

> I had one professor come to me and say, "There is no intelligent design, it's all about evolution." He said to me, "Nazareth, my great-great-grandfather was like a worm, and through millions and trillions of years, he had the legs stick out and the hands stick out and here we are today." I told him, "Well my great-great-grandfather was Adam, and he should have stepped on your grandpa a long time ago!"

That Nazareth speaks to and for a preselected conservative Christian audience does not mean he isn't sometimes funny. After a bit about how his infant daughter sleeps all day and cries all night, he announced, "I'm pro-life, but not at two in the morning." Actually, I may have been the only person in the room who laughed at that one. One of the most successful Christian comedians, Brad Stine, is so devoted to conservative politics that his performances often sound more like talk radio rants than comedy routines. But Stine is not a member of the Christian Comedy Association, and has, in fact, largely rebranded himself as a conservative, rather than Christian, comic. For the most part Christian comedians stay away from political material.

The equivalent of integrational musicians are the self-described clean comics, who range from dull to corny to hilarious, just as most stand-up comedians do. The ones I saw mostly stuck to familiar comedy tropes—airport security, cops and doughnuts, women and how they love to shop. Though I had feared that Christian comedy would be as amateurish and unbearable as Christian rock had been at the same juncture in its development, the level of talent was very much on par with mainstream comedy. Thor Ramsey, one of the stars of *Thou Shalt Laugh,* explained that while 1980s Christian rock was populated by Christians who decided to pick up guitars for the Lord, today's Christian comedy scene consists mostly of people who had years of secular club experience under their belts before they became Christian.

Curiously, the integrational comedians were at their best when they veered into separational territory, doing material about their lives as Christians. I hadn't expected that, but it made sense. I don't care whether comedy is clean or dirty, I just want it to be fresh. So while I didn't personally relate to the churchy subject matter, at least it hadn't been done to death on Comedy Central.

- People say, "I don't like the church, it's full of hypocrites." I wonder if the Church of Satan has hypocrites. "The only time we see you here is Halloween! Have you even sacrificed a goat this week?"
- I'm not afraid of death because I was raised Baptist and that's pretty much all we talked about. That and not dancing.
- We homeschool our kids. It's not that we don't like public school, we just don't want to get up that early. The hardest thing is seeing those bumper stickers: *My kid is an honor student at So-and-So Elementary School*. So I got a bumper sticker for my car: *My kids are homeschooled and we have no idea how they're doing*.

The father of Christian comedy is Mike Warnke, who emerged on the scene a few years before Isaac Air Freight, not as a comedian but as a repentant Satanist. Warnke became famous by spinning baroque tales of his life in a Satanic cult and his eventual salvation. Gradually he began leavening his stories of animal sacrifice, cannibalism, and virgin-rape with jokes about airplane food, dogs, and the difference between Baptists and Pentecostals. He released several comedy albums, but his stand-up career was always bolstered by his reputation as an authority on Satanism. Much of what America thought it knew about Satanists came from Warnke, who claimed that he had been a high priest with a coven of 1,500. During the Satanic ritual abuse panic of the 1980s, Warnke appeared on shows like *20/20* and *Larry King Live* to warn of the dangers posed by his former associates. At the end of his gigs, he would always take up a collection for his anti-Satanism ministry, which reportedly took in $1.5 million in 1986, its peak year.

In 1991, Jesus People USA's *Cornerstone* magazine published a twenty-four-thousand-word exposé—eventually expanded into a book—that meticulously and definitively revealed Warnke as a fraud. His career declined after that, but by proving that there was a market for Christian comedy, Warnke helped create an industry that would only begin to thrive after his downfall. Today, the quaint pre-Warnke humor of pastors with puppets has given way not only to stand-up comics, but to more elaborate acts as well. One is a parody band called ApologetiX, who describe themselves as Weird Al meets Billy Graham (for example, they redo "The Real Slim Shady" as "The Real Sin Savior").* Another is a hidden camera TV show called *Prank 3:16*, the Christian *Punk'd*. In one episode, the pranksters fake the Rapture, instilling panic in a poor girl who thinks she's been left behind.

The morning after the comedy showcase I returned to the Cornerstone Church for the opening session of the conference. At the registration table I picked up a badge with my name and the designation "press." I sighed. While I was willing to identify myself as a member of the media elite in one-on-one conversation, I was concerned about wearing the label in a room full of skeptical Christian conservatives. Soon I realized that the real problem was wearing it in a room full of aspiring comedians. Two different people got the hilarious idea to *press the badge* and wait for a reaction.

In fact, I was welcomed as warmly as anywhere I had been. Once again, being Jewish gave me a certain cachet, this time as both the theological older brother and as a member of a group that *does* have a reputation for being funny. A gregarious blond woman grabbed my arm to tell me how much she identified with Jewish culture. "My Jewish friends say I'm more Jewish than anyone they know!" she exclaimed. I eyed the three-inch silver cross around her neck and said nothing.

Dan Rupple began the morning with a comedian's prayer. "Father God, we're just trying to find a middle ground between being humble and being noticed, between being secure and desperately needing the approval and validation of nearly everyone around us." I'd been wondering about this very issue. Any comedian will tell you that great comedy comes from insecurity, self-loathing, and pain, while any Christian will tell you that Jesus helps you know joy and feel truly at peace. This, perhaps more than latent Puritanism, seemed the biggest impediment to Christian comedy.

---

*ApologetiX's funniest joke is unintentional. Their liner notes refer to the band Butthole Surfers as "Buttonhole Surfers."

"There is always a struggle between the comedian who is grossly insecure, and the Christian who is supposed to be secure in the loving hand of his almighty God," Rupple told me later, relaxing on a leather couch in the church Starbucks. "The reality is, we understand that we are secure spiritually, but our flesh is still very insecure—and I think it is that conflict that great humor can come from. Often people think the term *Christian comedy* is an oxymoron, 'cause there's nothing funny about being a Christian. I think it's really the exact opposite. I think it's hysterical what the Christian struggles with, trying to live out their beliefs in a world that is, for the most part, unbelieving. It's also, I think, quite humorous what some people go through to turn against God"—that is, to persuade themselves that pleasure or power or any other worldly measure of success is all that one needs out of life.

I mentioned what I'd learned about most contemporary Christian music—that it tries to avoid addressing the struggles of Christians in favor of painting a rosy picture of the Christian life. "I imagine that's harder to get away with in comedy."

"Sure. One of the staples of comedy is truth. Comedy has to have its basis in truth. It's an exaggeration of the truth. That's usually where the joke comes from, or from something's incongruity with the truth. Saying that it's all a bed of roses, you are not being truthful, and so I don't think you can be very effective as a comedian. Christian comedians are very, very prone to being very honest and candid with their struggles of what they are going through, probably much more than a musician. A musician has a little bit more luxury to romanticize."

On the other hand, Rupple said, comedians who are ruthless in exploring their personal struggles often pull their punches when it comes to taking on the behavior and teachings of the church. "Christian comedians need to be a little more dangerous. One of the roles of comedy in our culture is to challenge beliefs, challenge our sacred cows, shake things up a little bit. Be a little bit of an agitator through comedy to get us thinking and questioning. Sometimes Christians are a little hesitant to question their faith. I think it stands up to any scrutiny. If it is the truth of God, you know, bring it on."

Comedy can transcend entertainment, Rupple argued, but only if comedians are truly daring. "I think Christian comedians have been a little hesitant to do that. Even though I don't agree with their worldview or their style, I respect people like Lenny Bruce or Richard Pryor—and I even embrace some of their worldview. Pryor or Bruce or George Carlin, they are trying to convey truth, and sometimes they hit it. You know, they say things, and you're like, *You know what, he's right. That's right and we have to think that way.* A lot of times it isn't what I think is right, or the truth, and sometimes it's even offensive to my Christian beliefs, but I am glad someone's out there trying to say something."

"So what's holding Christian comedians back?"

"I think they are probably a little afraid of some elements in the Christian community that would be a little narrow-minded and just wouldn't quite get it," Rupple answered. "Sometimes Christians are not the hippest people. A lot of what we did with Isaac Air Freight was satire, and we spent a lot of time explaining 'No, don't you understand: I'm making fun of it. I am not endorsing, I'm making fun of it.' You just have to do the best you can and hope that the majority of the people get what you are trying to say. You don't want to offend anyone for the sake of offending them, but if you say something that's very true and it offends someone, it's probably because they're just not quite getting it, and maybe you can explain it later. That's what e-mail is for."

Not surprisingly, comedians have the same experience as musicians when it comes to Christian audiences: While they are overly judgmental regarding matters of doctrine, they are less demanding than they should be when it comes to talent. "The church audience to a fault is too forgiving, they are too kind, they are not near as discerning and critical as they should be. The very nature of our faith is to be forgiving and gracious, and so we do that with our artists. I think that has, in all the Christian art forms, slowed down the progress, because it's like, 'Eh, it's good enough for the church.'"

Rupple brought up another way in which performing for Christian audiences can make a comedian soft. "We use Christian jargon," he said. "*Praise the Lord. Hallelujah. Amen. Isn't God good?*—all these trite Christian buzzwords. At times, when it's genuine, when it's appropriate, that's fine, but I think we often use it as a safety net. Just like the blue comedian will use a profanity, we'll use *Praise the Lord* because we know it generates support and applause. It can make you lazy if you are not careful."

Every comedian I spoke with agreed that there are some jokes you can do in clubs that you can't get away with in church, but they handle this divide in different ways. "I try to do the same exact show, outside of giving an invitation" for an altar call, Nazareth told me. "I think Christian now, so whatever joke comes out of me now should be acceptable to Christians." Others, however, tailor their shows carefully.

Sherri Shepherd is one of the most successful Christian comedians in America. A year after this conference she would be hired as a cohost of *The View* on ABC. Shepherd told me that whenever she plays a church, her comedian friend Bone Hampton sits her down and explains which parts of her club act won't fly.

"There's so much stuff that Bone says all the time: 'You can't say that in church.' And I say, 'Why can't I talk about my breasts?' You see a woman with huge breasts, and I got a lot of cleavage, but I can't talk about it onstage? And he says, 'Christians don't want—they already have a visual, they don't want you to talk about it and maybe cause them to stumble,' and I'm like, 'You're kidding me.' So there's a lot of stuff that I do that I can't do in church." Not that she doesn't understand. "You have to respect the audience that you're in front of. They're paying you, so to assault them with stuff is disrespectful. But there's a lot of stuff that I have to remind myself, *That's not where these people are.* I did a Church of Christ—they don't dance, the women wear skirts—and that was a hard one for me. First of all I'm a black woman, I'm a little ghetto, I have to really be on my p's and q's, because even my Christian comedy, I call it *adult Christian comedy.* I don't even allow kids in my shows because I talk about adult stuff, even being a Christian."

And that's not all, she continued. "Sometimes you have to change up your material for white Christian audiences versus black Christian audiences. Black people sometimes are a little more liberal as far as what we can give to them, because a black person who goes to church, we've still got an uncle or a cousin that's been in prison, that's on drugs, that's crazy, so you can go ahead and talk about it. Sometimes I find that with white Christians they're like"—here she slipped into an uptight white accent—"'We've been delivered from that; we don't have to go there.'"

Still, Shepherd does understand the importance of limits. "I'm a Christian first and a comedian second," she said, "so there's some things I forgo saying that would be hysterical, because there's people out there that are watching, and I know they're looking at me and I'm a role model. So I'm gonna let that part die because there's a greater thing that I'm doing here."

Besides, she added, there are some things comedians can do in church that they can't do in clubs. "I love doing churches because I can talk about my journey with God. With secular comedy clubs, I'm not there to beat them over the head with a Bible, I'm there to make them laugh. Also, church audiences know the lingo. With churches I always talk about *submission,* because that's what a lot of churches teach: submitting to your husband. And so I can say, 'I'm trying to submit to my husband,' and the church ladies aren't going to go, 'Oh my God, what?!' But in a comedy club, if I say I'm trying to submit to my husband, I'm going to have a hundred women going, 'Is he beating you? Has he brainwashed you?' So I have to say, 'I'm trying to get along with my husband, I'm trying to be a good wife.' I basically say the same thing, but I take out Jesus and I change up stuff so they can understand it."

Thor Ramsey spent years playing clubs before he became a Christian. Now he plays churches exclusively, but only because the better pay and less grueling schedule give him more time to spend with his wife and daughter. "You'll know when you cross a line in the church by the reaction of the crowd," he assured me. "You will know you've crossed the evangelical boundary."

"Do church audiences heckle?" I asked. I tried to imagine how a Christian comedian handles hecklers. *How'd you like it if I came to where you work and forgave you?*

"No," said Ramsey, "but they always come up after and tell you if something struck them the wrong way. They'll heckle you at the end of the show. I do a whole bit on the *Left Behind* series, and I use the phrase *buck naked.* A guy actually e-mailed me. There's a verse in the Bible where Paul talks about 'coarse jesting,' and he felt my using the term *buck naked* was coarse jesting. At the time, I was all earnest. I e-mailed him back, giving him some examples of the Bible being real and not whitewashing things. You could say Adam and Eve were buck naked in the Garden and it would be biblical. Or there is the story of Onan spilling his seed on the ground. When people say that their pastor preaches through the Bible, I *know* they skip stuff. We went back and forth, and he actually ended up saying—this is an actual quote—'Just because the Bible talks about it, doesn't mean we should.' I go, *Boy, that's a mentality you can't argue with right there.* There was nothing I could do." He shook his head. "Now I've just got a policy: 'Thank you very much for your comments. I'll take them into consideration.'"

"That's the weird thing about Christian audiences," a comedian named Michael Rayner told me: "They will find so many bizarre things offensive when you're just joking around. Sometimes in my regular comedy club sets, I'll say, 'Usually the comedian tries to flirt with the cute girls, but I'm happily married. Me and my wife make sweet Christian love.' Now, the audience thinks that's really funny, that I say 'sweet Christian love.' But in a Christian audience, that's actually too scandalous sometimes, talking about sex with your wife. *Wow, that's scandalous!*"

Rayner is an L.A. guy with a bit of a nerd-chic aesthetic. "So many Christians are sort of *downer Christians,* you know what I mean?" he continued. Often, he said, he gets along better with atheists than with other Christians, in part because of his strong left-wing convictions. "I get so frustrated with how the Christian conservatives have taken over, and there just needs to be an antidote to their rhetoric," he said. "So much of Christian pop culture is just dreck, you know what I mean? It's some kind of preachy, weird message. The thing I hate even about Bible tracts is it's always the biker who's smoking and drinking and doing IV drugs that's going to hell and not the rich businessman who doesn't care about his fellow man, or some Enron executive who raped and pillaged a pension from the working class."

But here's the strange thing: Rayner doesn't use any of this in his set. He's a prop comic. He's more clever than most members of the breed—you may have seen him on *Letterman* spinning a McDonald's cheeseburger on an umbrella—but it doesn't afford him a lot of opportunity for social commentary. "Given your obvious passion about this, have you thought about doing comedy that addresses it?" I asked.

"I have. When I'm riffing with my friends, I do stuff that I will never do onstage yet, but I'd like to figure out how to do it. I want to be the Christian Lenny Bruce, to dispel Christian myth, to be kind of harsh and cruel and yet uplifting." An obstacle to this goal, he said, is that one of the stereotypes he wants to combat is that Christians have to be "angry and shouty." That means finding a way to get his opinions across without negating his message that it's wrong to force your opinions on other people.

In his personal life, Rayner said proudly, his non-Christian friends call him *the good Christian*, "because I never get upset when they have their opinions." Similarly, he often finds himself in Christian groups where it's assumed that everyone in the room "is a stone rah-rah Republican." But in either situation, he rarely raises an objection unless he can do it in a one-on-one conversation. "To me, it's always about the personal relationship with folks. Hanging out, chatting, and letting them see that you're a human being. Then if they're interested, that's when you say, 'This is why.' Right now, I'm reading a lot of books to try to figure out, where do I fit in this Christian left? I feel I'm a Christian leftist. I know it seems like an oxymoron, but . . ."

"But it seems like a great hook for a comedian, too," I pressed.

"Yeah, that's probably true. A lot of comics are openly atheist. Like, David Cross, I think, is very funny—very atheist. Patton Oswalt always talks about being an atheist. Even Penn and Teller, who do funny magic, *huge* in the atheist community. Penn does a radio show where he's almost like a proselytizing atheist—but I love him. And I want to be like him, where I'm a proselytizing Christian, but with logic and reason."

The conference broke for lunch, provided free by Chick-fil-A. (The evangelicals' favorite fast-food chain, Chick-fil-A is known for its explicitly religious mission statement and its affiliation with Christian conservative organizations like Focus on the Family.) Wandering among the tables, I talked to a number of comedians who challenged the very concept of Christian comedy, which was somewhat odd considering that they were all members of the Christian Comedy Association. "But if you say *Christian comedy* it ghettoizes you," explained one young man. "It's not good to be in a ghetto," he riffed. "You know what happened to the Jews."

I nodded slowly. "Yeah, it must have been really hard in Warsaw to land a sitcom."

"Maybe that came out wrong," he muttered.

Maybe, but minus the unfortunate analogy, the goal of joining the main-stream is paramount for a lot of Christian comedians today.

"Here's the old model," Dan Rupple told the conference when the break was over: "You beg for five minutes at a youth service, then you get evening services, then you join CCA, and finally you book Promise Keepers or Women of Faith and you've made it." But now, he declared, "God has said, 'I'm going to go out and gift my people so they can infiltrate the industry.'" Yet even as he urged people to set their sights on Hollywood, Rupple warned that anyone who did should expect to come under fire from other Christians. Recalling the opening scene of *Saving Private Ryan,* Rupple said, "The first guys in any battle are the ones that take the shots. And unfortu-nately too much of it comes from the body of Christ." Christians who have become successful in the industry are often accused of selling out.

Sherri Shepherd, who spoke next, said that too many Christians think the only reason to work in Hollywood is so you can inject Christian propa-ganda into the media. "If you work at the post office, you can't say, 'God bless you, would you like some stamps?' 'Jesus is good, would you like paper or plastic?' 'Have you accepted Jesus as your personal savior, and would you like fries with that?'" Instead, she said, Christians are needed in Hollywood for the personal connections they can make. "If we could get to Angelina Jolie. If we could get to Brad Pitt and lay hands on him." She paused. "Boy, I would *love* to lay hands on Brad Pitt. There are a lot of Christian women who would help me."

Echoing Michael Rayner, Shepherd said that forming genuine friend-ships with people like Brooke Shields and Queen Latifah allowed her to share the gospel with them in ways that didn't feel intrusive. "I told my girl-friends, I felt like the Lord had called me here to help them." Now, she claimed, "Queen Latifah is beginning her walk with God" (adding not-so-cryptically that "there's some stuff she's trying to step away from"). And then one day, she said, she found out she would be working with Andy Dick. The Hollywood-savvy audience laughed nervously. Dick is notorious for his drug-fueled, bisexual antics. "My girlfriend was so excited, she said, 'He might be your next project.' I said, 'Uh huh, I ain't heard nothin' from the Lord about that guy. He got two *E! True Hollywood Stories.*'" But Shep-herd hit it off with Dick, spoke to him about God, and even invited him to her church—where he showed up with his posse, having not slept all night. "He had a great time!" she marveled. "He turned to me and said, 'This is so much f-ing fun.' But he said the word. Fortunately they were praying and worshipping so loudly, no one heard him. I said, 'Andy, you can't say that in church,' but God said, 'But Sherri, he's *here.*'"

Dan Rupple closed the day with another film reference to express his perspective on the current state of Christians in Hollywood. In *The New World,* he said, the American Indians watch the arrival of the first Europeans warily. "Are they dangerous?" one asks. "Not yet," is the response, "but more will come."

After the conference, Rupple introduced me to his wife, Peggy, who works for the Mass Communication department of Biola University, a major Christian institution in Los Angeles. Biola MassComm is in the forefront of a movement to bring Christian filmmakers into Hollywood. For years, Christian movies have been, as even most Christians will admit, shoddy third-rate productions with heavy-handed messages. In recent years schools like Biola and Act One, a writing workshop run by a former nun, have been training Christians to value quality storytelling above overt evangelism. This new focus has coincided with Hollywood's recognition that the Christian market can be profitable—"chasing *Passion* dollars," it's called—and as a result, studios are increasingly turning to Act One and Biola to tap rising talents.

"We have a place at the table now," said Peggy Rupple. "We're amping up the craft and the quality and the integrity, and our students are interning at major studios. You don't know their names yet, but they're in the ranks." These young people, she implied, are not unlike the first missionaries in a foreign country; the goal is not to topple the government and impose a faith, but to spread it from the ground up. "It's a small start, but the thing we ask ourselves is, 'What's the best way to infiltrate Hollywood with the gospel?'"

"You know, all this talk about infiltration and invasion sounds a little, um, hostile," I observed.

"You never want to use that word in the secular realm because it sounds like you've got a major agenda on your hands," she agreed. "But when we use that word with students, all we mean is *we're going to be who we are.* We're going to be a light. You don't have to say *Jesus.* God is going to give you opportunities to witness, but your responsibility is just to be the best at your craft and to be an ambassador, whether that means saying his name"—she seemed to sense that she was going off message—"or just loving on 'em. Mainly just loving on 'em. And you just watch, you'll have opportunities. But subtly. Because if you say too much, you're gonna get kicked off the set. You're going to lose your platform. So you've got to have the mindset that you're in enemy territory." And then hastily: "In a sense. But we don't even teach 'em that. We don't use that phrase. We say, 'It's a place to love people.' It's a mission field. We think it's the biggest mission field out there. Some parents feel like they're sacrificing their children at the altar of secular entertainment; we just cast this huge picture of a mission field out there, and say, 'Your kids are taking a great opportunity.'"

Eager comedy fans filled the plush theater of the Cornerstone Church for the closing-night showcase. The lights dimmed and Thor Ramsey took the stage to emcee. The thing everyone asks first about Christian comedy is: *Is it funny?* The first showcase had been better than I'd expected, and if I'd only seen that I would have answered, in a noncommittal way, *Yeah, it can be funny.* After the closing showcase, I have to say, *I was really surprised by the caliber. I just didn't think it would be that good.*

But this was not really the biggest revelation of the evening. What I found more interesting was that I was getting the church show—the routines that many of these comedians wouldn't do for secular audiences because we wouldn't get the references or relate to the problems. In fact, I decided, this is precisely the material Christian comedians should be doing in mainstream clubs, and not just, as I'd felt before, because it's fresh. The best Christian comedians are the rough equivalent of transformational musicians. In performing honest routines that express their anxieties about what is most important to them—their faith, their practice, their culture—these performers have the potential to build bridges—to help non-Christians understand what it's like to be Christian in America in the same way that Richard Pryor helped white people understand what it was like to be black.

Sherri Shepherd's heartbreaking and delirious monologue about catching her husband in an affair had several moments that captured something I instantly recognized as a common evangelical myopia—the condition of believing that *whatever I happen to want* is the same as *God's plan for my life.* Even murdering your unfaithful husband can be a calling. "I didn't see any problem," said Shepherd. "I figured I'd just witness to people in jail."* Nazareth captured the same delusion from a different angle when he recalled saying his prayers as a young, single man. "I said, 'God, I want a beautiful wife, with a rich father, that memorized the entire Bible. But let your will be done.'"

Ramsey also turned out to be extremely likable onstage, a spiky-haired former hipster now happily going to seed with adulthood. And he was comfortable enough in his faith to take on the hypocrisies of Christian mass culture. In one routine, he offered a neat riposte to Nazareth's take on creationism versus evolution. "A few years ago, Christians started putting that little Jesus fish on our cars," he said. "Then evolutionists came out with a fish that has legs and the word *Darwin.* So we made a bigger fish *eating* that fish. Because that seems like the Christian thing to do." He let that sink in, then added, "I was on a plane the other day and I got into a conversation with the guy next to me. He turned out to be a Darwinist, and we had a disagreement about something, so I ate him. I think that was an effective witness."†

The performer who gave the most insight into evangelical culture was a cute, slender young woman named Kerri Pomarolli. Pomarolli performs in character as "Kerri," a ditsy blonde who is fluent in Christianese but alarm-

---

*When Shepherd got the gig at *The View,* it occurred to me that she might be a kind of antidote to her fellow Christian copanelist Elizabeth Hasselbeck, who had a reputation as a hectoring scold. Shepherd, I thought, could show the side of American Christianity that is relaxed, funny, and self-deprecating. And while she has done this, that aspect of her faith may always be overshadowed by a few stunning displays of ignorance. Once, while challenging evolution, she suggested that the world might be flat. Another time, she insisted that the ancient Greeks could not have lived before Jesus because she didn't think "anything predated Christians."

†Here's another Ramsey bit that caught my attention: "My wife and I had IVF six times. We have a girl. My wife calls her the miracle baby. Because she didn't have to have sex with me." Okay, not the funniest joke in the world, but I wouldn't mind if every evangelical in the country got to hear it. I hope he didn't get too many e-mails after the show.

ingly ignorant of actual Christian spirit. Bouncing onto the stage, she immediately began puncturing holes in the earnest shibboleths of the past two days, revealing the egotism that often disguises itself as modern evangelical piety. "I wanna be on *America's Next Top Model*?" she trilled in California uptalk. "Because we need more Christians in Hollywood?" A camera flash went off from the front row and Kerri vamped through a series of exaggerated fashion poses. The audience laughed and applauded, and Kerri affected a vain humility. "It's a gift from the Lord," she said.

Much of Kerri's routine revolved around her recent past as a single woman. "I am so ready to become a trophy wife," she said. "I mean, a pastor's wife. I will submit to not having to go to work. And I read Proverbs 31 and that did not speak to me at all." Okay, here a secular audience would need a crib sheet. Proverbs 31 describes "a wife of noble character" who "gets up while it is still dark" to "work vigorously" in the field. "What would I be doing in a field?" Kerri asked, dumbfounded. "I don't plow. And that's when I decided I'm really more of a Proverbs 32 woman. Like, 'She rises late and her kids make her breakfast.'"

Being single and trying to stay chaste, she went on, meant endless well-intended comments from her married friends. "I didn't meet my husband until I was fifteen," one says, "and I'm so glad I waited." Another friend called and said excitedly, "Guess what, Kerri? I'm engaged!" Kerri scrunched up her face. "Well I'm Christian, so I'm like, 'Praise the Lord'— in that fake L.A. I-hate-you voice. 'You're so blessed. Where did you meet him?' And she's like, 'Well, I was waiting on God, waiting on God—and then I signed on to SassySingles.com and two hundred and thirty-seven dates later, there he was: my gift from above!'"

There's something in the Southern California air that makes people want to pitch sitcom ideas, and as I made my way to the airport the next morning, one began to assemble itself in my mind: Thor Ramsey, easygoing Christian everydad, moves his family into a new house. On one side, his neighbors are a liberal gay couple. He likes them, but they're skeptical about him. On the other side are judgmental fundamentalists. They're thrilled to have another Christian around, but he thinks they're creeps. Hilarity ensues.

It's nothing groundbreaking, at least not on the surface. But maybe our culture war could be eased just a bit if the public face of evangelicalism was a good-natured, tolerant, *funny* ordinary guy instead of James Dobson. It would help secular liberals understand that they can disagree with the Christian agenda without fearing and disliking Christians. And it might force bitter religious conservatives to acknowledge that their vision of how to be Christian in America is not the only valid one. It might even give young Christians a healthier role model than Bibleman.

Besides, thirty years after *The Jeffersons* and ten years after *Will & Grace*, Christians are overdue for their turn to have the rest of us laugh with them, not at them.

13

Give me a man and let us fight each other

In a sweltering church gym in rural Georgia, a wiry young redhead in a torn jumpsuit balanced on the second rope of a fifteen-foot wrestling ring, wobbling comically and grinning a goofy grin. As the audience chanted, "Dirt! Dirt! Dirt!" Justin Dirt, "The Custodial Crippler," held aloft his trademark plunger, tipped it, and poured a plungerful of water into his mouth. The fans cheered. A boy in the front row waved a plunger he'd brought from home.

In the ring below, Dirt's tag team partner, the heroic Rob Adonis, lay in a heap as two burly heels—"Outlaw" Todd Zane and "War Daddy" Jesse Stone—loomed over him. Dirt dropped the plunger and with a flying leap, knocked Zane and Stone to the floor. There was a flurry of action—punches, holds, escapes—then the bad guys were on their feet again. They threw Dirt into the ropes, and when he bounced back in their direction, took him down with an illegal double clothesline. The audience booed. "You suck!" "Poke him in the eye!" "Break his ass!"

Dirt struggled to his feet, but before he could attack again, Stone grabbed him by the arm and hit him with something more powerful than a phony punch. "Forget this loser," he said, jerking his head at Adonis. "Join us! Join the Apocalypse. We can give you the respect you deserve." Dirt looked confused. The audience hooted: "Don't do it! Don't do it!" Stone sneered. "Do you want to live in the shadow of Rob Adonis your whole life? Or do you want to be a man?" Adonis raised his head from the mat. The spotlight caught the giant white cross on his black Lycra uniform.

The Custodial Crippler ran from the ring choking back tears. Rob Adonis grabbed a rope and pulled himself to his knees. "You'll never get him," he hissed at the villains. "Dirt is *saved*." Then Justin Dirt emerged from the curtains and dove into the ring once more. From the floor, Rob Adonis held out his hand for help. Dirt walked purposefully over to his partner— and then slapped his hand away and with a single kick to the head sent him back to the mat. As the audience exploded, Dirt tore open his jumpsuit to reveal a black Apocalypse T-shirt underneath. The heels laughed with glee as they led their new recruit out of the ring. Slowly, Adonis got back onto his knees and stayed there, head bowed, eyes closed, praying.

I was back on track. After the unnerving experience of finding out that liberal-baiting author Frank Peretti was a reasonable and considerate human being, I had charted a course for the fringes of the Christian pop culture universe, determined to seek out residents who had nothing in common with my world and were proud to say so—people who had no desire to distance themselves from *those other, really crazy Christians.* Instead, I'd mostly found more reasonable, considerate, and intelligent people who were, on balance, more like me than not.

And while this had been refreshing, it had also been a little bit disappointing. I still wanted to know how bizarre and antagonistic this alternate universe could get, and the Christian comedy conference had brought me too close to Hollywood in terms of both geography and sensibility. I needed to get back to the grassroots of evangelical America, where the merchants of popular culture have their sights firmly on the Kingdom of Heaven, without also keeping one eye on Blockbuster and Barnes & Noble. I needed to find a form of Christian entertainment so preposterous that even other Christians can't really believe it exists.

Something like Christian pro wrestling.

Christian pro wrestling, which combines the over-the-top violence and showmanship of the WWE with the message of Christ's humble love, is so insanely counterintuitive that, of course, there are at least four separate troupes dedicated to it. They ply their trade on portable rings across the Bible Belt, putting on shows for audiences in the dozens or hundreds—a far cry from the 50 million who watch the WWE on national television, but enough to demonstrate their appeal.

Not that it surprised me that wrestling would draw a crowd. I had been a fan myself as a young teenager in the days of Hulk Hogan, the Iron Sheik, and "Rowdy" Roddy Piper. Most Saturday mornings, my step-brother Greg and I would perch on his bed in front of the TV, shouting glee-fully at the antics on the screen. Of course we enjoyed the brawls, the leaps, and the cartoon punch-outs, but what I really remember is the characters. They were good guys and bad guys—*baby faces* and *heels* in behind-the-scenes jargon—who had bitter rivalries, nursed grudges, and wallowed in unearned pride. Without these soap opera plots, all the hair pulling and smashing each other with folding chairs would have been just mindless fake violence. Rob Adonis, the founder and star of Ultimate Christian Wrestling, promised me that such storylines were a UCW specialty—only all his stories had the same message.

A vicious sun scorched the outskirts of Athens, Georgia. The black road shimmered into the distance as the air conditioner in my rented Dodge Stratus whined in protest against the humid assault. Up ahead a billboard taunted, "If you think it's hot now, just keep taking my name in vain—God."

Turning onto a side road, I spotted the battered church sign announcing "Pro Wrestling Sat 8pm Free." I pulled into the parking lot of Harvest Church, a sprawling, low-slung building with all the charm of a strip mall. A door to a side wing was propped open and I stuck my head in.

The Harvest Church gymnasium is a windowless box with high ceilings and speckled gray institutional flooring. Just off center, framed by six rows of folding chairs, was a wrestling ring with a black skirt and red cables. A platform extended from one corner of the ring to the thick red curtains where the wrestlers made their entrances. Near the curtain, a barrel-chested man with a vanishing Caesar cut and patchy goatee knelt on the floor making adjustments to some piece of equipment. Rob Adonis looked up and waved me inside.

Indoors, the oppressive heat gave way to rank, sticky, torturous heat. Speakers blasted the crypto-Christian band Creed, and the arena-rock guitar riffs slogged through the muggy air. A single oscillating fan near the open door appeared ready to die of despair. Rob stood up to greet me as I climbed onto the platform. He was three inches taller than me and almost twice my weight—six-four, two hundred and ninety pounds with a fifty-six-inch chest, he volunteered later. He didn't quite live up to his ancient Greek namesake, but he was pleasant-looking enough, with an open, freckled face and warm brown eyes. I first took his white "America" T-shirt for Abercrombie or Old Navy, until I noticed that the flag had a Jesus fish where the stars should have been.

While Rob finished up what he was doing I watched some of his wrestlers practice for the evening's performance. These phony fighters were unquestionably genuine athletes. I hadn't been sure at first. The young trainees in their baggy shorts and Nikes looked reasonably fit, but the older stars, while clearly strong, were anything but buff. They were big and bulky with giant, round bellies, like refrigerators that had spent too much time in the refrigerator. In the ring, however, they were tough and agile, not only landing the moves but making them look natural.

The wrestlers paid attention to every detail. I watched a newcomer called Enigma practice a tricky combo with "Awesome" Austin Creed, a gregarious, handsome young black guy—the only African-American on the roster—whose character was modeled on Apollo Creed from the *Rocky* films. When they finally nailed the routine, Austin congratulated Enigma with a slap on the ass. "It's not gay," he protested preemptively. "We're playing a sport."

That was the first of several gay jokes I'd hear throughout the day, which was probably to be expected from conservative Christian men who wear skimpy, flamboyant outfits and roll around with each other on a mat. The surprising part was how good-natured the jokes were, made unselfconsciously and without any apparent malice toward actual gay people. Compared with other methods of channeling homophobia, impishly raising the question of whether another wrestler's impending wedding would be taking place in Massachusetts seemed downright healthy.

I can't remember when I was not a wrestling fan, that's how big a fan I was." Rob Adonis settled into a shapeless gray sofa in the dingy but air-conditioned backstage lounge. Rob was raised Southern Baptist in a family he called "as *Leave It to Beaver* as you can imagine." On weekdays, he's "Mr. Fields," a high school English teacher, but at UCW he's Rob Adonis, "The Modern Day Warrior."

"It's just so fun to get out here and do what we do," he said. "And then to be doing it for God on top of that, there's just no greater high. I have never in my life taken illegal drugs. I've never snorted a line of cocaine. I know a lot of people who have, and that's their business. If that's what they do, that's what they do. But I would challenge any of them to, man, get yourself in here and get high doing what we are doing, and I bet that line of coke will do nothing for you tomorrow."

Rob's wrestling career began in 1998, when he was twenty-two. There are hundreds of independent wrestling companies in the United States, and Rob spent five years touring the South with any that would have him. "It was very sinful in a lot of ways," he said. "There were pounds of cocaine in the back, kegs of alcohol, underage girls, pills, pot, everything you could imagine. But I was the guy who walked right past it all, put my gear on, wrestled, entertained, got my check, and moved right on." Then one night in 2003, Rob woke up with a vision. "I got the call that night, literally. I mean, it was a phone call. It was the clearest picture I've ever had in my life of what God wanted me do." He started putting together Ultimate Christian Wrestling the next morning, killing off, he said, a more lucrative career in secular wrestling.

Rob stressed the personal nature of this calling. "I don't see a thing in the world wrong with Christians wrestling secularly, if that's where you are," he said. "Because if God's not called you into the ministry to do this, you're just gonna be spinning your wheels here anyways. You've got a great guide up there that knows where he wants you and knows where you need to be, and if you just try to put yourself somewhere, then it's not going to work anyway."

Rob's vision for Christian wrestling had two parts. One was to use the sport's appeal as a way to attract people who had given up on church as hopelessly tame (or hopelessly lacking in sweaty men wrapping their legs around other men's necks). The other was to harness wrestling's narrative capacity to tell meaningful stories. Rob got me up to speed with the current angle. "We have got a bad-girl manager who just accepted Christ at the last show. So this is going to be her first appearance as a Christian, and you are going to see her struggle tonight as she tries to pull the guy she manages, 'Outlaw' Todd Zane, and tries to get him to see the beauty of faith and of salvation.

"When we portray stories in the ring, we are attacking the issues that are facing these people in the crowd. They are fighting battles with addiction. They are the spouse begging the other one to come to church, begging him to be involved in their kid's life, begging him to be the good parent. And we are trying to portray those dilemmas so that these people say, 'Man that's me; that is me all over.'" Each show ends with Rob breaking character to talk directly to the crowd. "We want to look at them and say, 'Tonight in this ring we portrayed some of your struggles. And let me tell you something, when you are tired of being tired, I've got a savior that will take all your burdens from you.'"

"But you're doing all this with fighting," I pointed out. "What about turning the other cheek?"

"Well, we have done the turning the other cheek thing, where we have had the guy get slapped on this side and then get slapped on this side—and then get attacked. But I believe there is a big difference between turning the other cheek and defending what's right. When there is an issue of pride on the line, then yeah, I should turn the other cheek, because my pride is worthless in the greater scheme of the world. But when it becomes an issue of my family's safety then I feel like protection is the only method. If it involves my wife, then protecting her is my number one priority. If it involves the ministry, protecting what we have done is my number one priority. We always hear the violence question—*How can you promote that kind of violence?*—but it's a show. We are in no way, shape, or form telling you to go beat somebody up with a Bible, and start a barroom brawl and preach at them. What we are really trying to do here is say that every day is a battle, every day is a wrestling match for you, whether you are wrestling with an addiction, whether you are wrestling with a marital problem, whether you are wrestling with the boss, or a child, or whatever. Everything in your life is ultimately a wrestling match. And you know, when the good guys win, they give the glory to God; when the bad guys win it's because the good guy faltered somewhat, and he didn't do the right things."

I asked how bad a bad guy can really be in Christian wrestling.

"Well, obviously we don't incorporate any profanity. There is not going to be cussing and swearing out here," said Rob. "We will threaten each other and say, 'I am going to get you' or 'Next week you're mine.' We'll throw people out of the wrestling ring, but we absolutely won't swear at them." He added that this was a principle of showmanship, not just Christianity. "If you have to cuss at the crowd to get over with them, you are not really over," he said. When he wrestled for secular clubs, the heels used to love playing Alabama, because it was so easy to get a rise out of people there. "If you crack jokes on those folks based around a lack of education, a lack of teeth, a lack of, let's say, sibling sexual ethics, they will become enraged and they want to fight you in the parking lot." Rob thought it was cheap. "What's beautiful about a bad guy is he has got to believe that what he is doing is right, no matter how bad it is. And so the best bad guys can walk out through the ropes, and just snarl at a guy in the crowd and he'll come unglued."

"Do you have other limits that make UCW different from non-Christian wrestling?" I asked. Rob sets the rules for the league, so what he says goes.

Rob answered right away. "There is a technique we have in wrestling which I am not a fan of called *gigging* or *blading* or *coloring* or *juicing,* which is where you intentionally cut your head. You know, you take the big chair shot and cut your head with a razor and you come up pouring blood. I've refused to do it from day one. Never done it. Proudly."

I wasn't surprised at that, but in a way it seemed arbitrary. You can hit someone with a chair as long as they don't bleed? "What was the objection?" I asked. "What made you draw the line there?"

"I think ethically for me—and this is hard to say because one of my heroes is Ric Flair and he was a big bleeder, always getting the big blond hair covered in blood—but I have always felt that I could get over with the crowd based on my ability to wrestle and entertain, not on my ability to bleed. I have wrestled shows with guys who couldn't wrestle a lick. They were terrible. I mean, they were awful, they didn't have any technique, they didn't know any holds—but they go get a table, they go get a ladder, and they go get a chair, and they go get some thumbtacks, and they would light it on fire, and you would hit them and they would come up and they got thumbtacks in their face and all over their chest, and they are bleeding all over the place, and they get the barbwire baseball bat, and they get a fluorescent lightbulb, and I'm thinking, *You know what, it doesn't take any skill to hit someone in the head with a fluorescent lightbulb and cut them open.* You can hand a monkey a big long fluorescent lightbulb and stand there and poke it in the eye and it will swing and hit you in the face and it will cut your face open. There's no skill."

"I'm confused," I said. "Is this a moral judgment or is it just a personal preference?"

"It's just a personal thing. I don't think there is anything . . ." Rob cut himself off. "Well, I don't know. It's obviously spoken against in the Bible, that you shouldn't purposely mangle yourself. Which is a problem with a lot of the kids nowadays that are cutters, that are releasing demons or whatever they say they are doing with it. I think that's wrong to purposely hurt yourself like that. While, granted, usually the pros they can gig and it's just a little nick, and they have taken four or five aspirin during the day, so their blood's thinned out, and so they can go"—he tightened his face muscles—"and, *pshhhh!* But at the end of the day it's not even worth putting a Band-Aid on it, it's so small. It's a little Neosporin, and it's over. So it's not really so much an ethical, moral issue, it's just nothing that's ever appealed to me. I have never been into the bleeding, the hard-core thing. I will *watch* it all day long," he added. "I've got those Japan tapes of Mick Foley and Terry Funk that explode with it, and I will *watch*. I mean, I think it's *entertainment,* it's just not my cup of tea for myself."

While I was letting my stomach settle, Rob added as an afterthought that most churches probably wouldn't allow it anyway, if only for health reasons. "Plus, you know, they are using us as a tool to draw people, and while the blood may draw some people, it'll also scare a lot of people away."

And then something occurred to him. "We have re-created the whipping post of Jesus." He pointed to a crumbling Styrofoam rock stored in a corner of the room. "We got ropes and we tied him up to that, and we used that Hollywood effects stuff that you rub it on their back, and all you have to do is touch it and it turns red. So you can take a little plastic whip, and we could hit the Jesus character with it, and it looked like we just ripped him open.* So we would do that for effects, but as far as using real blood, our policy has always been that we don't bleed on purpose."

---

*Later, Rob mentioned that he'd seen *The Passion of the Christ* "more times than I can remember."

If the special effects—and elbow drops—aren't always a hundred percent convincing, Rob said that audiences get so caught up in the drama that it doesn't matter. "Everybody pretty much knows that it's not a real fight," he said, "but it still amazes me how many of our fans, for two hours, they get so lost in it." He mentioned one storyline in which Justin Dirt falls for a bad girl. He proposes to her in the ring and she humiliates him, slapping him in the face and leaving him crying. "Later, she went to the bathroom and got confronted by these girls who were really angry. 'Why did you do that to him?'"

"Did she stay in character?"

"Well I don't know how she handled it because I wasn't in the girl's bathroom, but we don't encourage anybody outside of the show to put on any kind of a facade. We really try to tell people, 'Look, it's a show.' It's no different than if you went to the Fox Theater in Atlanta and you saw *Macbeth*. At the end of the play Macbeth is dead and Macduff is standing over the top of him with a sword. Well, if you were to go out to Denny's that evening, the actor that played Macbeth could be eating there—he's not really dead. We really try to let folks know this is a production. This is a ministry tool and a production.

"And it amazes me, because back when I first started wrestling, the goal was to try to get people to believe it—and they wouldn't. And now we don't really want them to believe after it's over. We want them to believe in the ministry, not believe in the wrestlers. We want them to believe in Christ, we don't want them to believe in me, because I can't do anything for you. I can entertain you, but I can't get you to heaven when it's over. I can't heal you. I can't rid you of your financial troubles. But God can, so believe in him. And it amazes me how many people, they want to believe so bad that they talk themselves into it."

People want to believe so bad that they talk themselves into it. Perhaps Christian wrestling did make a kind of sense.

Rob sat up a bit. "What we do, it's a real novelty to people," he acknowledged. "They look at it and they say, 'I just don't see how you can possibly pull this off. I want to come see it for myself.' And I'm good with that. Paul said become all things to all people. Some people say they don't like anything that's Christian and secular combined. I have heard people say that the only place for Jesus is in the pulpit. My response to them is: I don't know if you're talking about my Jesus Christ, because Jesus Christ is ageless, sizeless, and timeless; he is everywhere all the time. And if it takes me doing something a little off kilter to get you to come here and listen to the message, I will do that. I will be an idiot for God any day of the week."

"But it helps that you love the sport," I said. "If something happened and wrestling all of a sudden became uncool and everyone started going to see mime instead, would you pack this up and go do mime?"

Rob nodded his head seriously. "If God said, 'Go get *The Best of Marcel Marceau* and learn how to do the box and the wall,' I guess I'd be painting my face and walking around like this, because my commitment is to Christ, it's not to wrestling. My job is to minister to people and try to bring them the truth of what Christ did for us on the cross. My assignment is a schoolteacher. My assignment is Ultimate Christian Wrestling. God may move my assignment, but he is never going to change my job." Rob smiled. "To be honest with you, I can't wait—I mean, I am not ready to die today, but when I die, when I meet God, the first thing I am going to ask him is 'Where did you come up with this?'"

As evening arrived, the Harvest Church gym began filling up with high-spirited wrestling fans. Most were UCW regulars, less spectators at a sporting event than guests at a community party. Chubby children in the five- to ten-year-old range darted up the aisles. Teenagers in flip-flops rocked back on their chairs. Moms and dads in stone-washed jeans and extralarge T-shirts passed out juice boxes to toddlers. Oldsters in wheelchairs traded greetings and gossip. Almost all of the black people sat together in one section. I assumed they sat there every time. "Do you like secular wrestling too?" I asked one family. "Not as much as we like this," said the dad with a grin. "Too much cussin'."

I made my way backstage. A high school student with long bangs and a tuft of hair on his chin operated the A/V equipment. He wore a T-shirt that said "I have nunchuck skills." Another *Napoleon Dynamite* fan—evangelicals revere the cult comedy as proof that a PG film can be hip. In this case, though, there might have been something else going on. Later I caught sight of the kid's duffle bag, with two pairs of nunchucks sticking out of it.

Shortly before show time, the wrestlers gathered for a group prayer and "praise reports." Rob started with some good news. "My brother is getting baptized," he announced, "and also his girlfriend."

"His girlfriend or his wife?" someone asked.

"His girlfriend."

"Is his wife also saved?" a third wrestler deadpanned.

I found a seat in the audience. With a blast of Christian rock, the video screens flashed a title card announcing the "Ultimate Armageddon Tour"—is there any other kind?—and the first match began. This was the tag team match—Adonis and Dirt versus the Apocalypse—that would set up the evening's themes of friendship and betrayal.

I'd forgotten how much fun pro wrestling is. Preaching and potbellies aside, the UCW puts on a hell of a show. Drops, head butts, chin locks, slams—more moves than I knew names for. The crowd reaction only amplified the entertainment. If it didn't smack of redneck stereotyping, I'd have to use the words *whoop* and *holler*. During one match, I could have sworn that the entire room was chanting, "Suck my dick! Suck my dick!" Later I asked Rob, who assured me that they were only taunting one of the heels as a "southern fried chicken." Another recurring chant was that old wrestling standby, "U.S.A.! U.S.A.!" which seemed odd, given that every wrestler on the roster hailed from a four-state area. Apparently one of the heels agreed. Losing his cool with the chanting crowd, Colt Derringer turned around and bellowed, "I'm *from* the U.S.A.! Shut up!"

Although it was hard to reconcile the shouting and flailing with my image of Christianity, theologian Hugh S. Pyper of the University of Sheffield in England has noted that wrestling matches play an important role in the Bible, and that even the most raunchy secular pro wrestling is indebted to Christian themes. In a lecture to the Society of Biblical Literature, Pyper argued that "the popularity of both the Bible and wrestling stems from their ability to engage similar basic human reactions to perceived justice and injustice." The WWE's appropriation of terms like "Armageddon" and "Judgment Day"—or even "Austin 3:16"—is not accidental, he said.

Throughout Judges, and indeed in Genesis and in Samuel/Kings, narrative shapes and moral outcomes that offend a strict sense of fair play but take delight in the cunning trick, and the effective revenge, are played out. David himself, in the book of Kings at least, often operates by rules that seem closer to the WWE than to the Beatitudes.

There have even been several evangelicals in the WWE, most notably Shawn Michaels, who once wrestled with "God" as his tag team partner (they lost).

At the same time, Christian wrestling may be the form of contemporary Christian pop culture that most closely captures the spirit of the nineteenth-century revival meetings. It may be bizarre, but it is inarguably authentic and engaging. There is nothing crass or commercial about the UCW, which succeeds not on any slick production values or marketing, but on the infectious frenzy that it stirs up in its fans.

The altar call isn't the very end of the evening—there has to be something after to keep people in their seats—but for Rob Adonis, this is what everything has been building up to. "We've had a little shift tonight," he began, referring to the first match of the evening. "One of my best friends turned his back on me. But I'm not even gonna focus on that. I'm not gonna focus on that. What I'm gonna focus on is giving God the glory." About forty people came forward for the altar call that night, many of them young children. That fit Rob's estimate that at any given show, about 10 percent of the audience will *make a decision for Christ.* "We are well over twelve hundred and fifty-seven decisions that have been made in our ministry," he said. "How do I know God is in this? That's how."

This wasn't the first time I'd found that someone was keeping a running tally of souls saved at their events. Not only is the altar call a sacred ritual for evangelicals, it's often a form of score card. And yet it seems a profoundly flawed one. I was sure that most of the people at the show that night had been there before. Were there even that many new people to be saved? Or that many non-Christians coming to see Christian wrestling? Surely at events like this, most of the people who come forward have already been born again and simply want to take the opportunity to relive the emotional experience. There's nothing wrong with that, but I don't think they can be counted as new decisions. At the first altar call I witnessed, at SHOUTfest in Kansas, my sister-in-law and all her friends joined the procession to the stage. Was some second-rate band carving notches in the altar for them, even though they all attend a Christian school?

And even if some of the people who come forward have been genuinely moved to confess their sins for the first time, are they really Christians now? It's one thing to get caught up in the excitement of a wrestling match or rock show or even a traditional sermon, but what happens the next day or the next week? Do they read the Bible, go to church, talk to a pastor? Maybe. But maybe not. The fetishization of the altar call as a single moment of victory seems to obscure the need for the hard work that it must take to bring somebody to a genuinely meaningful faith.

At last it was time for the final drama of the evening, the spiritual wrestling match between the recently saved bad-girl manager and her star wrestler, "Outlaw" Todd Zane. Apparently, Zane was not thrilled about his manager's newfound religion. It probably didn't help that, like many new believers, she wouldn't stop badgering him. "Do you even believe in God?" she asked him as they came out. "Do you?" The manager was a petite blonde with long wavy hair, in tight jeans and a red blouse. Zane dodged the question. "I have to know," she demanded.

"Well I done told you, this is not the time or place, okay? Do not pressure me."

That seemed like a perfectly reasonable request. No doubt this matter could be discussed more fruitfully in privacy, without four hundred strangers whooping and jeering. But manager girl didn't see it that way. "What do you mean? Why *don't* you believe in God?"

"I haven't said if I believe in him or not!"

"Well you haven't said if you did!" They didn't seem to be getting anywhere, so manager girl tried another tactic: screaming louder. "I want to know if you believe in God. Answer me!" The crowd applauded wildly.

"Okay. All right. You want me to answer you?" Zane growled.

"Yeah, we do!" shouted a man in the third row.

"But it will not be the way that you want it," Zane said. "It'll be on my terms." He began, "When I was thirteen years old, I saw my grandparents, the people that I loved better than anyone I've ever known . . ." This didn't sound good. The crowd quieted down, suddenly respectful. "I was on a school bus, and I came down the road and there was a wreck, and the school bus driver saw who it was. And she looked back at me and she tried to divert my attention, but she was unable to because I recognized the car. I ran off the bus, and you know what? I saw my grandparents laying in the middle of a major highway, at a major intersection, laying there dead. Let me ask you something. Where was your God?"

In the audience, a few people muttered, but Zane pressed on. "At fifteen years old, I lived in a house with an alcoholic for a father. My mother finally had enough one day and she said, 'I'm gone.' I didn't see her for at least a year. Fifteen years old I was left to fend for myself. I ask you, where was your God?"

"He was there!" someone shouted. "He was right there."

"At nineteen years old I thought, *Well you know what, I done it all, I think I'll get married,*" Zane announced. There was a certain logic to that, I guess. "But you know what, I never had nobody show me what a family was, so how are they gonna think that I can manage a family? But I was gonna try, and we had a child, a beautiful girl. A beautiful girl. And you know what? My wife left me and she took my little girl with her. Once again I found that people that you love will walk all over you. You ask me if I believe in God, I ask you, where was your God?"

He thundered the last line, made it a challenge, and the audience took him up on it. "He was right there! He was right beside you!" This time, dozens of people shouted it, in much the same tone that WWE fans shout "Suck it!" Really, you've never heard such a hostile expression of comfort. Plus, they seemed so certain that this was the correct answer. It didn't even occur to them—or to Zane—to ask the obvious follow up: *Well then why didn't he do anything?*

Manager girl touched Zane's arm, and offered a tender reply, but her gentle words were out of synch with the mood in the room. "If this is an attempt to get me into your church, with your God, forget it," Zane snarled.

"Do you believe in God, Todd?"

"You want to know if I believe in God?" He worked the ring with the artistry of an accomplished heel. "You want to know if I believe in God?"

Manager girl was quiet, but the audience was on its feet. "Yeah!" "Answer the question!"

"I believe in myself!" he bellowed.

The crowd exploded with derision as the lights cut off. When they came back up, Zane was standing defiantly, arms folded, head down. Manager girl lip-synched a worship song to him. Over Zane's shoulder a spotlight came up on the ethereal figure of Jesus perched on one of the speakers. He wore a simple white robe and a very pained expression.

I didn't blame him. I thoroughly enjoyed the UCW show as a form of entertainment, and Rob Adonis seemed like a pretty cool guy with a good heart and a good sense of humor. But seeing a man's private struggle with doubt turned into an opportunity for a public shaming, I decided that maybe some forms of pop culture really can't be made authentically Christian.

14

Let a search be made for beautiful young virgins

U p to this point, I've mostly been writing about leisure activities and entertainment. There's no question Christian pop culture is easiest to notice when it takes the form of common amusements repackaged for godly purposes. But there is another important way in which evangelicals have embraced the methods and media of popular culture: as a tool for spreading a social agenda.

It is commonplace for large churches these days to have in-house recording and editing studios, where pastors can create polished videos to show during the service or in the rec room to the youth group. According to *Christianity Today,* 80 percent of all American churches have digital video projectors or display panels in their sanctuaries. High-tech sermons are meant for believers and have no direct impact on the world at large, but evangelicals frequently use the same media and marketing techniques to engage the culture in social and political conversation. The impact is often stronger and more lasting than when the same messages are transmitted through traditional intellectual argument. Widely distributed shockumentaries like *The Silent Scream* and *The Gay Agenda* gave crucial emotional power to the antiabortion and antigay movements of the 1980s and 1990s.

Today, any social issue worth its salt comes with an elaborate pop-culture component. That's especially true when the issue involves teenagers, as is the case with abstinence education. Abstinence education is the parallel universe version of sex education. Sex ed recognizes that half of all U.S. teenagers are sexually active, and handles this by encouraging them to wait until adulthood while providing information on how to protect themselves if they choose not to. Abstinence education teaches that people who are not married should not have sex, period. Unlike most Christian culture, which remains largely unseen by non-Christians, abstinence education has replaced sex education in more than one-third of U.S. public schools.*

The modern abstinence movement had its crossover moment in 1996 when a provision buried in Bill Clinton's welfare reform law budgeted $50 million a year for public school programs teaching that "sexual activity outside of the context of marriage is likely to have harmful psychological and physical effects," even for adults. Any program falling short of this absolute standard—or supplementing it with information about contraceptives—was now ineligible for federal funding. Under the Bush administration, abstinence-only funding has skyrocketed to $204 million a year. Total federal spending on abstinence has topped $1 billion in the last decade.

To find out how this happened, I headed back to Nashville for the annual convention of the National Abstinence Clearinghouse, an umbrella organization of groups with names like True Love Waits, Purity Promise, and Why kNOw. The convention was held at the theme-park-like Gaylord Opryland Hotel, a masterpiece of artificiality designed, coincidentally, by the same firm that designed the Holy Land Experience in Orlando. Under a glass atrium fifteen stories high, Mississippi Delta flatboats cruised an indoor river through nine acres of meticulously landscaped gardens. Aged-brick sidewalks meandered through miniature Victorian towns. It was a perfect little world that did not, in any meaningful way, exist.

I made my way to the more businesslike second floor, where the Abstinence Clearinghouse had reserved a suite of conference rooms, and gave my name to the chipper lady at the check-in desk. Although abstinence education curricula profess secularism to get in the door at public schools, virtually every group that publishes one is openly Christian and runs separate programs within the evangelical or Catholic communities. Even the

---

*More precisely, of the 86 percent of school districts that have sex-education policies, 35 percent mandate abstinence-only, according to a survey by the Guttmacher Institute.

medical-sounding term *abstinence* is a halfhearted replacement for the movement's original name of choice: *chastity*. In 2006, one abstinence group that had received more than a million dollars from the government was cut off when the ACLU pointed out it had been teaching, in its own words, that "a personal relationship with Jesus Christ [is] the best way to live a sexually pure life." Clearly, Christians consider National Abstinence Clearinghouse a parachurch organization; the 2003 convention was one of the events at which Icon Productions screened advance footage of *The Passion of the Christ* as part of its now legendary under-the-radar marketing campaign.

Just past check-in was the social hub of the convention: the exhibitor tables, where edutainers displayed the latest in chastity-ware. Most abstinence paraphernalia is straightforwardly practical—books, videos, and posters featuring lectures that would have to be called *stern,* despite the attempts to soften the blow with photos of smiling young people or bouncy electronic music. But there is also a range of products that put a more commercial spin on purity.

The abstinence movement has its own young adult novel, *If Only I'd Known,* and even a feature film, 2005's *Echoes of Innocence,* a supernatural thriller about a girl's attempt to defend her sexual purity from demons. But mostly it has trinkets: "Worth the wait" temporary tattoos; "Committed" necklaces. At the convention, a company called Wait Wear sold stop-sign panties and thongs that warned "No vows, no sex." There were T-shirts with messages like "Sex causes babies," "Herpes kills dates," and on a mock road sign, "Virginity Lane, exit when married." There was even a chastity spin on Testamints bearing the slogan "Sex is 'Mint' for Marriage." A gold-plated rose pin came with a card explaining its symbolism: "You are like a beautiful rose. Each time you engage in premarital sex a precious petal is stripped away. Don't leave your future husband holding a bare stem."

Some folks were clearly trying to pass off their remaindered antiabortion wares as abstinence products. The human fetus replicas, I was told, were meant to make girls aware that sex will get them pregnant. "I like this one because if you feel it, it's soft," said the young woman at the True Love Waits table, proffering a thirteen-week model. "A lot of them are hard plastic. This one feels like a baby."

Other products seemed equally tangential, like *The First Clean Sex Quote and Joke Book*. I figured it was there mostly because the author, Allen Unruh, is the husband of Abstinence Clearinghouse founder Leslee Unruh. Its abstinence message is actually a bit muddled. On the one hand, Unruh offers appropriate one-liners such as "Abstinence is one subject you should not practice in moderation." But then he also quips, "I had an aunt who waited so long for her ship to come in that her pier collapsed." I flipped a few pages and spotted a section titled "Women's Lib."

One women's libber started out a speech: "Where would you men be without us women?" A guy in the back shouted, "In the Garden of Eden!"

One guy said, "I'm sure glad my wife joined women's lib. Now she hates all men, not just me."

I checked the copyright date. It said 2004.

Perhaps the most revealing product was a children's book called *The Princess and the Kiss*. It tells the tale of a princess with a "special gift" from God that her parents hide and protect for her until it can be claimed by her husband. When the girl worries that she will never meet a man worthy of the gift, her mother comforts her that "even if no husband came, the gift would be hers to treasure forever."

Fairy-tale weddings are central to the mythology of the chastity movement. Pictures abound of young brides in white gowns. A wedding without chastity hardly counts. At one convention seminar, Thomas Sullivan, an official with the federal Administration for Children and Families, said that with premarital sex so common, "A lot of clergy I talk to don't like to officiate at marriages because they consider them shams, an excuse for a party."

The perfect wedding fantasy, and its psychosexual subtext, is reinforced at formal-dress "purity balls," an event created by Leslee Unruh where fathers present their teen and preteen daughters with rings while the crypto-couples exchange vows. The men promise "before God to cover my daughter as her authority and protection in the area of purity," while the girls pledge "to remain sexually pure until the day I give myself as a wedding gift to my husband."* Not all Christians are comfortable with this. The web site of Christians for Biblical Equality, the feminist evangelical group I discovered at Cornerstone, frets that purity balls—and I would add the chastity movement in general—cast "women as objects to be managed by men: first by fathers then by husbands." The dehumanizing effect of the movement's virginity fetish finds its ultimate expression in texts like *Sex: The Spiritual Laws*, a book by a minister named Dale Conaway, which asserts that the hymen is God's sacred seal. "If the seal is broken, it can reveal an intruder was present and that product tampering may have taken place."

But we're getting way ahead of ourselves, because for the chastity movement, saving sexual intercourse until marriage is a last resort; the ideal is for people to save even their first kiss for their wedding day. When I read *The Princess and the Kiss*, I assumed the titular gift was meant as a child-safe metaphor. It wasn't. One of the seminars I attended at the convention was "Why We Saved Our Kiss for Marriage," led by the daughter and son-in-law of Allen and Leslee Unruh. For purity purists, any affection beyond holding hands is inappropriate for the unwed. One reason to avoid kissing, kids are told, is that it leads inexorably to more. Beyond simple good-night kisses, "passion becomes like a car with worn-down brakes speeding downhill," says one junior high school curriculum. In a brochure I picked up, "prolonged kissing," even with lips closed, is compared to being "locked in a death grip." Abstinence leaders aren't shy about using fear of death to enforce their standards. Another curriculum says French kissing can be put you at risk for AIDS if you've been flossing or "eating crunchy foods," and a third adds that compromising injuries "may even be caused by overly enthusiastic open-mouth kissing."†

---

*If you think this ceremony is icky, consider the advice from Focus on the Family that when teens start to feel sexually aroused, they should picture the faces of their parents. Or Jesus.

†In reality, there has been exactly one confirmed case of HIV transmission through kissing. Both partners had advanced gum disease.

○ ○ ○

The truth about abstinence-only education is that it doesn't work. In 2007, after the Nashville convention, a nine-year government-mandated study found that teenagers who took abstinence classes were just as likely to engage in sex, beginning at the same age, as those who did not. The conclusive, nonpartisan research took some wind out of the movement's sails. It was still reeling from repeated surveys finding that eight out of ten parents want their kids to have comprehensive sex education, as well as from a 2004 report in which Democratic Congressman Henry Waxman found that eleven of the thirteen most commonly used abstinence curricula contained misleading and inaccurate information. Among the claims flagged by Waxman were that half of gay teenagers have HIV and that touching another person's genitals "can result in pregnancy." An article on the Abstinence Clearinghouse web site dismissed the Waxman report as a product of "the 1960s mindset in which 'free love' is acceptable and morality is diminished."

But taking some time to read through these curricula myself, I found that Waxman's report only scratched the surface. The specifics of abstinence education vary from curriculum to curriculum. Not all are offensive, though you could argue that even the better ones are naïve in their faith that all teenagers can be convinced to say no. But many paint a ludicrous picture of sex as something inherently and irredeemably dangerous—a gleaming butcher's knife in the hands of a toddler, as an illustration from a curriculum called *Sex Respect* depicts it. In a supplemental *Sex Respect* video, a student asks, "What if I want to have sex before I get married?" The instructor's response: "Well, I guess you'll just have to be prepared to die. And you'll probably take with you your spouse and one or more of your children."

Abstinence curricula work hard to persuade children that even if they make it to adulthood and marriage alive and disease free, premarital sex will still ruin their chances for long-term happiness. "Most men and women prefer to marry individuals with little or no sexual experience," claims the movement's quasi-offical guidelines, adding that "individuals who lack sexual self-control prior to marriage may have difficulty remaining faithful during marriage." In *Sex Respect,* one forty-two-year-old woman laments having had sex with her fiancé before their marriage. "Even though I knew it was wrong, I tried to make myself think it was right because we were engaged. That didn't help. The guilt still haunts me every time I have sex now, and I've been married over twenty years."

This zero-tolerance approach becomes genuinely dangerous with the suppression of information about contraception and preventing sexually transmitted disease. To qualify for federal funding, abstinence programs may not mention contraceptives at all, except to discuss their failure rates. The abstinence ed line is that advocating chastity while discussing condoms sends mixed messages; that teaching safer sex encourages promiscuity. That has a common-sense appeal, but studies have found that traditional sex education does not cause students to have sex sooner or more frequently.

Abstinence curricula take seriously their mandate to discuss the failure rates of condoms, frequently going well beyond fact and leaving teens with the impression that if they do have sex, it's better not to use protection. "For condoms to be used properly," says the curriculum *Choosing the Best,* "over ten specific steps must be followed every time, which tends to minimize the romance and spontaneity of the sex act." The first step is allegedly "inspecting the condom for holes and leaks before using." The last: "immediate washing of the genital areas with either rubbing alcohol or dilute solutions of Lysol."*

Other "facts" thrown around by abstinence proponents are that pornography causes brain damage and that premarital sex depletes a chemical necessary for forming permanent a bond with one's spouse (the doctor who came up with this theory was later appointed to run the Bush administration's women's health programs). At the Nashville convention, one speaker said he wanted to "strangle" reporters who turn to public health experts to debunk abstinence education. "I'm sick and tired of hearing the words *medically accurate,*" he said unironically.

A number of abstinence groups had brought young people to the convention to testify about how well their products worked. Out in the lobby, I eavesdropped as a towering, handsome young man shared his story with two girls. While he was once sexually active, he explained, he managed to

---

*Later editions struck that particular bit of advice.

avoid catching any diseases—a fact he regarded as a small miracle, given what he'd learned in abstinence class. Eventually he went on a sex fast. "I tried it for forty days, then another forty days. And I noticed my basketball game was getting better." One of the girls nodded. "Secondary virginity," she said. "That's the path I'm on."

One of the primary goals of the convention was to teach abstinence educators how to communicate with today's young people. "What you need to work on most is your packaging," model-turned-activist Lakita Garth told the group, "because you already have the truth. Abstinence is the bomb message." Faced with blank stares, she added, "For those of you who don't know *the bomb,* remember *dynamite?*"

The problem is that today's kids can tell immediately when something has been packaged for them, and they tend to resent it. Speaker after speaker failed to appreciate this. Keith Deltano, who described himself as "Chris Rock with an abstinence message," despite being an unfunny white guy, took the stage with what he described as "an antirap rap song." By this he meant either that the song challenged rap music's traditional celebration of sexual promiscuity, or that anyone who heard it would never want to listen to rap music again. Deltano's advice on how to reach children included organizing events at public schools, and then letting every kid into the auditorium, even if they didn't have the required parental permission slip. "You say, 'Keith, that's lying,'" he told the room. "No, lying is telling kids that condoms will protect them when HIV is running rampant! I have no guilt." The audience applauded enthusiastically.

In the full-court press for sexual purity, abstinence promoters usually end up endorsing limits on almost everything teenagers like to do. *Teen Virtue* magazine warns girls not to get their belly buttons pierced because it sends "a signal to guys that you may be willing to compromise sexually," even if you aren't. *Represent* magazine, a publication of the abstinence group Operation Keepsake, forbids listening to emo music, apparently due to the correlation between sexual activity and low self-esteem: "It may provide an outlet for the singer, but for those of us who subject ourselves to this music, it's potentially a dead-end, a cycle of hurt." The *Revolve* BibleZine is even wary of guys and girls getting together to pray. "There are exceptions, but usually it's pretty sketchy," says one guy. "I'd avoid it until you're engaged."

What do actual teenagers make of all this? In *Shaking the World for Jesus,* Heather Hendershot studies the letters section of *Brio,* Focus on the Family's magazine for teenage girls, and finds that "readers do not merely internalize the chastity directive without substantial questioning, negotiation, and varying degrees of resistance." Among the *Brio* readers seeking "loopholes" are a girl who wants to know if it's "okay to fantasize about your wedding night and what sex will be like after you're married," and another who says, "I have pledged to remain sexually pure until marriage. But what if Jesus comes back before I get married?"

The abstinence movement is grounded in what Hendershot calls "essentialist notions of gender." One group I found runs separate programs for boys and girls that starkly delineate the narrow range of choices available to each sex: the boys' is called "Protector vs. Predator," the girls' is "Treasure vs. Target." In accepting this dichotomy, Hendershot observes, the chastity movement has constructed a thorny paradox for itself. On the one hand, it teaches that by their very nature, boys are aggressive and girls are submissive. This is the subtext of all those warnings against kissing: Once started, real men can't stop and real women won't. "How can boys still be masculine while resisting their active sexual urges," Hendershot asks, "and how can girls still be feminine while resisting the urge to passively submit?"

One solution is to construct "self-control" as the macho alternative for guys. "Be a *strong* man," says one poster. "It takes strength to keep your passions under control." Perhaps not coincidentally, promiscuity is generally presented as the essential trait of gay men, helping to paint "lack of control" as effeminate. Girls, meanwhile, are generally placed in the role of helpers, whose primary purpose is to dress and behave in a way that will not trigger lust in boys. The notion of female sexual desire is rarely considered; you will never read about girls who "struggle with masturbation" as boys do. When female desire does come up, it is usually presented as aberrational. The *Sex Respect* curriculum notes that guys will sometimes have to say no to their dates, because "the liberation movement has produced some aggressive girls." First equal pay for equal work, now hot, steamy sex. What'll they want next?

There are exceptions to these attitudes within the broader chastity movement. Author Lauren Winner wrote a sophisticated book for adults called *Real Sex: The Naked Truth About Chastity* that espouses a very conservative view of sex while also critiquing the church's reductionism on the subject. And an artist who calls herself the Pink Nun construes abstinence as an explicitly "feminist" stance. "I'm saying, 'Don't let yourself be sold as an object to just be played with,'" The Pink Nun has said. Her shirts feature slogans such as "I am not your slot," over an image of a woman's spread legs with a toaster where her vulva should be.

But these voices are not represented in the Abstinence Clearinghouse, a determinedly reactionary organization. When Allen Unruh spoke, he took the opportunity to rail against a television ad he'd seen in his hotel room the night before that implied that test-driving a car is as sensible as test-driving a relationship before marriage. "I want you to call GM and tell them: 'I understand you're promoting fornication to sell automobiles!'" he said. Leslee Unruh's own topic was more serious: AIDS in Africa. Most of the world understands the need for condom distribution in countries like Uganda that have been ravaged by AIDS. The mainstream conservative approach is known as *ABC*: Abstinence, Be faithful, use Condoms. ABC is the official policy of the Bush administration and of World Vision, the evangelical charity I'd seen at Cornerstone and Bibleman. "Abstinence Clearinghouse will never be ABC!" Leslee Unruh thundered. She told us she'd been meeting with Clearinghouse-approved AIDS workers around the world and that they had uniformly denounced the policy. "Tell American mixed-message people, keep your condoms at home," Unruh claimed she was told.

Unruh, a gnomish woman with a tight smile and stiff helmet of blond hair, is proud of her reputation as someone who never compromises. "I was asked a couple of weeks ago, 'Wouldn't you like common ground? Wouldn't you like to invite people to the table?' We are the table now. We set the table. And we are not budging!" When not leading the abstinence movement, Unruh is an important figure in pro-life circles. She reportedly helped write the South Dakota legislation banning all abortions in the state without exception. In fact, there is a lot of crossover between the two movements. Abstinence school curricula frequently ask young students to, for example, draw pictures of themselves in the womb. Many antiabortion crisis pregnancy centers have launched abstinence education components—partly because of the federal grants available, no doubt, but also because of the theology that grounds both. One center that has sponsored public school visits by Keith Deltano teaches that "pregnancy is not the root problem, but a symptom of a lifestyle that is outside of God's will."

The convention ended with a banquet and the presentation of the annual Abstie Awards. To my disappointment, these were given to leading advocates of abstinence education, not to people who had the least sex. Entertainment at a function such as this is a delicate matter. There was a Christian comedian—a prop comic—and a song from former Miss America Tara Dawn Christensen, who made purity her pageant platform. That probably seemed like a safe choice, but Christensen's bodysuit caused some consternation among my tablemates. It covered her from ankles to wrists, but it was awfully sheer and lacy, though completely opaque. When one woman at the table began singing along, her friend joked, "All you need is the outfit." The woman replied, "I'm saving *that* for my husband."

By the end of the convention I was so addled by abstinence propaganda that even the hotel ice cream parlor, Sweet Surrender, sounded disreputable. On my way out of the hotel, I noticed that a gallery on the bottom floor was putting on a tribute to Norman Rockwell, featuring life-size, three-dimensional recreations of his famous paintings. Out of curiosity, I wandered through the homey displays—Doctor Dowd examining a little girl's doll, the old swimmin' hole, the soda shop. Before long, I was caught up in the soothing coziness of it all. In the picture-perfect one-room schoolhouse, I squeezed behind a desk and soaked in the nostalgia for an America that never existed. For a few minutes, at least, it was easy to see the appeal.

15

Train the younger women to
love their husbands

God has a plan for Linda Dillow's life: to clean up the mess made by the abstinence movement.

She doesn't put it that way, exactly. Dillow, a young-looking grandmother of five from the suburbs of Colorado Springs, is staunchly in favor of chastity until marriage. But she is also acutely aware of the unintended consequences of how that's been taught. "The church has erred greatly," Dillow told me. "You can't just say to your children, 'Stay away from this—and then get married and all of sudden turn around and delight in it.' It's kind of hard to shift gears in one day." This is why God called Dillow to become the Christian Dr. Ruth, sharing with married couples the good news of hot, healthy, holy sex. "Christians have become wrapped up in tradition," Dillow fretted. "There's this fear that if you teach what God teaches in the scripture—which is a free, wonderful, exciting sexual relationship in marriage—if you teach that, people will take license, and sex will get out of hand. They will give in too much to their desires. I think there's a fear of what will happen if you say 'God is for freedom.'"

To combat that fear, Dillow and her friend Lorraine Pintus founded Intimate Issues, a pro-sex ministry that hosts conferences for women and couples seeking a richer love life. They have also written two books that promote the joys of marital sex, *Intimate Issues* and *Intimacy Ignited*. These are not mere *tab A goes in slot B* manuals, but advice books to "fire up your sex life." And they are only two entries in a flourishing genre that includes titles such as *Sacred Sex, The Glorious Pursuit, Sheet Music,* and *His Needs, Her Needs.* "Some women," write Dillow and Pintus, "have spent so many years 'damming up' their sexual passions in an attempt to remain pure that they find it difficult to suddenly open the floodgates and allow sexual feelings to flow." The Christian sex advice movement is dedicated to unleashing that flood.

Dillow knows what much of the world thinks of Christians: They're prudes, they're frigid, they fear and discourage sexual pleasure, especially in women. And she admits that Christians have only themselves to blame for this perception. "Augustine, who wrote a lot of wonderful things, had a very warped view about sex," she said. "Even Martin Luther, who was married, said, 'Intercourse is never without sin, but God excuses it by his grace.' Women today don't know these statements, but I think the whole attitude has filtered down to them." But what was historically true is no longer universal.

In the 2007 HBO documentary *Friends of God,* megachurch pastor Ted Haggard declares that "evangelicals have the best sex life of any other group." It's a darkly comic moment, given that by the time the film aired Haggard had confessed to indiscretions with a male prostitute, but the scene is revealing in other ways too. In it, Haggard stops two men outside his church and asks them, "How often do you have sex with your wife?"

"Every day," they both answer.

Then Haggard says, "Out of a hundred times, when you have sex, what percentage does she climax?"

And the men answer, "Every one."

Regardless of whether they're telling the truth, it's an exchange that undermines stereotypes about fundamentalists. Here are Christian men not only rejoicing in sex, but identifying female pleasure as a defining element of what makes it great. And whatever Haggard's own sex life was like (Dillow and Pintus may now wish he hadn't blurbed their first book), research bears him out. A University of Chicago survey has found that 32 percent of conservative Protestant women report reaching orgasm every time they make love, compared with 27 percent of mainline Protestants and Catholics and only 22 percent of unaffiliated respondents.

Are these the same people who issue dire warnings about French kissing? Switching gears doesn't begin to describe the transition from absti-nence ed to Christian sex advice. "Relax. Let go. Give in to your erotic feel-ings," urges *Intimacy Ignited*. "Allow yourself to become *intoxicated* by your mate's sexual touches." What a difference a wedding band makes. Yet not every Christian understands this. In *Intimate Issues*, Dillow and Pintus quote a typical woman who says, "Because I want to be godly, I can't allow myself to be too earthly—and sex is definitely earthly. I allow myself to experience pleasure—but only so much."

From the perspective of most evangelical sex counselors, this attitude is not just unnecessarily strict, but antibiblical. "Spiritual intimacy is actually found in the midst of the relational, fleshy delight of sexual union," say Dil-low and Pintus.

> Why else would God take the ultimate sexual act, sexual intercourse between a husband and wife, and liken it to the ultimate spiritual experience, the union of Christ and the Church (Ephesians 5:31–32)? Just as a husband and wife experience deep joy as they lose themselves and merge into oneness at the moment of sexual cli-max, we experience ultimate joy as we become one with Jesus Christ in a union that leads to incomprehensible joy. Sexual intercourse mirrors our relationship to God and causes us to worship Him for giving us this good gift.

The canard that conservative Christians believe sex is only for procre-ation is explicitly refuted by several writers. Citing scripture, they identify numerous reasons God created sex. Procreation is one, but the Bible also encourages sex as way to strengthen marital bonds, as a defense against indiscriminate lust, and as a means for dispensing comfort. And judging by the allocation of space, the main reason God invented sex is pleasure. Sex-ual pleasure gets an entire book of the Bible: the Song of Solomon.

At the Christian comedy convention, one of the comedians had a rou-tine about it. "I was told Song of Solomon was about Christ and the Church," he said, letting his jaw drop. "Have you *read* the book? It's got naked people running through the woods." And more than that. The Song of Solomon is indisputably one of the greatest love poems ever written, a feast of sensuality and eroticism. If you haven't looked at it recently, here's an extended passage, in the King James translation.

> *Thou hast ravished my heart, my sister, my spouse; thou hast ravished my heart with one of thine eyes, with one chain of thy neck.*
>
> *How fair is thy love, my sister, my spouse! how much better is thy love than wine! and the smell of thine ointments than all spices!*
>
> *Thy lips, O my spouse, drop as the honeycomb: honey and milk are under thy tongue; and the smell of thy garments is like the smell of Lebanon.*
>
> *A garden inclosed is my sister, my spouse; a spring shut up, a fountain sealed.*
>
> *Thy plants are an orchard of pomegranates, with pleasant fruits; camphire, with spikenard,*
>
> *Spikenard and saffron; calamus and cinnamon, with all trees of frankincense; myrrh and aloes, with all the chief spices:*
>
> *A fountain of gardens, a well of living waters, and streams from Lebanon.*
>
> *Awake, O north wind; and come, thou south; blow upon my garden, that the spices thereof may flow out. Let my beloved come into his garden, and eat his pleasant fruits.*

Evangelical gatekeepers have often struggled with how fully to embrace the Song of Solomon. In 1997, Christian bookstores banned an album by the band Vigilantes of Love because it included a rock 'n' roll paraphrase ("I wanna attack your flesh with glad abandon / I wanna look for your fruits and put my hands on them"). Dillow and Pintus offer a corrective. *Intimacy Ignited*, which they wrote with their husbands, takes couples through the poem verse by verse, using it as a practical guide for lovemaking. When

Solomon's bride says, "Let his left hand be under my head and his right hand embrace me," Dillow and Pintus helpfully point out that the Hebrew word translated as *embrace* has the sense here of *fondle*. When she says "his fruit was sweet to my taste," they note that, like the passage I quoted above, "this phrase may be a veiled and delicate reference to an oral-genital caress." At the same time, they make the larger point that not only does God approve of all this, but that God's approval is the reason for doing it. Not oral-genital caressing necessarily, but whatever makes you both happy.

Like most Christian pop culture, the pop sexuality movement has lagged behind its mainstream counterpart, though not quite as far as you might think. The first Christian sex advice books began appearing in the 1970s— "wrapped in cellophane and stocked on the top shelf in Christian bookstores," says Tim Alan Gardner, the author of *Sacred Sex*. Many of these early works were written in response to, and repudiation of, "women's liberation." The most famous, and still the genre's only crossover success, was Marabel Morgan's *The Total Woman,* which sold over 10 million copies and was the bestselling nonfiction title of 1974. Morgan is best remembered as the woman who advised wives to greet their husbands at the door in skimpy, even bizarre, outfits; her books weren't the only thing wrapped in cellophane. But her more significant contribution to the culture was her broader message that "it is only when a woman surrenders her life to her husband, reveres and worships him, and is willing to serve him, that she becomes really beautiful to him."

Within the evangelical subculture, the most popular and influential early sex manual was *The Act of Marriage,* written in 1976 by Tim and Beverly LaHaye. Until *Left Behind,* this book was what Tim LaHaye was most famous for. Despite its coy title, it is frank about sex—for its time, shockingly so. Its dry, textbook tone allows it a forthrightness previously unfound in euphemism-heavy Christian marriage manuals.

> Gradually, the husband should move his hands gently down his wife's body until he contacts the vulva region, mindful to keep his fingernails smoothly filed to avoid producing any discomfort (which could cause her heating emotions to become suddenly chilled).

The LaHayes were among the first popular authors to promote the idea that pleasurable sex fulfills, rather than sullies, God's plan for marriage. God, they note, created the clitoris, whose only function is sexual arousal. They were, however, a bit more grudging than today's authors are. Sex is spiritual, they write, because "everything a Christ-controlled Christian does is spiritual. That includes eating, elimination, spanking children, or emptying the trash."

For a generation of Christians, *The Act of Marriage* was one of two books that nearly every couple received as a discreet wedding gift. The other was *Intended for Pleasure,* a 1977 book by physician Ed Wheat and his wife. Wheat's book echoed Morgan's in its advice to women. A chapter for wives instructs, "Look pretty. Keep smiling. Don't complain." But even then, the patriarchal edifice was beginning to crumble. "A wife gladly submits to a husband who loves in God's way," writes Wheat. "But neither can *demand* the appropriate response from the other. It must be a gift."

Thirty years later, gender stereotypes certainly remain—"man was created with a need; woman was created to fill a need," write Dillow and Pintus—but as a practical matter, the emphasis on mutuality has become central. In 2007, sex therapist Christopher McCluskey told *Christianity Today* that husbands sometimes come into his office saying, "We're here because you're a Christian counselor and my wife is withholding herself from me. I want you to address this from the scriptures and instruct her that she's in sin because her body is not her own."

> Does he have scriptural basis for every argument he's making? Yes. Is he right? No. He's totally missed the spirit of the act, though he could back up every point with Scripture. I tell him, "Everything you're saying may be right by the letter of the law, but it's so far from the spirit of the law that you're the one who's in sin, because you've totally missed the spirit. And if you force your wife to submit to you in giving you her body, Satan will be glorified through what you do."

The relevant biblical injunction is from 1 Corinthians: "The wife's body does not belong to her alone but also to her husband. In the same way, the husband's body does not belong to him alone but also to his wife." So while Dillow and Pintus frequently tell wives that they may never refuse their husband's sexual advances, they also inform husbands that "giving authority of your body to your wife means there will be times you must deny your own sexual desire so you can serve her." That the viability of such an arrangement requires a marriage in which there is perfect mutual empathy is precisely the point.

Of course, this ideal is undermined considerably by the larger context. Virtually all sex advice books are written for women, so women are getting their side of the message far more often. And while Dillow and Pintus tell wives they should not be afraid to "aggressively take the initiative," a more common sentiment is the one pastor Wendy Treat expresses in *Sex: Let's Talk About It*: "Begin to see your husband as Tarzan. See him as the man God brought into the world as your conqueror."

Treat does not have the same stature as Dillow and Pintus, but her book is perhaps more revealing about the audience for Christian sex advice. "Too often," she writes casually, "couples complete the sex act, and the husband goes to sleep while the wife rolls over and cries for hours." This heartbreaking picture is only compounded by the recognition that while Treat thinks she is offering a solution, she is probably part of the problem. One reason wives can't enjoy sex, Treat says, is that they had too much of it before they got married. "I've not met one woman who had sex before marriage who was not ashamed of it," Treat writes. Not coincidentally, here's how Treat handles the topic in her own family: "I explain to my children that sex before marriage will eat you up inside, because God has written in your heart the right thing to do. If you go against His plan, it just hurts you. It is painful and ugly. I have always taught my children to feel badly when they do anything against the Word." So the crying jags are God's punishment for sin. Or maybe too many women had mothers like Wendy Treat.

Treat is the embodiment of a tone-deafness that still plagues Christian counselors when it comes to sex, even when their intent is admirable. "Men, love your wife's frame," she writes. "Don't wish she had bigger breasts. I've heard so many comments on breast size through the years, and they are all so ignorant. Breast tissue is just fat. God made each woman with the right amount of fat. So receive it. Love her frame. Don't covet another kind of frame. Let her breasts satisfy you at all times." How could you not?

The refreshing thing about Dillow and Pintus is that they would never tell husbands that their wives' breasts are "just fat." Following the Song of Solomon, they encourage couples to develop a "private love language" to refer to their bodies.

> Instead of *garden,* one husband used the word *flower* to refer to his wife's vagina. She would call him at work and say, "I have a bouquet of flowers for you tonight," or she would hug him in the kitchen and say, "Honey, the flower is in bloom tonight."

Other recommended sex codes include "Would you like to fly with me?" "Let's go sailing," and "Let's play a board game. I'll be the board and you play the game." Dillow and Pintus acknowledge that this "may seem silly, but maybe a little silliness is what's needed." Especially if half of the couple has been crying herself to sleep.

It is easy for worldly readers, steeped in the depravity of ungodly sex, to find some of Dillow and Pintus's advice quaint or nauseating or even a little poignant. Still, Dillow and Pintus have built a well-deserved following because they emphasize the enjoyment of sex, urging couples to bring "spice and variety" to their lovemaking and reminding them that "intercourse is only one of many ways to have sex." If this seems underwhelming in its obviousness, consider that the authors are working in a community that reveres John Piper, the coeditor of a 2005 anthology called *Sex and the Supremacy of Christ.* Piper is not known as a sex guru, but he is enormously influential in evangelical culture in general. A sixty-two-year-old pastor and author, he is regarded by some as one of the movement's leading intellectual voices, and is often cited as an inspiration by Christian rock stars trying to sound smart. Piper is also a strict Calvinist who believes in the "total depravity" of mankind. He embraces his theology's traditional asceticism, but, with a stroke of marketing genius that reveals why he's so popular, has renamed it "Christian hedonism."

In Piper's book, "to engage in sex is to call God as witness to hold us accountable for our covenantal commitment." *Forget board games, honey. Let's go to the bedroom and call God as witness to hold us accountable for our covenantal commitment.* To understand Piper's view of the enterprise, here is how he begins *Sex and the Supremacy of Christ,* which was written at a time when the newspapers were full of kidnappings and murders of Americans in the Middle East.

> There is a connection between the beheadings of Jack Hensley and Eugene Armstrong and Nick Berg and Paul Johnson and Kenneth Bigley in Iraq, and this book on *Sex and the Supremacy of Christ.*
>
>> I look at them and I see their hands and their eyes. And I think of my hands and my eyes and my death and my faith. And then I hear the words of Jesus put it all in perspective, and in relation to sex.
>> You have heard that it was said, "You shall not commit adultery." But I say to you that everyone who looks at a woman with lustful intent has already committed adultery with her in his heart. If your right eye causes you to sin, tear it out and throw it away. For it is better that you lose one of your members than that your whole body be thrown into hell. And if your right hand causes you to sin, cut it off and throw it away. For it is better that you lose one of your members than that your whole body go into hell. (Matthew 5:27–30 ESV)
>
> In other words, there is something far more important than to keep your eye or your hand—or your head—namely, to receive eternal life and not to perish in hell. And Jesus links it with the war that we are waging not in Iraq but in our hearts. And the issue is sexual desire and what we do with it.

It is hard to know what to say about someone who, when seeing a video of a fellow human being having his head sliced off, thinks, *I just hope he never masturbated.* (And that's not mentioning that even if Berg was the most sexually pure man on earth, he's still going to hell, because, you know: Jew.) But it is this dim view of sex that Dillow and Pintus are working against. Piper's coeditor, Justin Taylor, endorses the Martin Luther quote that Dillow lamented in our conversation. "There *is* sin bound up with the sex act," he writes, "but marriage is the matrix for the redemption of sex." For this segment of the evangelical community, *puritanical* is a compliment. In the closing chapter of *Sex and the Supremacy of Christ,* Baptist theologian Mark Dever argues that the Puritans simply valued sex more than us. He quotes approvingly a seventeenth-century admonition to "strive more against your own flesh than against all your Enemies in Earth and Hell," and endorses the belief that marital sex is "to be used and enjoyed in moderation with the glory of God as the ultimate end."

When I contacted Linda Dillow to ask if I could attend one of her $50 Intimate Issues conferences, she was hesitant. "Women listen differently if there's a man in the room," she said. Finally she agreed to my presence at Calvary Church in Lancaster, Pennsylvania, as long as I stayed out of sight, in the sound room at the back of sanctuary. From this post, surrounded by an impressive array of computers, CD burners, and mixing boards, I looked down through thick glass at the large hall where more than three thousand women sat attentively in their seats. Some had come from as far away as Canada and Idaho.

The stage was tastefully decorated with white flowers and green candles, and Dillow wore a matronly flowered dress. She smiled easily as she worked her way through a homey PowerPoint presentation. "My husband warned me when I started this ministry that men would have two reactions," she told the crowd. "First, they would think, *What kind of woman would write a book like that?* I said, 'Okay, I can handle that. What's the second thing?' And he looked me in the eye and said, 'What is she like in bed?'"

Through the speaker in the sound room, I heard the audience laugh knowingly at these hypothetical men and their one-track minds. Dillow and Pintus kept the mood of the conference light and sisterly. They projected corny cartoons onto the sanctuary's video screens, and half-joked that long Sunday mornings in church are the perfect time to practice Kegel exercises. Intimate Issues conferences cover much the same material as the book, but they give women a chance to bring their questions directly to the authors, and to see that they are not alone in their concerns and curiosity.

The question Dillow and Pintus get more than any other is "What's not okay in bed?" The modern evangelical view is that unless scripture prohibits something, husbands and wives should do whatever they enjoy. That sounds simple enough, until you get into specifics. Dillow and Pintus list ten prohibitions from the Bible, found mostly in the book of Leviticus. Several are straightforward: adultery, homosexuality, bestiality, prostitution, incest. But others raise as many questions as they answer. What is impurity? What constitutes lustful passions or coarse talk?

"God doesn't in the scriptures say, 'All right, these acts are acceptable,'" Dillow told me. "It is a matter of interpretation, so you obviously are going to have different perspectives." Her own is to examine "the whole intent of all scripture. The message Christ brought is: *You are not under the law; you are under grace,* and that we are given a lot of freedom to decide what is beneficial for us, what is loving between *this* husband and *this* wife."

Christian sex counselors usually find that talk like this quickly brings out the specific question that couples really have in mind: *What about oral sex?* The simple answer is that other than those two allusions in the Song of Solomon, the Bible doesn't say. That leaves sex advisers a broad range of possible responses. Dillow and Pintus are careful to say that couples should decide for themselves what they're comfortable with, but make it plain that they think it's pretty swell. Other writers are more circumspect. I asked Dillow why that is, and she answered, "Because of the homosexual thing."

On the topic of oral sex, Wendy Treat says curtly that "the Lord left it to your conscience." The LaHayes say, without further clarification, that "if it has a place in marriage, we would suggest it be limited to foreplay." Ed Wheat is silent on fellatio, but he observes that some couples turn to "oral stimulation" when the wife is unable to achieve orgasm through intercourse. He opposes this on the somewhat strained logic that God designed male and female bodies so that with a lot of practice it is possible for some women to sometimes achieve orgasms through vaginal intercourse, and that he would not have done this if he wanted couples to take a "shortcut." In other words, the fact that it's difficult proves that God wants you to work hard at it—to the exclusion of the method he made much easier just to taunt you. "Also," Wheat adds, "oral-genital sex definitely limits the amount of loving verbal communication that husband and wife can have as they make love."

Consistent with this position, Wheat also condemns female "self-stimulation," except as part of a learning process. "As soon as she is consistently able to reach a climax, the couple should resume regular sexual intercourse. Otherwise they may fall so into a pattern of manual stimulation that she may be hindered in learning to enjoy orgasm during intercourse." And that's when both people are present. Masturbation as solo sex is even more fraught. Dillow and Pintus are forgiving on the subject, saying that as long as fantasies about people other than your spouse are not involved, it is a "personal issue." Kevin Leman, in *Sheet Music,* actually advocates it as a way to get comfortable with your body. "It's not wrong to enjoy the pleasurable sensation of brushing your hair," he writes. "If you can touch every other part of your body, why not touch the most sensitive parts?"

But other authors are happy to tell you exactly why not. "It may cause you to feel that you don't need a spouse or that a spouse can never fulfill you like you think you can fulfill yourself," says Treat. The LaHayes simply assert that "no married man should relieve his mounting, God-given desire for his wife except through coitus."

Masturbation with visual aids, everyone agrees, is a major sin. "Pornography is a mistress, an adulteress," say Dillow and Pintus. "Her goal is to rape your husband's soul and lead him to the grave." But what constitutes pornography? Treat says soap operas are nothing more than "cheap pornography" for women. *Sex and the Supremacy of Christ* says the same of romance novels, reserving special ire for the insidious Christian romances that deceive women into thinking that their lust is honoring God.

The disputes pile up quickly. Dillow and Pintus say vibrators may be "beneficial"; the LaHayes say they "might prove dangerous in overstimulating and establishing an appetite for a level of stimulation their partner could not provide naturally"; and Treat sniffs, "They didn't have such equipment when the Bible was written." Dillow and Pintus say "perhaps we should all run to Victoria's Secret and buy a suitable 'dancing outfit'"; Piper intones, "Victoria's Secret is Victoria's Lie." A "quickie," say Dillow and Pintus, "satisfies and whets the appetite." No, says Wheat, "only lust and self-gratification are done in haste." At least there's one thing everyone can agree on. "What about anal sex?" asks Leman. "It's kinky, and I believe it's wrong. This is one area where I tell men they need to let go of this expectation or fantasy." No one will try to argue that the Bible expressly forbids it, but most are happy to do so on the Bible's behalf. Tim Gardner, in *Sacred Sex,* says anal sex is sinful because it is "motivated by needs to debase the self." Dillow allows that couples must make their own decision, but she strongly advises against it for "medical reasons." Not, of course, because of the homosexual thing.

Interestingly, the Internet may be eroding the authority of Christian sex experts. Online, evangelicals have begun to build their own communities for sharing advice about sex that bypasses the delicate sensibilities and culturally determined taboos of even the more open-minded professionals. The largest of these is a web site called The Marriage Bed, whose bulletin boards offer not pronouncements from on high, but energetic conversation. Participants are clear in desiring biblically correct advice, but they are equally clear that they do not need to be soothed or lectured. Some participants will explain why they find anal sex humiliating while others endorse it with great enthusiasm. This is the site to check if you're looking for the Christian case for women using strap-on dildos on their husbands ("If the only access to the prostrate is through the rectum, and I know for a fact that my pressing on the prostrate increases his pleasure, than perhaps it *is* okay in God's eyes for me to do that for the man He's given me") or men ejaculating on their wives' faces ("It's part of our nature to want to be creative with where we 'release' our most basic creative force, and I can't help but want to be creative, I was created in my Creator's image"). When you're finished researching, recommended sex toys can be purchased at specialty Christian sites where the proprietors remove the packaging so that men aren't tempted by the cover models and that don't carry anything that looks anatomically realistic.

Once I began exploring the Christian sex subculture online I found that there is even a parallel universe fetish: domestic discipline. The concept of the submissive wife is, while controversial, familiar in Christian marriage literature, promoted in books like *Liberated Through Submission* and *Me? Obey Him?* So it's not too surprising that a passionate subculture reads the Bible as encouraging, or even mandating, sexual bondage and discipline. Enthusiasts gather on several web sites and bulletin boards to discuss, for instance, the differences among "play spanking," "punishment spanking," and "maintenance spanking" (to "remind the submissive to behave [and] reinforce roles in the relationship").

"I can't see putting something like that alongside the definition of love" in Corinthians, said Dillow when asked about domestic discipline. "Does

God discipline us? Yes. But, you know, Christ wouldn't get out a whip." Still, she acknowledged, "We are all very influenced by our cultural biases."

As someone who is interested in what the Bible has to say about sex but doesn't feel the need to apply it, I found myself interpreting scripture far more strictly than most modern evangelical authors do. Begin with the simple premise that marital bliss is a holy state that people should aspire to. In 1 Corinthians, Paul makes it quite plain that married sex is "a concession" that Jesus allows only if the alternative is unmarried sex. The ideal, says Paul, is "for a man not to marry," adding, "I wish that all men were as I am"—celibate. It's hardly a passionate endorsement of the Song of Solomon.

I also noticed that Dillow and Pintus's list of biblical prohibitions ignores one stated very clearly in Leviticus: "If a man lies with a woman during her monthly period and has sexual relations with her, he has exposed the source of her flow, and she has also uncovered it. Both of them must be cut off from their people." I asked Dillow why she overlooked it.

"That was true in the Old Testament," she replied. "It was a very different time. The New Testament says Christ is the end of the law. We don't wash our hands in a certain way before we eat. We don't follow the six-hundred-and-some rules of the Levitical code. So that would be one."

"But that could be said of almost any of the things you list in your book," I replied. "How do you know which rules were for a different time and which rules are for all time?"

Her answer was that if a prohibition is reiterated in the New Testament, it stands. But even here, she and her colleagues are inconsistent. Incest is never explicitly mentioned in the New Testament, nor is bestiality. Are these Levitical taboos also made acceptable?

At the conference in Lancaster, Dillow took a few moments to warn women that there is a dark side to sex as well. As surely as it is God's gift, it is also "Satan's tool to destroy you, your husband, and the country." In *Intimacy Ignited*, Dillow and Pintus write that "every Christian couple, whether they acknowledge it or not, is caught up in a greater drama—a heavenly battle involving the armies of God and the armies of Satan." Each side is using sex as a weapon, which is why it's important to be on guard.

For the audience, Dillow repeated a story she relates in her books.

Recently while eating dinner in a restaurant in Denver, a woman saw a group of people at another table praying. As she was leaving the restaurant, she stopped by the table and said, "I noticed earlier that you were praying. You must be Christians." The man at the head of the table replied, "No, we are Satanists. And we are committed to praying for the destruction of Christian marriages."

In my soundproof room, I laughed out loud. On top of everything else, Christians have their own parallel universe urban legends (Dillow's follow-up that she knows the story is true because she's heard it "three different ways from three different parts of the country" only confirmed my classification). But my mirth evaporated when Dillow introduced a guest speaker, a younger woman who tearfully described her experiences as the victim of Satanic ritual abuse. The details of her account were as horrific as they were unquestionably false. And yet she genuinely believed them, as did, as far as I could tell, the entire audience. Outside the evangelical bubble, Satanic ritual abuse was debunked many years ago;* inside it stands as a warning of the worst that sex can be.

This is the most extreme example of the Christian sex advice movement's disconnection from reality, but it is probably the natural outcome of the movement's basic failure to accept the evidence of the world around it. There were many ways in which I admired the advice in these books and conferences. Despite lingering gender stereotypes, these books, especially Dillow and Pintus's, offered generally sound and worthwhile information. Many marriages, not just Christian ones, could be improved by less television and more foot massages. Still, it was hard to get past the authors' firm pronouncements about the horrors that are *inevitably* brought down on marriages by such commonplace "transgressions" as having a sexual history or fantasizing about movie stars. To say, as these books do, that this behavior renders you incapable of loving your spouse deeply, fully, and

---

*See, for example, Debbie Nathan and Michael R. Snedeker, *Satan's Silence: Ritual Abuse and the Making of a Modern American Witch Hunt* (Basic Books, 1995).

without shame, is insulting to 99 percent of married Americans. Or at least it would be if it weren't manifestly false.

The LaHayes have an answer to this. As evidence that masturbation is wrong, they write, "feelings of guilt are a nearly universal aftermath of masturbation unless one has been brainwashed by the humanistic philosophy that does not hold to a God-given conscience or, in many cases, right or wrong." It's perfectly impenetrable circular logic. Guilt proves that God objects and lack of guilt proves that you've rejected God.

In a way, understanding the flaws of the Christian sex advice movement helps make plain a problem that many people have with conservative evangelical philosophy in general. Can all the mysteries of sex and marriage really be answered by a two-thousand-year-old book? There is wisdom in the Bible, certainly, but how reliable is it as a universal instruction manual?

Paradoxically, by trying to read the Bible as all-encompassing, pop Christianity actually diminishes it. There's something disappointing about reducing the transcendent poetry of the Song of Solomon to a mere self-help book. One typical sentence of *Intimacy Ignited* says that when the Song describes Solomon's naked body, "God is saying, 'It is right and good to dwell on *your husband's* body'" [emphasis in the original]. But the Song of Solomon *isn't* about us (except in the sense that any great love poem is "about" the person who reads it). Back when I was reading different versions of the Bible, I got a chuckle out of how the *Personal Promise Bible* rendered a line in the Song as "Gina's two breasts are like two fawns." Read that way, the ridiculousness becomes clear. But this pop reductionism is precisely what Dillow and Pintus do in *Intimacy Ignited*. While there is no doubt that many, if not most, couples can benefit from sex advice, perhaps it would be better to leave the Bible out of it, for the sake of the Bible as much as anything.

Of course, when it comes to hermeneutics of the Bible that are simultaneously too expansive and too reductive, the main victim of evangelical culture is not the Song of Solomon—it's the book of Genesis, and the story of creation.

16

The opposing ideas of what is falsely called knowledge

P erched heavily on a white stone wall, a cast-iron stegosaurus watched expressionlessly as a backhoe tore up a patch of land that was supposed to have been left green. "We've been doing some more research in the last few months which has already indicated we have to add extra parking," Mark Looy shouted over the rumbling. "The lobby is probably also going to be too small. That outdoor area with the pillars, that's going to be glass-enclosed now. That becomes a portico, a kind of pre-lobby for people to gather, get their tickets. Our projections are for more than two hundred and fifty thousand guests in the first year, and so we had to do some expansion."

Looy (pronounced *loy*) is a gracious, well-fed man with a halo of snow-white hair and matching moustache. He is a vice president of Answers in Genesis, America's largest and most influential creationist organization, and handles "ministry relations"—publicity—for AiG's $27 million Creation Museum in northern Kentucky. The glitzy museum, which officially opened in May 2007, is the premier cultural institution of young earth creationism, the belief that God created the universe and everything in it between six and ten thousand years ago. When I visited in September 2006, AiG was scrambling to finish construction. As Looy led me through the parking lot, he proudly called my attention to the landscaping that was transforming forty-nine acres of Midwestern flatland into a pleasant, if not quite Edenic, park.

We stepped aside for a minivan, and I noticed the motto on its license plate: "Kentucky: It's that friendly." Above that, the driver had affixed the familiar medallion of a giant Jesus fish devouring a smaller Darwin one.

The Creation Museum is seventy thousand square feet of state-of-the-art edutainment, built by set designers with places like Universal Studios on their résumés. Looy watched my reaction happily as we entered the lobby, a walk-through jungle diorama under a soaring forty-five-foot ceiling. A burbling waterfall plunged over a ramble of fiberglass rocks into a glass tank stocked with fish and turtles. On the shore, mannequins of bronze-skinned people lounged under artificial trees while dog-sized dinosaurs frolicked in the bushes around them. Across the hall, a forty-foot sauropod swung its animitronic neck to and fro among the hanging vines.

A museum visitor—possibly one of the charter members whose donations bought them advance admission—pushed his wide-eyed toddler down the corridor in a stroller. From the lobby display alone she was already learning so much. *Long ago, dinosaurs and people were friends.* In another room, the girl would even have a chance to scramble onto a triceratops and sit in its leather saddle.

"This is fanciful, right?" I asked Looy. "You're not really saying that people rode on dinosaurs?"

He raised a bushy eyebrow. "What would be fanciful about humans domesticating wild animals?"

Here's how entrenched creationism is in America: According to a 2007 *Newsweek* poll, 13 percent of self-described *atheists or agnostics* believe that "God created humans pretty much in the present form at one time within the last ten thousand years or so." Young earth creationism is the most commonly held belief about the origin and development of life, with 48 percent of all Americans embracing it. Another 30 percent believe that humans developed over millions of years but that the process was guided by God. Among evangelicals, 73 percent subscribe to young earth creationism, while 18 percent believe in a long process guided by God.*

---

*This poll is broadly consistent with many others taken over the past twenty-five years. However, it is important to keep in mind some flaws in all of them. Pollsters almost never

A century and a half after *On the Origin of Species,* the creation-evolution debate is still regularly in the news.* Usually we hear about the creationist movement in the context of legal, educational, and political battles: the lawsuit against a Pennsylvania school district that had mandated the teaching of Intelligent Design; the officials in Georgia who required science textbooks to carry stickers saying "evolution is a theory, not a fact"; the 2007 Republican primary debate where three candidates declined to raise their hand when asked if they believed in evolution. But while all this is important, I suspect that creationism has flourished for the very simple reason that it is very simple.

"When you look at the Bible and you look at the evidence, it makes sense," says a young mother in the documentary *Friends of God.* "It's just easy to explain to your children." Evolution, on the other hand, only makes sense if you understand biology, and biology is not particularly easy to explain. As a result, most nonevangelicals don't really learn about the development of life until late high school or college, while evangelical kids start learning creationism—and anti-Darwinism—before kindergarten. By the time evangelicals are taught about evolution in school, they are well prepared to resist it. Although some surveys show that denial of evolution is correlated with lower education, analysis by sociologists Otis Dudley Duncan and Claudia Geist finds that this is due to the number of poorly educated but less religious people who happen to join devout Christians in

---

include a third option, old earth creationism, which holds that there is no conflict between Genesis and "deep time." It seems likely that at least some people who believe in this identify themselves as young earth creationists for lack of a better answer. Perhaps more important, it is impossible to know what people mean when they agree with the statement that God "guided" the development of life. Do they have in mind supernatural intervention, or do they mean that evolution is an entirely natural process but that God is the source of all natural processes? Believers in the latter sometimes say that God works *through* evolution. This concept, known as theistic evolution or evolutionary creationism, is closer in substance and spirit to evolutionary science than to special creationism, and we'll hear more about it later.

*Although the debate did not actually begin until the 1920s. As Edward J. Larson shows in *Summer for the Gods,* most American Protestants, including some of those who literally defined fundamentalism, accommodated evolution and an old earth for decades until fossil discoveries made it clear that the theory applied to humans, not just other animals.

their skepticism of Darwin. Among firm religious believers alone, denial of evolution correlates with *high* education. And given that "creation science" is now taught in nearly 190 evangelical colleges, note Duncan and Geist, "the positive relationship of creationism to education among the very religious may become even stronger in the future."

Today, creationism is a thriving commercial enterprise as well as an educational one. By studying tax returns of the ten largest creation organizations, blogger Jim Lippard found that Americans spent at least $22 million on creationism in 2004, up from $13 million in 1999. Much of that money went to lectures and academic texts, but no small amount was spent on what can only be called creationist pop culture.

There are hundreds, if not thousands, of books about creationism, starting with board books like *A Is for Adam,* aimed at children as young as two. As kids get a little older, the lessons become more complex. In *What Really Happened to the Dinosaurs?* Answers in Genesis president Ken Ham writes, "If Adam had not sinned, death would not have been in the world, and friendly dinosaurs would still be around. Sin is such a terrible thing, isn't it?" Authors of creationist children's books are not afraid to take detours when opportunities arise. In retelling Genesis, *My Creation Bible* says, God "made the first woman, Adam's wife was she. A man and a woman, that's what marriage should be."

Older kids get chapter books like *Life in the Great Ice Age* and *The Lost World Adventures,* which places "characters created by Sir Arthur Conan Doyle in the explosive setting of the creation/evolution debate." This is the age where attacks on evolution begin in earnest. Books like *Someone's Making a Monkey Out of You* and *Skeletons in Your Closet* present evolution as a chronicle of scientific blunders and frauds; for creationists, the Piltdown Man fiasco remains the most significant event in the history of evolutionary science.*

Creationist books for adults are more sophisticated, though even these occasionally veer off into high weirdness. *Alien Intrusion: UFO's and the Evolution Connection* debunks stories of flying saucers and alien abductions by

---

*The Piltdown Man fossils, "discovered" in 1912 and promoted as evolution's "missing link," were not widely exposed as a hoax until 1953.

explaining that they are nothing more unusual than demonic attacks. Alien visitors are often said to communicate messages about evolution, which seals the proof of their Satanic origin.

Those who don't like to read can buy creationism DVDs or listen to the syndicated radio drama *Jonathan Park,* about a renegade paleontologist whose Indiana Jones–style adventures are "based on real places and scientific discoveries." There are also CDs of children's songs with titles like "Darwin's Mistake" and "I'm a K.I.D. (Not a Monkey)."

Answers in Genesis has its own in-house troubadour, Buddy Davis. One of his country-bluegrass ballads instructs kids on the proper way to challenge Darwinist authorities. When faced with a park ranger who says the Grand Canyon was formed by "a little bit of water and a long, long time," Davis sings, " 'Were you there?' was all I said / He swallowed hard and his face got red."

This same devastating attack also works on college professors, and it is not simplified for the sake of the lyrics. "Were you there?" is indeed the question that Answers in Genesis advises asking anyone who claims to know anything about the prehistoric past.

Other creationist products include a T-shirt showing a Darwin fish bowing before a Jesus one (it probably knew its alternative was being eaten) and a board game "designed to help fight the brainwashing of an entire generation. It clearly shows that the modern Darwinian theory of evolution is arguably the greatest hoax of modern times." Creation vacations have become an industry of their own, with cruises, summer camps, and nature tours that present antievolutionary interpretations of natural wonders like the Grand Canyon, Yosemite, and Death Valley. Creationist docents offer unauthorized tours of natural history museums and science centers.

Among the creationists' own museums, the Answers in Genesis museum is the newest and most elaborate, but there are several others.

- Dinosaur Adventure Land in Pensacola, Florida, is as much theme park as museum, with dozens of rides and games. Don't expect any downtime: Bible tracts hang over the urinals. The park remains open even though its founder, Kent Hovind, is currently serving a ten-year prison sentence for refusing to pay taxes.

- The Mt. Blanco Fossil museum in Crosbyton, Texas, exhibits model fossil bones of a giant human, proving that the biblical account of such creatures is accurate.*
- The Creation Evidence Museum, in Glen Rose, Texas, has a "hyperbaric biosphere," designed to prove founder Carl Baugh's theories that earth's preflood atmosphere caused plants and animals to grow larger and live longer than they do now, and also turned the sky a lovely shade of pink.

Before my trip to Answers in Genesis, I had the opportunity to visit two other creation museums. One was at the Santee, California, headquarters of the Institute for Creation Research, the country's second-largest creationist organization; a series of dingy rooms traced the six days of creation and their aftermath through the use of black lights and plastic animal figures. The other museum I visited was a side attraction of *The Great Passion Play* in Eureka Springs, Arkansas, which also takes visitors on a walk from the Garden of Eden through the Great Flood. The Eden room consists of model dinosaur skeletons in front of a painted mural. The audio tour assures visitors that "this garden exhibit pales in comparison to the actual Garden of Eden."

This is a disclaimer the Answers in Genesis museum will not have to make. Its displays may not be as stupendous as the ones designed by God, but they are good enough that no apologies are necessary. In the lobby, I looked again at the dinosaurs outnumbering any other creature, including man. *What is it about creationists and dinosaurs?* I wondered.

"Evolutionists probably use dinosaurs as much as anything to promote their worldview," Mark Looy said. "At science museums, the kids go to the dinosaurs. They bypass most of the other stuff. And we're going to use dinosaurs as a teaching tool, to show that the Bible is true." Before I could

---

*"There were giants in the earth in those days; and also after that, when the sons of God came in unto the daughters of men, and they bare children to them, the same became mighty men which were of old, men of renown." (Gen. 6:4, KJV)

ask how, specifically, dinosaurs show that the Bible is true, Looy added a comment that I felt answered the question as well as any: "And frankly, it's an attraction for kids and kids will bring their parents. So there's a marketing aspect too."

Looy promised me a better look at the museum later. A group of pastors would be arriving soon and I could join them for a tour. First, though, he wanted to introduce me to Ken Ham, the founder and president of Answers in Genesis. As we walked through the warren of cubicles and filing cabinets in the private section of the building, Looy told me more about the philosophy of the museum. "To hold the interest nowadays of young people, you got to have visuals, entertainment," he said. "Just a few weeks ago I was at the Field Museum in Chicago. They had a lot of young people there and they were all watching the videos. They weren't standing there and reading about the so-called ape-men, you know? Most people just breeze through a museum unless something really catches their eye." The Creation Museum, he said, would have about sixty video kiosks, hologram-like illusions, and a special-effects theater, where a video spin through history is accompanied by shaking seats, sprays of water, and gusts of wind.

Looy knocked on the door of a corner office, and Ken Ham rose from his desk to let us in. In contrast to the chatty, avuncular Looy, Ham is a somber, imposing figure. Born and raised in Australia, he speaks in a clipped, heavily accented baritone that conveys a combination of boundless suspicion and macho authority. His hooded eyes and lycanthropic chin-curtain beard complete his aura of Old Testament prophet.

Ham gestured to a chair and I sat down. Looy made himself comfortable on a nearby love seat. Ham sat behind his elegant desk, framed by a giant window overlooking the museum grounds, a row of fossils displayed on the sill. It was an office intelligently designed to induce admiration, envy, or both. According to AiG's tax returns, Ham was paid $121,764 in 2004, plus $63,808 for expenses.

Ham came to the United States in the late 1980s, and worked at the Institute for Creation Research for several years before founding Answers in Genesis. A creation museum had been a dream of his since his early days in Australia. "There are people who will come to a museum that you couldn't blow into church with a stick of dynamite," he said.

"So you hope to attract non-Christians as well as Christians."

"We definitely will. The whole aim of the museum in an ultimate sense is to stand there and say the Bible is true, it is God's word. Its history in Genesis is true, and we can defend it. We can use observational science to confirm that history. And if its history is true, we are going to challenge you that the rest is true—its message of the gospel, its message of Christian morality." He leaned back in his chair. Through the museum, he said, "we can make some clear statements to the culture and do it in a professional way, without hitting people over the head. It's not an evolution-bashing place, and it is not taking the Bible and bashing anyone on the head."

"That would be refreshing," I said.

Ham didn't smile. "We have tried to maintain the highest of integrity, not to be in attack mode, to be positive in what we say. And we will actually represent evolutionists faithfully, not like some of the secular museums do with creationism. They make claims about what creationists believe that are just simply not true. The natural history museum in New York actually attacks creationists, and calls what they believe *myth*. You know, *the myth of the global flood*. We are not going to do that with the evolutionists. We are just going to present what they say very, very carefully from their own books and materials, and we are not going to attack them like that." He put his palms flat on his desk. "I see a lot of misreporting saying that we're blaming evolution for social ills, or blaming evolution for abortion or gay marriage. That's simply not true."

I started to talk about the other creation museums I'd seen and read about, but Looy interrupted. "Some of those we don't have any affiliation with, because their science might be a little bit suspect." For example, he said, the Creation Evidence Museum, with the hyperbaric biosphere, has "drawn conclusions from fragmentary evidence. They say it's convincing evidence, when we would say it's tentative evidence."

"Do you deal with Intelligent Design at all?" I asked.

Looy shook his head. "We are here to proclaim biblical truths," he said. "I mean, we don't hide anything. Some of the ID people do. They don't tell you who the creator is. There's a kind of caginess we don't care for."

The pastors gawked at dinosaurs in the lobby, waiting for Carl Kerby to kick off the museum tour. Kerby is one of Answers in Genesis's most-requested lecturers and the creator of its extremely impressive web site, which claims more than 1.6 million visitors per month.

"What we want to show here at the museum is how to put on biblical glasses to understand evidence," Kerby told the group as he led us to the first room, where two animatronic paleontologists debated the significance of their finds. "The difference we have with evolutionists isn't the actual evidence, it's the interpretation of evidence," he said. "We'll have a replica of the skeleton of Lucy," the famous *Australopithecus afarensis* discovered in 1974. "Those are the bones," said Kerby, talking fast. "That's the facts. But then you'll go to a museum and you'll find the reconstruction. Well that's the *interpretation,* because quite honestly they didn't find any of the hands!" Kerby became excited. "They didn't find the foot bones from Lucy! Well when you go to the museum, you're going to see human hands, human feet! That was *not found.* That's actually *misleading.* Is our problem with the facts? No, most of the time our problem is with the reconstruction."

The museum's "creation walk" begins in the Garden of Eden, which, predictably, is teeming with dinosaurs. Not just lumbering sauropods either, but swift-footed velociraptors and towering Tyrannosaurus rexes. Not that Adam and Eve need to be afraid. The way Answers in Genesis reads the Bible, there was no death in the world before man's sin, so all these dinosaurs—not to mention the lions and tigers and bears—were vegetarians. Kerby was fairly obsessed with the idea that because God said that his creation was "good," that could only mean that animals did not hunt and eat other animals. This seemed like a strange moral judgment to make about nature, but Kerby disagreed. "If there is a God that used millions of years of death and suffering to get to where we are today, he's responsible for all these ugly things."

Kerby led us to a scene of Noah's Ark under construction. The exhibit went into great detail about exactly how Noah could have fit all the animals into the ark, including dinosaurs (he brought babies). No doubt creationists sometimes wish they could say the dinosaurs went extinct in the flood; that would certainly be convenient, especially since the flood is supposed to be responsible for all the fossils in the world. But that would contradict the Bible, which says that Noah "kept alive" two of *every* animal. So instead, Answers in Genesis teaches that dinosaurs died shortly after the flood, when the transformed habitat made it difficult for them to find food. The distinction between being killed in the flood and dying as a result of the flood seems moot, at least from the dinosaurs' point of view, but this doesn't seem to bother creationists who must set the bar for "kept alive" pretty low. When Noah leaves the ark, God tells him to release the animals "so they can multiply on the earth and be fruitful and increase in number upon it," so apparently this whole transformed habitat problem took God by surprise too.

While the walk through biblical history was eye-opening enough, the Creation Museum also deals with the present day. A room called Graffiti Alley is festooned with spray-painted messages like "Modern World abandons the Bible" and "Today man decides ~~truth~~ whatever." At the end of this passage is the Culture in Crisis room which shows the walls of a church being smashed by a wrecking ball labeled "millions of years." Videos show a boy surfing the Internet for pornography and a girl going into an abortion clinic. I wondered how Ham could complain that accusing his group of blaming evolution for social ills was a misrepresentation, but later I found a brochure saying that the problem wasn't evolution per se but rather "the harmful consequences of evolutionary thinking." A clever loophole. If the museum doesn't pan out, perhaps Ham can go into law.

The final room in the museum is the chapel, where members of Answers in Genesis wait to pray with anyone who is moved by what they've seen. One young pastor in our group was very impressed with this. "It's like how other museums dump you out into the gift shop," he observed.

Back at the lobby, Mark Looy rejoined us to open the doors of the planetarium. The Creation Museum has a planetarium. As I walked in, I looked up to see if it was just a big hole in the ceiling.

In all my travels through evangelical culture, I never felt more acutely that I was in a funhouse mirror universe than while sitting in the creationist planetarium. Leaning back in a comfortable seat, I watched the digitally projected stars spin around the black dome above me. Anyone who has ever sat through a planetarium show would recognize instantly the dulcet-toned narration and majestic but unobtrusive orchestral score. The computer-generated planets would sharpen into focus and the narrator would offer some familiar observation about their size or composition or orbit, and I would almost forget where I was. And then the voice would say something like, "The moon's scarred surface is vastly different from that of the Earth. That's because God created the moon for a different purpose than the Earth. The moon was created to be the lesser light that rules in the night. It's not designed for life as the Earth is."

Since most of the informational videos and signage weren't yet installed in the museum rooms I'd seen, the planetarium was the first time I got to hear much detail about AiG's creation science. Problems stacked up rapidly. Some required an understanding of science to spot, such as the claim that the Earth and moon would have been touching 1.5 billion years ago if they'd really been around that long. But others would stand out for anyone who even had an *interest* in science. "The next planet out from the sun also presents challenges to secular thinking," viewers are told at one point. "Neptune is almost a twin to Uranus. It's nearly identical in size, mass, and composition. It even has a similar color. Yet Neptune has much greater internal heat than Uranus. This is a puzzle for secular formations scenarios—but it's not a problem for biblical creation." Later I confirmed that this did in fact mean what it sounded like: If something is a "puzzle," that makes it a lethal problem for scientific inquiry (as opposed to what scientific inquiry exists to solve); on the other hand, creationism has no puzzles because God can do whatever he wants—create man, make a planet that looks just like another planet but with a different core temperature, *whatever*. If science is the search for answers, creationism is the elimination of questions.

And yet when so much effort, expense, and expertise have been devoted to persuading you that everything you know is wrong, it's easy to succumb. After the museum tour and the planetarium show, I felt like a character in a *Twilight Zone* episode. When I arrived here I felt like I had entered a world that had gone mad. Now I couldn't help wondering if I was the crazy one after all.

The day at the museum ended with a luncheon for the pastors and a PowerPoint presentation by Ken Ham. Although he knew I was in the room, he was talking now for his loyal followers, and the conciliatory language he'd used in his office was gone.

"There is a battle in our culture over the word of God," he said. "That battle goes back to the Garden of Eden and the first temptation: *Can you really trust God?*" The pastors muttered their assent between bites of barbecue pork. "Secular culture's aim is to evolutionize Christians," Ham continued, showing a slide of a Christian family walking into a machine labeled "secular culture" and emerging on the other side as ape-men. Evolution, he went on, is an intentional attack on Christianity. He illustrated this with a cartoon of two castles perched on islands in a sea. One was built on a foundation labeled "evolution" and was flying the flag of "Humanism." Rising above it were balloons representing "abortion," "homosexual behavior," and "school violence." The other castle, "Christianity," was built on a foundation of "creation," and it was under assault. While humanist pirates fired cannons at Christianity's foundation, the Christians were asleep at their posts, or aiming their cannons at the balloons instead of the structure they were attached to. Then Ham flipped to a slide labeled "The Solution." This cartoon showed the Christians blasting the foundation of evolution. The "Humanism" flag was on fire and the humanists were jumping ship. Any reticence Ham had about attacking evolutionists had apparently been overcome.

I realized with some surprise that Ken Ham scared me. I wasn't physically afraid. I didn't think he'd haul off and punch me if I told him that I was a humanist. But his grim affect and coldly irrational imitation of rationality struck me as borderline sociopathic.*

I looked up to see Mark Looy hurrying over to my seat with a giant grin on his face. "Look at this," he said, handing me a computer printout. "This just came off the Internet." It was an Associated Press article headlined, "Skeleton Sheds Light on Ape-Man Species." Scanning it quickly, I saw that researchers had discovered a nearly complete skeleton of a young *Australopithecus aferensis*; they were calling it "Lucy's baby." "The fossil find," said

---

*Later I read an essay Ham wrote for *Creation* magazine on the second anniversary of September 11: "After the 9/11 attack, I had someone say to me: 'I'm glad I wasn't in the World Trade Center—I would have died.' I replied, 'Well, don't worry, your turn is coming.'" Who thinks that way? Who thinks Jesus *wants* them to think that way? Ham's essay goes on to chastise the country for mourning the victims of 9/11 while forgetting that on that same day "more human beings were killed (murdered) by a different sort of terrorism"— abortion.

the report, included part of a hand and most of a foot, "providing the first time scientists have found an *aferensis* foot with the bones still positioned as they were in life."

Considering that this find undermined, and would possibly demolish, Carl Kerby's attack on the Lucy reconstruction, I didn't quite understand Looy's excitement. Clapping me on the back, he explained that I was missing the point—it wasn't about the science, it was about the battle. "With our web site," he said, "we can have a response up in half an hour. In the past it would have taken us weeks to publish something. The evolutionists would have had this story to themselves." He grinned some more and then said, "We'll publish something more thorough after we've had a chance to examine the evidence." I almost admired the way he made it sound like an afterthought.

After the lecture, I went up to talk to Ham again. I told him I was a little bothered by his lecture, especially the slides. "You did say you weren't going to go on the attack," I reminded him.

His jaw tensed slightly under his beard. "They're symbolic," he said, comparing his talk to the Bible itself. "Paul uses a lot of militaristic language."

"I know you're not actually advocating violence," I replied, "but what happened to being positive?" I held up a copy of an Answers in Genesis newsletter Looy had given me. The front page headline was "Evolutionists target children." An accompanying cartoon showed a white-coated scientist using a dinosaur Pied Piper to lure kids to evolution. I asked Ham, "How is this any different from what you're doing with dinosaurs here?"

"It's not."

"So why portray the evolutionists as villains?"

"We don't," he said, looking me in the eye. "That's perfectly neutral language."

I skimmed the article. "What about this part where it says, 'This traveling "science" exhibit is designed to indoctrinate young children'? You wouldn't mind if someone said that about you?"

"No. There's nothing negative about *indoctrination*." Now his voice grew sharp. "The problem is what they're being indoctrinated into."

"You call evolution 'morally bankrupt,'" I pointed out, my voice rising to match his. "That's not an attack? Have you ever seen a publication from a secular science museum say anything remotely similar about creationism? Or a major newspaper, for that matter?"

"All the time. We get that *all the time.*"

Mark Looy popped his head in between us. "Got everything you need?" he asked me.

The Creation Museum may not dump guests into the gift shop at the end of their tour, but of course there is one. It's called the Dragon Hall Bookstore. "Could dragon legends be based on fact?" asks the museum guide. "Evidence that Noah's descendents encountered dinosaurs is the theme of our Bookstore and Gift Shop." I browsed the shelves numbly, barely registering the medieval motif. *Dinosaurs were dragons,* I thought vaguely. *Dragons were real.* Why not? After a day of spiritual and intellectual battering, I didn't feel capable of making firm judgments about such things. After all, *Was I there?*

In his office, Ham had told me that in addition to attracting outsiders, he hoped the museum would be "a rallying point for Christians" that would "equip them for creation evangelism." For Answers in Genesis, creationism is not primarily an explanation of the origins and history of the world, it is a tool for spreading and defending the faith. Professional creationists don't take much solace from the fact that three-quarters of evangelicals already accept special creation; if that acceptance is too passive, too uninformed, it is essentially useless.

I wonder, however, if Answers in Genesis has overestimated how much "information" amateur creationists should really have. For decades now, ordinary evangelicals have been more than satisfied with their home-brewed and half-baked creationist beliefs. On its web site, AiG has a page of "Arguments we think creationists should NOT use," because they are either dubious or flat-out wrong, even by the minimal standards of creationism. This page is necessary because creationists, in fact, use these arguments *regularly,* as anyone who has ever written about evolution can attest from his folder of angry e-mails. One of these ridiculous contentions—"If we evolved from apes, apes shouldn't exist today"—is so popular that even Larry King has used it when interviewing evolutionary scientists. AiG patiently explains what's wrong with it, but in attempting to dispel ignorance, it only allows doubt to creep in. If creationists are told by other creationists that arguments they'd found so convincing for so long are actually bogus, what's to stop them from bringing a new skepticism to all creationist arguments—in other words, from doing real science?

Indeed the very premise of the creation museum—that creation science is an all-encompassing discipline that must be applied to the entire history of the universe—undermines the fundamental appeal of creationism, its simplicity. It's one thing to say "God created man; I'm a K.I.D. not a monkey." But you have to leave it at that. The museum does the opposite. It demands belief in a whole range of other things that, especially in aggregate, become increasingly difficult to swallow *or* understand. You have to believe that Noah really, literally had two of every kind of animal on the ark. Which means you have to think about what a *kind* is, and how they all fit, and how they got there from all over the world, and what they ate on the ark, and how eight people cared for them all, and how this ungainly ship stayed afloat, and what the animals ate when they came off the ark, and how they dispersed around the world again, and, of course, what really happened to the dinosaurs.

But don't stop there. Every detail of the Tower of Babel story has to be held to equal scrutiny, and plate tectonics, and distant starlight, and giant humans. It goes without saying that professional creationists have answers to all these questions, and no doubt there will be many visitors to the Creation Museum who will find them satisfying. But if there's one thing I've learned in my travels, it's that despite what too many secularists think, evangelicals are not stupid. An intelligent person might accept a story about the origins of man because they lack the working knowledge to understand its flaws and have never really had to think about the broader implications of that story. But when pressed to affirm that their simple belief requires equal acceptance of beliefs that are much more complex— and in drastic opposition to the "common sense" that was the appeal of the original belief—surely there's a chance, at least, that they will begin to reconsider.

Evangelicals will not, of course, abandon the central tenet of the Nicene Creed that God is the "maker of heaven and earth, of all that is," but nor do they need to. Theistic evolution—the idea that evolution is the natural process that is the mechanism of divine creation—is accepted by most mainline denominations. If I'm correct that young earth creationism, in flexing its muscle, is inadvertently exposing its weaknesses, then the cultural moment is right for theistic evolution to make inroads among evangelicals. In this context, it's heartening that *Christianity Today* named as one of the best books of 2006 *The Language of God,* an argument for theistic evolution by the noted geneticist Francis Collins. And maybe attitudes are not as hardened as we all think. According to a CBS News poll, about half of all young earth creationists agree that it is possible to believe in both God and evolution. That's a kind of open-mindedness. Perhaps all that is needed is the establishment of theistic evolution organizations with the same resources and pop culture savvy of creationist ones.*

Theistic evolution holds that God reveals himself equally through his words, in the Bible, and his works, in nature. Denis O. Lamoureux, a professor at St. Joseph's College in the University of Alberta, writes that "science discovers how the Creator made the world, while Scripture offers the ultimate meaning of the creation." As such, it is a kind of blasphemy to dismiss scientific findings that don't accord with the Bible.

Because theistic evolution honors natural processes as the work of God, it refuses, when faced with thorny scientific problems, to fall back on supernatural miracles, as creationism inevitably does. For example, here is how G. Thomas Sharp of the Eureka Springs Museum of Earth History answers the question, in his audio tour, of how the animals got to, and survived on, Noah's Ark: "A great hindrance in understanding is to impose upon biblical reality a natural explanation. I think it is quite possible that God guided the animals into their stalls, where they went to sleep."

Of course it is. But then, it would have been equally possible for God to shrink all the animals down so Noah could fit them in a shoe box, or to lift them all into the air and let them hover in a stasis field for forty days, or to cause wicked humans to drop dead without inflicting the flood on the rest of the planet in the first place. The *God can do anything* explanation is really

---

*The intelligent design movement, which is well funded and organized, is often confused with theistic evolution. One key difference is that while theistic evolution says religion does not *conflict* with science, ID says religious principles can be *confirmed* through science.

the opposite of an explanation, and creation scientists know it. That's why they use the "biblical reality" gambit only as a last resort.

Most young earth creationists never accepted the nineteenth-century *omphalos* hypothesis, which argued that the world appears to be ancient because God made it to look that way. Understanding the vast logical, and theological, problems with this proposal, creationists prefer to use other methods to explain away radiometric dating, for example. But lately, the hypothesis has enjoyed a renaissance as an explanation for starlight that appears to have been traveling for billions of years before reaching our eyes. That starlight, it is claimed, was created *already in transit* to us.

By contrast, theistic evolution's equal trust in *the two books of God,* the Bible and nature, frees Christians to do real science. In a 2007 Internet debate between writers Andrew Sullivan, a moderate Catholic, and Sam Harris, a staunch atheist, Sullivan wrote,

> I believe that God is truth and truth is, by definition, reasonable. Science cannot disprove true faith; because true faith rests on the truth; and science cannot be in ultimate conflict with the truth. So I am perfectly happy to believe in evolution, for example, as the most powerful theory yet devised explaining human history and pre-history. I have no fear of what science will tell us about the universe—since God is definitionally the Creator of such a universe; and the meaning of the universe cannot be in conflict with its Creator. I do not, in other words, see reason as somehow in conflict with faith—since both are reconciled by a Truth that may yet be beyond our understanding.

If American Christianity could be won over to this view, it would have profound implications for matters beyond science (in this, Answers in Genesis and I are in agreement, though, as with the fossil record, we interpret it differently). In theistic evolution's willingness to accept gaps in human knowledge, I see a reflection of Romans 11:33: "How unsearchable his judgements and his paths beyond tracing out!" And to say that we can't know the mind of God with any certainty is to recognize that we must be wary, at the very least, of imposing moral codes in his name; it is to embrace the quality that Sullivan identifies as *humility*:

You ask legitimately: how can I, convinced of this truth, resist imposing it on others? The answer is: humility and doubt. I may believe these things, but I am aware that others may not; and I respect their own existential decision to believe something else. I respect their decision because I respect my own, and realize it is indescribable to those who have not directly experienced it. That's why I am such a dogged defender of pluralism and secularism—because I believe secularism alone does justice to the profundity of the claims of religion. The attempt to force or even rig laws to encourage others to share my faith defeats the point of my faith—which is that it is both freely chosen and definitionally dealing with matters that cannot be subject to common consensus . . . Humility requires relinquishing the impulse to force faith on others, to condemn those with different faiths, or to condescend to those who have sincerely concluded that there is no God at all.

It took a few hours after leaving the Creation Museum for my head to clear enough to understand how utterly bizarre it was. Even if there were other creationists out there who were nuttier than Ken Ham—Kent Hovind with his tax-evading dinosaurs, Carl Baugh with his pink sky and giant humans—the ingenuity and sophistication with which Answers in Genesis pursued its agenda pretty much had me persuaded that my quest for the strangest and most hostile manifestation of Christian pop culture had come to an end.

And then I recalled one small exhibit I had seen at the Institute for Creation Research in California. It was a short video titled *Effects of the Copernican Principle*. In it, a creation scholar makes the following remarks:

The great Copernican cliché . . . is that Copernicus dethroned humankind and dethroned Earth from its special place at the center of the universe. It was a demotion. Carl Sagan talks about the great series of demotions for humankind beginning with Copernicus. But if you think about it, to be demoted means to be taken down a notch. The pre-Copernican Earth couldn't be taken down a notch, it was

already at the very center, the low point of the universe. The philosopher Pico said, "We live in the filthy and excrementory parts of the
lower world." And so to move the Earth from that place to the status
of a planet was a *promotion* not a *demotion*.

Such a heavy-handed defense of heliocentrism seemed gratuitous in
this day and age—unless, of course, there were still dissenters somewhere
arguing that God's chosen planet *must* be at the center of everything. Sure
enough, a little hunting turned up the Association for Biblical Astronomy, a
tiny but fiercely dedicated organization that holds that science—and a literal reading of the Bible—reveals that the entire universe revolves around
the earth.

The president of the association, Gerardus Dingeman Bouw, holds a
PhD in astronomy from Case Western Reserve. When I called him up to
find out how large the geocentrist movement is, Bouw warned me that I
should not trust certain individuals who are not affiliated with the ABA.
"What frustrates me," he said, "is that people become interested in geocen-
tricity, and they have talent, and then they decide to use those talents in
promoting their own ideas, which are usually ineffective and not—well,
they're off the wall, let's put it that way. They are not based on hard science."

I had a moment of quiet despair. All my efforts to seek out the darkest
corners of this parallel universe had finally brought me to geocentricism,
only to find out that even geocentrists insist on distinguishing themselves
from *those other, really crazy geocentrists*. Maybe it was time to call it quits.

17

Their visions are false and their divinations a lie

A cobblestone street on the Brooklyn waterfront, Halloween 2006. Nightfall in New York City never brings total darkness, but it comes close here in this canyon of old warehouses. The choppy blackness of the East River holds the ambient glow from the Manhattan skyline at arm's length, and the great underbelly of the Brooklyn Bridge casts shadows on the shadows. This was once an industrial neighborhood; the buildings housed actual wares. Today, they've been converted into multimillion-dollar lofts, art galleries, and gourmet chocolatiers.

When I began my yearlong expedition into the Christian parallel universe, I hadn't expected to end up here, in my own backyard. Early on, I had decided that my adventures should culminate in a look at the strangest, scariest, nuttiest manifestation of Bible-thumping culture. I began bookmarking web sites of fundamentalist ministries whose brand of pop culture was a *rejection* of pop culture, making special note of those that reserved their most venomous remarks for pop Christianity.

I found churches that declared rock 'n' roll "a vehicle for demon infestation," and fumed that there can no more be Christian rock than Christian adultery; one pastor discovered occult messages on Amy Grant albums. I read warnings to "tread with extreme caution and discernment in your local Christian bookstore," because it's likely to be pushing "gnosticism, relationalism, pantheism, self-atonement," and other heresies. I saw concerns that Christian comedy is risky, because "surely the awfulness of that place where lost souls are tormented eternally in its flames should not be made light of in any way."

I found King James onlyists, who declared any other version of the Bible to be a "*per*-version." I saw BibleZines denounced for being soft on sex, drinking, and gambling, while promoting pagan environmentalism ("Somehow, I missed the verse that says 'Honor God, then respect the planet,'" rails one minister. "But I do remember the verse where the Lord says He is going to completely burn up this planet."). I studied scientific proof that Hell is a physical place in the center of the Earth.

Pushing on, I came to denunciations of "false teachers," like Rick Warren and Billy Graham. I learned that Promise Keepers approves of "psychological approaches and techniques" (and is wobbly on Catholicism). As for the ex-gay movement I encountered at Cornerstone, apparently it's too soft on sodomites, as it urges people not to protest sodomite parades, send Bible tracts to their sodomite children, or shun their sodomite children's sodomite partners. Even Christmas trees, I discovered, are a form of idolatry, and Santa Claus is none other than Satan himself; his elves "suck human blood like vampires."

And Halloween, well . . . Halloween is fundamentalists' favorite time of year. Sure it's a nightmare of demonic paganism, but it's also hell house time. Hell houses are Christian haunted houses—shock-and-gore theatrical extravaganzas designed to scare kids into accepting Jesus by dramatizing the fiery wages of sin. The first one was opened in the 1970s by Jerry Falwell, who now knows if he got it right. In the 1990s, the idea was branded by a Denver pastor named Keenan Roberts, who created a do-it-yourself hell house kit. Roberts's hell house is a series of scenes showing the horrors of abortion, gay marriage, drugs, teen sex, and other activities that lead directly to the inferno. The $300 kit includes a script, a 263-page instruction manual, and a sound effects CD. Roberts claims to have sold eight hundred over the years. I began investigating hell houses to visit. I also looked into similar productions that show what life will be like for those left behind after the Rapture.

Yet the more I read up on these extremists, the more irrelevant they sounded—not just to my life and my secular world, but to the evangelical world that I'd been exploring. Out of the hundreds of people I'd met, I couldn't imagine more than a dozen even setting foot inside a hell house. It was easier to think of people who would condemn these productions as grotesque distortions of their faith. Obviously there are many thousands of American Christians who embrace such undistilled fundamentalism, but I could no longer think of it as the purest, most authentic expression—the secret id—of evangelical pop culture. Instead it seemed more like the crazy aunt in the attic—part of the family that few were willing to totally disown but that most were at least a little ashamed of. I decided not to go to a hell house.

And then a hell house came to me. A local theater company had purchased one of Roberts's kits and was staging a hell house in Brooklyn as a work of anthropological drama. A couple of years earlier a group of Los Angeles comedians had used Roberts's script to do a hell house spoof, but the Brooklyn producers wanted to do something different. With Roberts's blessing and advice, they were staging a hell house "with nary a wink or roll of the eyes," as the *New York Times* review put it. Instead of parachuting into the parallel universe one last time, I would stay home while a slice of that universe was dropped into mine. I wondered if there would be some sort of matter-antimatter explosion. To make the mix even more combustible, I invited along the evangelical I'd met whose worldview seemed most opposed to that of the hell house: Jay Bakker, the liberal son of Jim and Tammy Faye.

The show was being staged at a Brooklyn arts institution known for its avant-garde productions. When I arrived, the lobby was crowded with fashionable young people eating grilled eggplant maki and edamame hummus with pita chips. A few gathered around a small television to watch a video of Keenan Roberts explaining the hell house concept to his fellow pastors. "Hollywood does not set the standard for what I believe," he said into the camera. The hell house shows God's standard, and through it, "we're made into even more flaming evangelists." Someone behind me giggled. "The hell house ministry," Roberts concluded, "is all about communicating truth and love."

I sat down at a small table with a couple of young gay guys and their female friend. They weren't sure what they were in for. "I didn't realize until I Googled it that people actually do this for real," said the woman. "I thought it was a joke." Jay Bakker showed up just as we were called to begin the tour. He looked at the demon guide ushering guests into the hell house, a cackling black-robed figure with red skin and a pointy goatee. "Do we have to do this?" he asked quietly.

Our group, twenty-five or thirty of us, shuffled half-blind through the narrow, curtained labyrinth as one harrowing scene after another unfolded before us: a school shooter under the influence of Dungeons & Dragons; a girl committing suicide because she'd been raped by her father (he, apparently, gets off the hook); a gay marriage, followed by the "wedding reception," where one of the men is in a hospital, dying of AIDS ("Pretty soon Steve will be gone forever in eternal fire with all the other perverted, twisted, sin-infested souls," says our demon guide. "Oh we've got your alternative lifestyle—in HELL!"); a teenage couple in bed, while the demon eggs the boy on ("Kill the virtuous flower's virginity. Murder her morality. Choke every ounce of purity right out of her!").

Finally, the demon led us to hell itself, where tormented souls clawed at the walls of their fiery cells.

"I can't believe I got drunk!"

"He told me I was born gay, and I believed him!"

"Allah told me it was the right thing to do!"

Then an angel appeared and beckoned us into a white room for an altar call with Jesus himself. At this particular production, no one came forward. We were let out into a room done up like a church basement, with powdered doughnuts and a praise and worship band. "Can I pray with you?" volunteers asked each guest. Jay Bakker tapped my shoulder. "I have to get out of here. *Now.*"

Out on the sidewalk, Jay fumbled with his Zippo and lit a cigarette. He seemed jittery, bouncing on his toes as he smoked, and shaking his head. "If someone was even considering looking into Christianity, would you still feel that way after seeing that?" he seethed. "You'd be like, *fuck that.*"

"I guess you're supposed to be scared into it," I said.

He exhaled smoke. "That erratic behavior causes people not just to fear hell, but fear the people."

"Did this remind you of your childhood?" I asked.

"Well, I never went to anything like this, but it did put a visual on all the stuff they always told you in church. I remember going to clubs and going out dancing, and I had a fake ID, and everybody was like, 'You're going to go to hell if you do that. You can't love God and love the world.' I got to the point where I was like, 'I don't want to have anything to do with God anymore, because this seems like bull.' When I saw Jesus at the end tonight, I felt like raising my hand and asking Jesus, 'If you really love us, why is this the option—to serve you or torture us for eternity?'"

The irony, said Jay, is that when he says things like this, people accuse him of not being sufficiently Christian, when it's clear to him that it's things like hell house that are un-Christian. "Maybe they forget that their stereotypical characters represent real people, and they're telling them, basically, *you guys are worthless.* When they put down gay marriage, they're devaluing people's love for one another and their relationships with one another. In our church, we work with kids who have been through almost every issue in that room. I've had one of our kids who got arrested because they thought he was going to become a school shooter. Then he tried to hang himself, and he failed. Now he has brain damage. I've had kids of ours get shot. I've had girls who had abortions. I've got a lot of gay people in the congregation. To me, it devalues them as people to say, 'You're bad, you're wrong, and you're going straight to hell.' It's a mind-boggling message. Doesn't *gospel* mean *good news*? That wasn't good news: *Hey, by the way, if you're not going to hell, at least the majority of your friends are going to go there, and it's going to be awful and horrible.*" He mimicked a saccharine preacher's voice: 'That's how much God loves you.'"

He went on, "I was trying to look at it from their perspective, and I thought maybe what they're trying to do is get other Christians fired up to go out and try to save their friends. I felt like I can understand that because I grew up in that a little bit. *Don't let your friends go to hell.* It's supposed to be out of love, because what could be more loving that saving a friend from hell? But ultimately it's driven by fear. And if you're a teenager and you think all this is true, of course you're going to make your whole teenage life about trying to keep your friends out of hell. And what you do is alienate yourself from them by telling them how horrible and wrong and bad they are."

It was getting chilly, so we went into a bar. ESPN played silently on a flat-screen TV, while the jukebox doled out alt-rock anthems for a dollar apiece. I ordered a beer for myself and Diet Coke for Jay. He slid the paper off his straw. "How sick is it," he asked, "that everyone in hell is a teenager who made a bad choice? Where are the sweatshop owners and the politicians who are sending thousands of young men to die for their own power? Do you know what I mean? That would be more of a hell house to me—the preacher in the pulpit who is controlling people out of fear and hatred."

"Well, they seem to hate teenage culture in general, don't they?" I said. "Look at the rave scene." In that room, a demon spun house music as a guy slipped something into a girl's drink. When she passed out on the floor, he yelled, "Let's rape her!" and the entire club full of ravers circled her like vultures. "Even without the drugs and the rape," I said, "it looked like just going to a rave itself was halfway to hell."

"It's out of touch with reality," Jay agreed. "To me, the worst was the abortion scene." It was indeed gruesome. The walls were splattered with blood. A cheerleader—still clutching her pom-poms—screamed in pain while a doctor shoved a vacuum cleaner tube between her legs. "I want my baby!" she cried, but it was too late. The doctor pulled a hunk of raw meat from inside her and flung it across the room with a wet splat. Jay shook his head sadly. "I was ready to leave right then. First of all, that room with the dirt and the blood everywhere was more what it would look like if abortion was *against* the law, you know what I mean? But it wasn't the imagery as much as it was the message that made me sick to my stomach. I mean, what if you'd had an abortion? It sends this message of no hope. You're just torturing people. They have no idea of why people are in that situation."

"My guess is they don't give much thought to girls who might actually have gone through an abortion," I replied. "They're just making a political point."

Jay nodded. "It's almost like reprogramming for Christians—almost like brainwashing, to remind them, *This is what we do, this is what we believe.*" But he disagreed that the motive was entirely political. "The important thing you learn when you grow up an evangelical Christian is that the devil is around every corner. That's what they want to drive into kids' heads." He laughed. "Of course, a lot of what I preach about is the type of thing a guy who put this on would not tolerate at all. I fully expected us to be a room in hell: the Revolution Bible Study Room!"

"That raises an important question," I said. "For a lot of people who were in the audience tonight, this kind of thing, hell house, is what American Christianity is about. They have no idea—I certainly didn't—that there are places like Cornerstone, for instance. I think anybody who went to this show would actually be really comfortable at Cornerstone. It's music they might like, and it's people who are more like them than not. I guess what I'm wondering is, which one represents the future of the church? Because I think we're coming to a point when the parallel universe of Christian pop culture is going to collide with secular pop culture. And when that happens, will they enhance each other or will they explode?"

Jay drained his soda and ordered another. "I think it's going to be hard for them to converge, no matter what," he said. "Places like Cornerstone . . ." He weighed his words carefully. "Christians seem to be so welcoming, especially in their music festivals and things like that, but they still have a lot of rules and regulations."

He didn't elaborate, so I mentioned that I'd expected to see him at Cornerstone when I was there. "You've been a number of times, right?"

"Yeah," he smiled ruefully. "Years and years in a row."

"Then what happened?"

"Well, one year I said *bullshit* and they got really upset about that." Then he'd gotten into a public theological debate with one of the JPUSA big shots about whether Christians ought to "long for holiness" (Jay's point was that when you accept Christ you are holy, whether or not you, for example, say *bullshit*). And finally he went public as a gay-affirming pastor. For whatever reason or combination of reasons, he hadn't been asked back. "I actually feel like an asshole talking about all this stuff," Jay said. "To me, it's just water under the bridge. I would love to speak at Cornerstone. I love the people there. There's more good than there is bad. I just don't want to see people go through that with Christianity, and I don't want to fight with Christians anymore over petty stuff."

"Not all of that stuff is petty," I observed.

"Yeah. But there were also things like friends of mine getting yelled at. They yelled at one girl because she had a bikini top on. 'We can't have that here on the grounds, because it's causing boys to lust.' I'm like, 'It's one hundred and twenty degrees out here. Why don't you tell guys to get control of their own eyes?' We had people report us to the festival because we had a poster of Johnny Cash giving the finger and they wanted us to remove it. Even, like, major punk rockers with mohawks and stuff would

come up. They'd have stuff banned from our booths, or they'd yell at us."
Meanwhile, Jay had problems with other people's booths. "Like, there was
a shirt that said, 'Liars go to hell,' which I got upset about. My assistant pastor almost went and got in a fistfight about a shirt that said something
about gay people. The reason I kept going back is because I have some kind
of hope that God has called me to help the church become more tolerant."

"I know what you're talking about," I said. "I saw all that stuff too. But I
also saw stuff that made me think the church is becoming more tolerant." I
mentioned my conversation with Aaron Weiss of mewithoutYou. "At least
compared to other places I've been, Christians at Cornerstone seemed
pretty open-minded."

"Well, you're right. I think it's starting to happen because a lot of those
bands that go to Cornerstone, well, now they're actually able to play in normal clubs and play in the general marketplace, so I think their eyes are
being opened, that *these are good people.* They're not in that false reality anymore."

As we talked more, Jay acknowledged that his own bad experiences at
Cornerstone may have made it hard for him to recognize that the festival,
while not perfect, actually is part of a positive trend in Christian culture. At
the very least, it's a more vital trend than hell houses, he said. Progressive
Christianity, postmodern Christianity, "grace" Christianity is on the rise,
Jay said. "The fundamentalists, I think they're losing their influence. I think
they've peaked. And if they haven't peaked, it should be in the next couple
of years." For one thing, he said, hell houses and Jesus camps can't compete
with authentic cultural expressions. "I mean, as funny as that hell house
was, it wasn't really that entertaining. It was kind of disturbing. It was kind
of long and slow."

It was also doomed, he said, because it was contrary to God's word.
What connects with young people, Jay said, is "Christians living in the real
world," not fearing it. "Because really, when Jesus was talking about turning away from 'the world,' he was talking about the Roman government
and the religious leadership. But then fundamentalists went, 'You're listening to metal! You're going dancing!' That wasn't what Christ was talking
about at all. What he was saying was exactly the opposite. It was more like,
'No, you need to go dance; you need to go enjoy your life. You don't need to
conform to these guys who are putting impossible standards on you.'"

◌ ◌ ◌

David was a seventeen-year-old with an acoustic guitar and an army cap pulled low over his brown bangs. I met him in a church in the deep South, where he was volunteering for one of the ministries I'd come to write about. On his downtime, he sat picking out tunes by his favorite Christian rock bands, and we got to talking about his feelings about Christian culture. In many ways, he took a pretty conservative line. Christian singers, he said, should definitely sing about Jesus. "God's given them that talent for that purpose, and I believe if they don't do that, the singer might wake up one day and find he can't sing as well." He complained about musicians who spouted off about politics—"I'm not really into politics"—and singled out secular bands like Green Day and Yellowcard, whose music seemed to him little more than anti-Bush propaganda. He even hinted that they were only successful because liberal radio stations promoted them so heavily.

And then he began playing a song by the band he called his absolute favorite: mewithoutYou. "Um, it's kind of funny you should mention anti-Bush propaganda," I said, "because they're pretty anti-Bush."

"I'm not sure they're anti-Bush so much as antiwar," David said. "But, yeah, I guess that's true." He played and thought some more. "You can never really escape politics in music. But there's room for different views, even among Christians." One of the things David admired about mewithoutYou is that "they play all kinds of places, not just churches." Christians, he said, are too sheltered. He told me he worked part-time in a Christian bookstore, and he always wondered about Christian novels where "you've got these evil guys running around killing people, but they won't curse."

I mentioned that I'd talked to Christian authors who would love to let their villains curse. "We wouldn't sell that book," he said. "But I think we should."

When I began exploring evangelical pop culture, I had expected to discover a covert delivery mechanism for conservative ideology—and there is no shortage of that. But I also found important ways in which Christian pop culture can be a force for moderation. Perhaps this should not have been such a surprise. Creative people—artists, authors, performers, musicians—are often the most open-minded members of any society. Although there are still many Christian products being manufactured by hacks with an agenda, the market is shifting to favor genuine artists. As that happens, it is shifting to favor tolerance and reflection. The effect is still small, but I think it is real, and maybe it can be encouraged.

It would be easy enough to look back on the worst aspects of evangelical culture that I encountered—the insipid ignorance and radical right-wing politics couched as God's love—and end this journey determined to combat Christianity's incursions into the pop culture marketplace. But while I saw much that was deeply repugnant to me, combat seems like the wrong stance. Better, I think, to focus on supporting and encouraging the best aspects of Christian culture and watching the worst wither and die naturally.

This perspective stems largely from having seen firsthand what had never really sunk in when I'd encountered it in the form of statistics: that American evangelicalism is a tremendously heterodox society that is not well represented by its shrillest component, the religious right. According to the 2004 Pew Survey on American religious and political attitudes, only half of white evangelicals are "traditionalists." The other half are mostly "centrists." Centrists, liberal journalist Frances FitzGerald explained in *The New York Review of Books,* "are no more conservative than Americans generally except on abortion and gay rights, and even on these issues they are far more moderate than the traditionalists." A small but not insignificant percentage of evangelicals are "modernists," like Jay Bakker and Aaron Weiss (though they would say they are the true traditionalists).

Having met these people and seen their growing discomfort with the way their faith has been represented to the nation over the past two and a half decades, I've come to conclude that they are the ones who will bring about the demise of the religious right—probably the only ones who can. The recent vogue for neoatheism notwithstanding, nontheistic rationalists are grossly outnumbered and outgunned. Picking a fight with fundamentalists may be emotionally satisfying, and morally and academically correct, but we're going to get our teeth kicked in. Moderate Christians, however, have a fighting chance at quelling fundamentalism, and at least as much at stake in doing so.

It is often said that the strident tone of the new atheists turns off potential allies to the "secular cause." That may be true, but I don't think it's terribly important. What is of greater consequence is that by framing the debate as *any religion* versus *no religion,* atheists force religious moderates to side with fundamentalists—to forge alliances based on a single shared concept about the existence of a supernatural deity when they might actually have more in common with people who share their beliefs about other things, such as the nature of society and the respect that should be accorded to one's fellow man. After all, secularism as a sociopolitical model is not exclusively the property of the nonreligious.

If, in a struggle against intolerant fundamentalism, centrist and modernist evangelicals are the true natural allies of secularists, mainline Christians, and members of other faiths, then pop culture can be the forum in which we negotiate our common cause. Repeatedly during my excursions into what I've been calling a parallel universe, I met Christians who lamented, to varying degrees, that a separate universe even exists. As an outsider who has come to support the ascendancy of moderates within evangelicalism, I find myself sharing the goal of erasing that barrier. As evangelical artists forgo the safety of the Christian bubble for the greater risks and rewards of competing in the mainstream, I hope the mainstream will make a similar effort to explore this "crossover" Christian culture.

This will strike many people as counterintuitive. Before I began this project, the idea that the influence of conservative Christianity could be checked by encouraging the further spread of Christian pop culture would have seemed ridiculous. But from what I've seen, it is precisely insularity that breeds intolerance. Even if mainstream radio doesn't expand its embrace of Christian rock and Christian comedians never get their own sitcoms, Christians are going to continue to create Christian culture. When their only audience is other Christians, though, the feedback loop amplifies narrow-mindedness and inhibits self-examination.

What's more, the existence of a separate Christian bubble gives fundamentalists greater influence on Christian culture than they deserve based on their numbers (or their ideas). That's because the Christian subculture is dependent on gatekeepers, who by job description are more conservative than either the artists on one side of the gate or many consumers on the other. Thanks to the clout of the Christian Booksellers Association, Christian publishers will not publish and Christian authors will not write very many books that Christian bookstores will not carry. And the owners of

Christian bookstores, for the most part, reject books that offend the sensibilities and ideologies of their most conservative customers.

But imagine now that mainstream cultural outlets were more open to
Christian culture. In response, perhaps, Christian authors—and musicians
and comedians—might find themselves playing to a wider, much less conservative audience. They might then be moved to experiment with more
broad-minded material. This in turn might whet Christian audiences'
appetites for more such material, or at the very least encourage a healthy
debate that the current gatekeepers generally suppress. Mike Delaney, the
CD vendor I met at Cornerstone, said progressive Christians can transform
Christian culture slowly and organically, the way Jesus said the kingdom of
God is like a small amount of leaven in a giant mass of dough. By opening
ourselves up to Christian pop culture, the mainstream will help to mix the
batter.

It would be particularly valuable for mainstream radio—or more realis-
tically, given corporate radio's built-in limitations, mainstream music magazines, blogs, and concert venues—to embrace transformational Christian
musicians. Not only would they be serving secular audiences by introducing them to genuinely good music they would not otherwise have heard,
but they would also be encouraging the subset of Christian music that is
most correlated to humility and (lower-case *l*) liberalism within evangelicalism.

Secular consumers may be understandably wary of having Christian
content foisted on them, but ignoring Christian pop culture is not a solution to the spread of conservative Christianity. Our ignorance of Christian
culture not only causes us to misunderstand, misinterpret, and misjudge
our Christian neighbors, it also precludes our effectively challenging those
aspects of Christian culture that may be properly judged as offensive. To the
extent that we hope to change Christian culture, we have to understand and
appreciate it. Think about the situation in reverse: Is there anything more
ridiculous than a fundamentalist's rant about a TV show he's never seen?

When I talk about embracing Christian pop culture, I should be clear
that I don't have in mind the cynical form of top-down embrace that we frequently read about in the newspapers, in which Hollywood studios try to
tap into the church market by releasing a Bible-inspired film or shoehorning
an evangelical character into a TV show. ("Christians are the new gays,"

more than one person told me, rolling their eyes at the condescending voguishness evangelicals are currently enjoying in Hollywood.) Rather I'm thinking of a more genuine exchange of cultural equals.

Many younger Christians are already aware of the transformative power of such exchanges. They call it *lifestyle evangelism*—the idea that the most effective way to share the good news of Jesus Christ is not to talk about it or hand out tracts or do anything else overt, but merely to live the best life one can and be the best person one can. No other form of witness is more powerful, goes the theory, than modeling good Christian behavior and, more important, radiating the joy and serenity that comes from knowing Christ. Lifestyle evangelism is especially popular among Christians in the arts, who say that touring with secular rock bands or working on secular TV shows gives them a chance to influence, by example, society's tastemakers.

Personally, I'm not sure how successful it really is in leading people to *Christ,* but I can attest that it's a very successful method for generating positive feelings about *Christians.* The evangelicals I've felt the most fond of, the most comfortable around, and the most commonality with—regardless of political, social, or philosophical differences—were the ones who never tried to sell me on Jesus yet always seemed to be trying to live the life Jesus desired of them. The paradox of lifestyle evangelism is that while it might sound like a Christian's loving, friendly actions are all driven by an ulterior motive, it only *really* clicks when they're able to let go of that motive. The people who made the best case for Christianity were the ones who were genuinely unconcerned with whether I ever decided to become a Christian or not.

While evangelical detractors of lifestyle evangelism would read what I just wrote as proof that the method is a failure, most people can surely see that a way of behaving toward others that generates goodwill is inherently preferable to one that generates hostility or condescension. And the lesson for nonevangelicals who want to build bridges with evangelical moderates is that we can engage in lifestyle evangelism of our own. We can live in a way that will persuade traditional Christians that liberals, humanists, Muslims, New Agers, gays, feminists—what have you—are people with deep moral integrity, a viable and fulfilling worldview, and beneficial contributions to make to society.

Mocking fundamentalists will never accomplish anything. Part of the marketing genius of fundamentalism is that it has a built-in immunity to criticism, in the form of Jesus's promise that insults and persecution are both inevitable and a blessing. But it is not immune to instruction by example. Even if we can't win the hearts of fundamentalists, we can win the allegiance of more reasonable people away from them. Some of us can, and should, practice this with our Christian friends and colleagues, but for most people, especially from the most polarized segments of society, the place in which we come together is the arena of popular culture. Besides, while individuals may be set in their ways, culture is endlessly mutable, and the pop culture that the next generation of Christians grows up with need not reflect today's entrenched ideologies.

And since this is a reciprocal process, the same is true of secular pop culture. As Christians make their mark on the mainstream, the rest of us will feel their influence. If our response is hostile, it will only, as I've just argued, feed the growth of the most mean-spirited strain of Christian pop culture, and mainstream culture will be warped accordingly. But if we are welcoming, we help nurture a form of Christian culture that can in turn enrich our own. I loved American pop culture going into this project, and for the most part I still do. But the best aspects of Christian culture—the unabashed celebration of the transcendent, the challenge to crass materialism, the commitment to personal responsibility—helped me see more clearly what is too often lacking in secular entertainment and media. Jesus's radical message of brotherhood, selflessness, and dignity may be just the antidote to our contemporary ethos of shamelessness and overindulgence.

Evangelicalism and pop culture are two quintessentially American innovations that have never outgrown their worst impulses. Both James Dobson and Paris Hilton still exist. As our alternate universes begin to merge, we can either brace for an explosion, or we can open ourselves to the possibility that the new integrated universe will be better, richer, and more humane for everyone. And at least as much fun.

Acknowledgments

Now that I have written a book, I will never again skip the begat sections of the Bible. Those long lists of names are there for a reason.

This sprawling project was only possible because hundreds of people graciously agreed to let me and my notebook into their lives. If they had any doubts or suspicions, few showed it. I hope the results have rewarded their trust. For every person named in this book there are at least a half dozen more who provided invaluable assistance and insights. I am grateful to them all. And I must extend special thanks to a few people who, when I asked for their shirts, handed over their coats as well: Jay Bakker, Dan Bartow, Lori Lenz, Chris "Grandfather Rock" MacIntosh, Mark Powell, and Chuck Wallington.

I am deeply grateful for the efforts and support of everyone at Scribner, especially Brant Rumble and Nan Graham. And I can't praise highly enough my agent David Kuhn, who saw the potential for this material (as well as the title) before I did. Sections of this book were polished to a shine even before there was a book to put them in. For that I thank Chip Rowe at *Playboy,* and Leo Carey and Susan Morrison at *The New Yorker.*

A handful of trusted friends and family members read this book at various stages and kept me on the right track with their candid feedback. I am especially fortunate that one of them was the talented writer and editor Alexandra Ringe. The others were Jake Freydont-Attie, Bart Meyers, Alice Radosh, Allis Radosh, Ron Radosh, Lindsay Robertson, and Jared Stamm. Glenn Branch of the National Center for Science Education helped immensely with the chapter on creationism.

Two accomplished authors, A. J. Jacobs and David Shenk, were generous with their hard-won wisdom and made the process of producing my first book far less stressful than it would otherwise have been.

Numerous people offered tips, leads, and logistical support. Thanks to: Robin Abrahams, Mike Attie, Eric Berlin, Jason Bivins, John Duclayan, Sharon Duclayan, Myla Goldberg, Jim Hanas, Francis Heaney, Andrew Hearst, Jed Heyman, David Cay Johnston, Billy Kingsland, Melissa May, Dave Moore, Rob Nassau, Stephen Sherrill, Steven I. Weiss, and Lynne Yeamans. Thanks also to Ted Panken and to the staff of Transcriptiondesk.com for transcribing dozens of hours of interviews; to Dave Anderson for the author photo; and to Kevin Shay for his work on the web site for this book, GetRaptureReady.com.

Finally, words cannot express how much I owe to my wife, Gina Duclayan. Gina read and commented on every draft of this book, and I came to value her opinion more than anyone else's, including my own. She encouraged me, advised me, challenged me, inspired me, and put up with me. She picked up the slack when I worked long hours and took long trips. Also, her breasts are like two fawns.

Printed in the United States
by Baker & Taylor Publisher Services